MARKETING
———►———►———►— *Across Cultures*

"There has been an urgent need for a book on this most relevant Marketing topic. Other authors have attempted to write a list of 'do's and don'ts' but without any credible rationale. In one step, this new book rewrites the theory of global marketing with a new practical logic. The myriad of cases and anecdotes makes this both pleasant to read as well as being informative and rigorous. Highly recommended."

Ken Burnett, Management Consultant and International best-selling writer on Marketing

"This is the definitive text on marketing across cultures. It breaks new ground and reflects original thinking applied to the dilemmas of international marketing. It provides powerful insights and practical approaches that encompass the new "3-R's" of recognition, respect, and reconciliation. Based on solid research in the real world, the authors have made a significant contribution to the field."

David C. Wigglesworth, Ph.D.,
President, D.C.W. Research Associates International

"The authors show with numerous insides how easily we fail to connect if we neglect the less tangible cultural filter's trough which our intentions and messages are interpreted. A very hand's on guidebook touching the less tangible part of our marketing toolbox: how to connect between cultures."

Raymond van Buuren, Country Manager of Publicis Italy

"Becoming confused on a higher level is one of the best things that can happen to a person! This book helps me get up the stairs not one-by-one but in leaps and bounds!"

Henk Vlessert, Corporate Strategist, N.V. Interpolis, The Netherlands

"Developing communication, in particular brand advertising, for multinational clients, always lead to the same dilemma: creating global scale and ensuring local relevance! Fons Trompenaars and Peter Woolliams' unique approach successfully shows how to transform this tension into another winning place: it is not about compromise any more. It is all about elevating the brand to the next level."

Valérie Accary, BBDO Europe

FONS TROMPENAARS
PETER WOOLLIAMS

MARKETING
⟶⟶⟶⟶ *Across Cultures*

CAPSTONE

First published 2004 by
Capstone Publishing Ltd (a Wiley Company)
The Atrium
Southern Gate
Chichester
West Sussex PO19 8SQ
England
www.wileyeurope.com

CIP catalogue records for this book are available from the British Library and the US Library of Congress

ISBN 1-84112-471-0

Typeset by Forewords, 109 Oxford Road, Cowley, Oxford

Printed and bound by T.J. International Ltd, Padstow, Cornwall

10 9 8 7 6 5 4 3 2 1

This book is printed on acid-free paper responsibly manufactured from sustainable forestry in which at least two trees are planted for each one used for paper production.

Contents

For Geert Hofstede

Thank you for teaching us the basics of cross-cultural management.

We will not forget that our work is built on the shoulders of giants.

INTRODUCTION

Marketing across cultures

Many business historians often start from the perspective of a world without organizations and even question why they should exist. They consider the exchanges between the individual buyer and seller and how these can be achieved at the lowest cost. Coase argued, as far back as 1937, that creating an organization only made sense if the transaction costs resulting from purchases in the market were greater than the costs of setting up and running the organization (Griffiths and Wall, 2004).

However, technology and globalization have shifted the balance towards the market and away from hierarchical organizations. Individuals could obtain all they needed (needed, not wanted, as discussed later) through the marketplace by initiating the transaction themselves. Markets are the means whereby buyers and sellers can be brought together and thus work best to the benefit of all except when they become inefficient. On the other extreme, the communist centralized planning model placed all transactions within the organization.

In western thinking, a free market has the following features (Colebatch and Lamour, 1993):

- There are a large number of buyers and sellers – so the buyer has a choice of suppliers.
- The buyers know what they want.
- They are able to pay for it.
- They act independently of each other.
- The sellers are each free to enter or leave the market.
- Information about products, services, and processes is free and accessible.
- There are no overhead costs in the actual transaction – simply the price.

The market model is based on the assumption that social activity derives from the private dealings between individuals or groups.

Hierarchies work best when the transactions between the parties:

- are certain,
- occur frequently,
- require specific investments in time, money, equipment, and technology, and
- are not easily transferred to the open market.

These fundamental models that lie at the extreme ends of a bipolar spectrum have been debated and explored at length by western economists. However, as we shall demonstrate throughout this book, when we begin to include other cultures as either buyers and sellers, or both, not only do these basic models fail the marketer because of cultural differences, but an entirely different logic is also required, one that transcends this bipolar western thinking.

In western thinking, marketing has become an all-embracing business discipline. The Chartered Institute of Marketing in the UK defines marketing as: "The management process that identifies, anticipates, and supplies customer requirements efficiently and profitably." This implies both an external orientation – looking outward and studying the nature of existing and potential markets – and an internal orientation, to ensure an organization manages its resources effectively in order to meet those needs. Strategic marketing is the process of ensuring a good fit between these extremes.

Marketing as a discipline had (and still has) less significance when goods are scarce and demand exceeds supply. In such an environment, an organization can sell all it can make, so why bother to spend time and effort in trying to understand customer needs? In addition there may be little motive for being efficient if an organization has a monopoly. The East German Trabant car pleased very few of its purchasers, yet some manufacturing plants had waiting lists of up to 20 years. This was in sharp contrast to the West German market, where increasing competition resulted in excess supply. Western manufacturers then had to modify their products to reflect consumers' changing desires. A lower sales price, higher product quality, and other benefits could only be achieved by efficient production. With the reunification of Germany, the Trabant came to an abrupt end, as western manufacturers seized the opportunity presented by an extended and, in effect, new marketplace.

Production orientation sometimes returns to an otherwise competitive market – such as during periods of bad weather, strikes, acts of terrorism – or simply changes in consumer tastes or demand, like ice cream on a hot day at a beach café. However, the situation which organizations faced more frequently was one of increasing competition and thus many had to "shout louder" in order to entice customers to buy what they had produced (Palmer and Worthington, 1992). Little or no thinking was applied to identifying the benefits to the customer of the products that were being offered on sale; there were no attempts to identify customer needs in order to define what should be produced. Sales techniques such as promotions and personal selling were developed to emphasize what was on offer. Heavy advertising and promotion of package holidays during the 1970s and 80s was based on this mentality. This shift towards sales orientation still did little to focus on satisfying customer needs.

Marketing orientation developed as competitive markets shifted in the buyers' favor. If a product had benefits that a customer wanted, then the customer would buy. As Peter Drucker stated in *The Practice of Management*, published in 1973:

The aim of marketing is to make selling superfluous. The aim of marketing is to know and understand the customer so well that the product or service fits him [*sic*] and sells itself. Ideally, marketing should result in a customer who is ready to buy. All that should be needed is to make the product or service available.

This marketing orientation first achieved prominence in industries manufacturing products that were largely undifferentiated; it was their route to survival. Much of the theory was developed from Anglo-Saxon and US-led research, and is heavily biased towards these cultures. Even services in the public sector became increasingly attracted to this approach. Hospitals, schools, and government departments all began talking in terms of business objectives. Hospital patients became "clients" and rail passengers became "customers." However this was often driven more by governments allocating resources to service providers that were popular, rather than cost efficiently creating a "have and have not" society.

Thus we have arrived at an era in which marketing has become a business ideology, with the customer as the locus. However, with the internationalization of business, marketing professionals and strategists have become increasingly aware of the need to include culture as a fundamental component in their thinking. To their anguish, established theories break down and are insufficient when organizations are faced with new global markets with different cultural orientations.

The first serious book on the subject of the cultural aspects of marketing was written by Jean-Claude Usunier in 1997. It was published more than 20 years after warnings by two other Frenchmen, André

Laurent and Michel Crozier, about the limitations of Anglo-Saxon approaches to management and organization theories.

Usunier's book, however, only scratches the surface. His main stance was to compare the differences between cultural systems in which marketing activities unfold. This is very similar to what we will later describe and explain as the multi-local approach: that is, to offer different products or services adapted to each destination culture. Usunier does not resolve the dilemmas that a truly trans-national approach requires. Like many other writers, he also refers to culture as a factor affecting business, like other socio-political, financial, ecological, and legal factors.

Culture, based on our research at Trompenaars Hampden-Turner, is not like this; it is not simply a factor like most processes in the transactional environment.

To provide a reliable, generalizable framework that can help the modern marketer, culture must be considered as the context within which all transactions with stakeholders take place. For the trans-national organization it changes the entire landscape because it is *not* just another factor to put into the equation. It is the dominant factor, one that pervades all relationships and behaviors and, importantly, "meaning." Culture challenges the fundamental strategy of marketing, customer relations, definition of product, price, and advertisement. In short, culture is all pervading.

It is not unexpected that marketing, as a discipline, has lagged behind other business disciplines in recognizing the need for it to be rewritten to account for culture. This is partly explained when we remember that it is one of the organizational disciplines that is heavily influenced by (abstract) economic theories. And economists seek general laws that apply universally across (national) boundaries. They prefer to focus their research on similarities rather than on differences.

For example, in *On the Principles of Political Economy and Taxation* (1817) Ricardo described how countries can take advantage of international trade by concentrating on the relative advantage they have with certain products. A frequently quoted example concerns sheets and wine, in England and Portugal respectively. Here the international trade opportunities were better than in their respective home markets. The English wanted Portuguese wine and the Portuguese wanted the output from English cotton mills.

This approach is too simplistic as it implies, firstly, that tastes, preferences, and habits are transferable between countries; secondly, it also implies that there is (real) free trade between nations. As far as these examples go, we obviously know better today. Even now, when wine has become a global product, it still takes the French at least ten times longer to chose the right vintage and grape combination than it does the Dutch, who tend to be more focused on price. Although free trade is talked about a lot by both the European Union and President Bush, the actions of politicians actually reveal the contrary. The clash of cultural identities is perhaps one of the most dominant issues that results in political leaders losing any kind of integrity or respect in the international context, while remaining surprisingly popular (among their supporters) at home.

Unfortunately, even in the more recent and culturally sensitive marketing frameworks published, such as that of Porter (1995), culture is still regarded simply as an add-on. Porter says that competitive advantage is not often generated when national competition is highest and assumes that the factors which determine national predispositions – like miniaturization for the Japanese, consistency for the Americans, style for the French, and taste for the Italians – are also successful internationally. Obviously the international success of Toyota, McDonald's, Chanel, and the pizza might support this, but there are many examples where successful national competition fails to guarantee international success. This is mainly because of the different tastes and preferences of customers in different destination cultures.

WHY DILEMMAS, AND DILEMMAS OF MARKETING? A NEW MODEL OF MARKETING COMPETENCE

Richard Boyatzis' seminal book *The Competent Manager* (1982) generated a paradigm shift in the quest to identify the characteristics distinguishing superior from average managerial performance, in attempts to identify and construct the "competent" manager. But there is still no agreed definition of the word "competence." Some, such as Boyatzis, define this as "an underlying characteristic of a person." Others, such as Woodruffe (1993) for example, define competency as "a set of behavior patterns that the incumbent needs to bring to a position in order to perform its tasks and functions with competence." And yet others use the terms skill and competence interchangeably.

For example we could consider hotel staff who need to be trained in how to deal with guests as customers. We might then say that a member of staff had the competence to deal with guests and provide customer satisfaction. Or we could consider that even after such training, competence to provide customer satisfaction is how staff actually perform, not simply what they know. They have to perform effectively on a continuous basis, as a result of which they can satisfy the customer even when facing new situations not encountered during their training. Competency, in this respect, is what people actually do, not simply what they know.

And this brings us directly to marketing. What are the competencies needed in order to be effective in marketing in today's ever-globalizing world?

Evidence from our research at THT enables us to build a new conceptual framework relevant to the future of marketing. It is based on these assumptions:

1. Knowledge and understanding is stored within corporate cultures, especially in the relationships between people and the relationship between the organization and its market.

2. Marketing strategy consists not of one infallible master plan, or "grand strategy," but in hundreds of trials and tentative initiatives.

3. Learning occurs when we eliminate the less successful trials and intensify and explore the more successful ones by continuously monitoring feedback from activities. Successful insurance is an unending inquiry into what helps customers and rewards the organization.

4. Management of change is based on adding value rather than throwing away the value of the old situation.

Our approach to understanding a corporation is to investigate its dilemmas. As we have previously noted, the word dilemma is from the Greek, meaning "two propositions." In our findings all cultures and corporations have developed habitual ways of resolving dilemmas, of being – for example – both well centralized and highly decentralized at the same time. The success of a company will depend, among other things, on both the autonomy of its parts and on how well the information arising from this autonomy has been centralized and coordinated. If you fail to exploit fully centralized information, your scattered operations might as well be totally independent. If various business units are not free to act on local information, then your HQ is subtracting, not adding, value. Any network only justifies itself by fine-tuning the values of decentralized action and centralized intelligence, which is then fed back to the various units.

In this book we will focus on how, by recognizing and respecting cultural differences, marketing professionals have to face a variety of dilemmas in order to be effective.

There are two worlds, each as real as the other. There is the world of facts, of atoms, in which we give statistical expression to hard data. These consist of exclusive categoriziations, either/or, this or that, yielding thousands of annotated objects. Then there is another world, reflective of our languages, a world of information or difference, with no necessary connection to physical objects. These are differences of value, aim, feeling, opinion, perception; a world of contrasts that are binary. Marketing is of this latter world. As we increasingly drown in more and more of our own data, we urgently need an alternative logic in order to generate meaning and knowledge.

This kind of information typically has two ends, equally vital to development and survival. Errors need corrections if continuous improvement is to occur. Results need to be framed by questions if knowledge is to accumulate. Differences need to be integrated. Competing needs to have its results shared cooperatively if learning is to come about. Rules need exceptions for increasingly enlightened legislation. Local, decentralized activities need to be thought about globally and centrally if strategies are to improve.

We improve and prosper not by choosing one end over the other, but by reconciling the values at both ends and achieving one value through its opposite. Two desirable aims are in creative tension – and hence dilemmas, pairs of propositions, must be reconciled.

The opposites that marketers must deal with, like growth and decay, put tension into their world, sharpen their sensitivities, and increase their self-awareness. The problem cannot be "solved," in the sense of eliminated, but it can be transcended. Small and family businesses need stability and change, tradition and innovation, public and private interest, planning and laissez-faire, order and freedom, growth and decay. Successful marketers get surges of energy from the fusing of these opposites.

Dilemma reconciliation could easily be described as good judgment, intuition, creative flair, vision, and leadership. Yet all these capacities have proved elusive when people try to explain them and they tend to vanish as unexpectedly as they first appeared.

Thinking in dilemmas

A dilemma can be defined as "two propositions in apparent conflict." A dilemma describes a situation whereby one has to choose between two good or desirable options, for example: "On the one hand we need flexibility while on the other hand we also need consistency." So a dilemma describes the tension that is created due to conflicting demands. In dealing with such apparently conflicting propositions, there are several options.

Ignoring the others

One type of response is to ignore the other orientation. Stick to your own standpoint. Your style of decision making is to impose your way of doing things either because it is your belief that your own way of doing things and your values are best, or because you have rejected other ways of thinking or doing things because you have either not recognized them or have no respect for them.

Abandon your standpoint

Another response is to abandon your orientation and "go native." Here you adopt a "when in Rome, do as the Romans do" approach. Acting or keeping up such pretences doesn't go unnoticed. Others may mistrust you and you won't contribute your own strengths to the situation you are in; it's like trying to impress on your first date.

Compromise

Sometimes do it your way. Sometimes give in to others. But this is a win–lose solution or even a lose–lose solution. Compromise cannot lead to a solution in which both parties are satisfied; something has to give.

Reconcile

What is needed is an approach where the two opposing views can come to fuse or blend, where the strength of one extreme is extended by considering and accommodating the other. This is reconciliation.

At their simplest, values are seen as opposites, and we tend to see only the differences.

However, one value cannot exist without the other. Errors need corrections for continuous improvement.

CENTRALIZATION   DECENTRALIZATION

Competing proves beneficial only when the results can be cooperatively harvested. Rules need exceptions for increasingly enlightened
legislation. Local, decentralized activities need to be thought about
globally and centrally.

We can now break the initial line into two axes and create a value
continuum. "Value added" is probably too narrow a term, because
only seldom do values stack up like children's wooden building
blocks placed on top of each other. Values come in all shapes and
sizes and must be reconciled or integrated into larger meanings.

Bridging these opposites
in a creative way could be
called an upward spiral.
You could also describe it
as innovative learning, or
creating value. Marketers
succeed and prosper not
by choosing one end over
the other, but by reconcil-

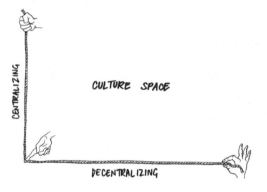

ing both and achieving one value through its opposite. Two
desirable aims are in creative tension; hence dilemmas must be reconciled into new integrities.

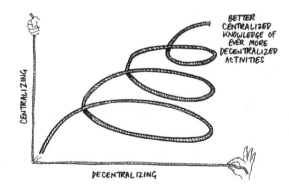

Clustering dilemmas of marketing

To show how this reconciliation can be achieved, we first need a way of clustering dilemmas so that we can offer a robust, generalizable framework in order to reconcile each type of dilemma. First, therefore, we have to describe our model of cross culture, which itself differentiates between norms and values of different cultures.

Culture, like an onion, comes in layers. The outer layer covers everything you can see and hear. Take any airport far away from home. When travelling from the airport into town you'll probably see the same things everywhere: factories, office buildings, traffic, food outlets, housing, and people. You only need to look a bit closer to see the differences. All the things that are visible and audible belong to the "outer layer of culture." This layer is thin. It can be peeled off easily, revealing a deeper layer. You simply notice that people in other cultures behave differently. The reasons why they do so are in the second layer: the domain of "norms and values," "good or bad," "right or wrong." You will never be able to see a norm, nor shake hands with a value. You can only observe their power on the surface level in the behavior of people. You may feel uncertain interpreting certain behaviors; what's good or normal in your culture may be wrong or strange in another. Is it bad when people shout? How should you interpret the feelings of customers who show no emotion? What impact would it have if you were to be late for an appointment with a client?

To understand marketing across cultures, we need to look for an explanation for all these differences in the core, the innermost layer. Every culture has its own history, often a long one. There have been disasters and plagues, shortages of food and labor. There have been influences from other cultures, war, migration. And then there's nature, sometimes wild and dangerous, sometimes willing and generous. And don't forget "other people": old people, young people, friends, and enemies. Throughout the centuries mankind has faced similar basic problems concerning other people, time, and nature. Each society has solved these problems in its own unique way and each solution is called a "basic assumption." Culture is the result of all the basic assumptions a society has developed over the centuries in order for it to survive. Only if you are familiar with these basic assumptions can you really understand a specific culture.

Basic assumptions are all in the heart, passed down from generation to generation. They're in your head as well and they got there unnoticed. Basic assumptions are very important for understanding cultural differences. They can be measured by dimensions, and at THT we distinguish seven basic cultural dimensions. Each one is like a continuum, covering all possible combinations between two contrasting basic values. Someone from a different culture will have a cultural profile that is different to yours. But remember that differences are just differences; in music an F-sharp is no better or worse than a B-flat – they are just different. Exactly the same can be said about cultures.

When we set down a product or marketing plan from one culture in another, the underlying assumptions of the culture in which it is placed will give it new meaning. This meaning is often puzzling and disturbing to the culture that invented it. The meaning of explicit "artefacts of culture" is completely dependent upon the underlying assumptions of implicit culture.

The seven dimensions model is described in Chapters 2 and 3 and is intended to provide a framework for exploring commonly shared problem areas in a structured way. Tensions arising from these cultural differences generate the dilemmas that marketers have to face.

They arise from the meaning of relationships between people, time orientation, and nature.

When marketers know the personal cultural profile of both their target customers and themselves, and can respect the differences, they are well on the way to developing cross-cultural competence and being much more effective.

So future marketers who are plying their function across cultures need to develop and then demonstrate an "adequateness" (*adaequatio*) for dilemmas – "that is, the understanding of the knower must be adequate to the thing being known" (*adaequatio rei et intellectus:* Plotinus, AD 270). To clarify, some people are incapable of appreciating a piece of music, not because they are deaf, but because of lack of *adaequatio*; the sense of hearing perceives nothing more than a succession of notes, whereas the music is grasped by intellectual powers. Some people possess these powers to such a degree that they can grasp an entire symphony simply on the strength of reading the score, while to others it is just a noise. The former is *adequate to the music but the latter is inadequate*.

For all of us, only those patterns and dynamics in organizations exist for which we have sufficient "adequateness." Effective marketing managers need to possess adequateness for reconciling dilemmas. For example, they won't try to win an argument with a customer; real leadership isn't about winning arguments.

What marketing has to achieve is the creation of wealth through the relationships between people and what they value. A product or service is a distillation of reconciled values offered to customers through relationships. (On a larger level in our dangerous world of polarizing differences, where hatreds have grown murderous, we must bridge new chasms if these are not to engulf us.) Effective behaviors that result in the reconciliation of contrasting values, we call transcultural competence, although this can include differences that are not necessarily rooted in the cultures of nation states. Through the integration of values into ever larger systems of satisfaction we can develop our new theory of marketing.

A NEW THEORY OF MARKETING

In this book we will offer a framework for rethinking the marketing approach for the transnational organization. We will look at some of the basic aspects of marketing – such as customer relations, market research, branding, etc. By treating culture as a context rather than a factor, we will consider the dilemmas faced by organizations when locating themselves in new markets.

For this purpose we need to extend the earlier definition of marketing. It now needs to include the system of activities which facilitates human interaction and information between products/services on the one hand and markets on the other. Therefore it goes beyond the original, Anglo-Saxon, meaning of how to get a product or service into a market.

There has been much discussion as to whether markets will ever globalize. Even when products and services tend to become more similar over time, and there is no doubt that this is happening, customers seem to have different reasons for buying similar products. Indeed the cultural factor is so dominant that some authors doubt there will ever be a converging taste across all customers, around the world.

In 1986 Michael Porter was very precise in observing dramatic change in international trade patterns. He concluded that within business, multidomestic home markets were themselves developing into global markets. In this respect, Usunier agrees with Porter that this development is much more of a "push" from organizations trying to integrate their production processes on all levels of the value chain, than a pull from the consumer (Usunier, 1997).

Obviously these trends have been dependent on the continued lowering of trade thresholds such as GATT and recently the European Union. In a freely competing world market, many organizations are forced to enter the international competitive arena in order to create synergies and lower costs by economies of scale. Add the internationalization of media to this process and there is little that can stop the push for an organization to internationalize.

It is difficult to ignore the fact that this process of increasing global competition has been increasing over the last three decades or so. Macroeconomic data support the proposition that international and regional trade has increased significantly faster than the accumulated GNPs of those countries trading. Economic integration across cultural boundaries and, therefore, global competition has increased significantly as a result. Similar macroeconomic data suggest that this situation has occurred even more so in many regions – Europe in particular, with the fall of the Berlin Wall and the integration of European markets. Nonetheless similar patterns are also unfolding in the Asia-Pacific region and in North and Middle America (NAFTA).

The reasons for this type of globalization have typically been based on internal business economic strategies. The first phase, in the 1960s and 70s, was initiated by multinationals who delegated much of their authority to their local generating companies in order to be as close to the market as possible. The country managers, being lords of local fiefdoms, exploited their authority by emphasizing that decentralization was the most relevant strategy in order to have the ability to able to react properly to their unique local market circumstances. Then in the 80s, under the doctrines of McKinsey and the like, a big centralization move was initiated. It was claimed that multi-local approaches needed to be replaced by centralized processes in order to achieve any global economies of scale. Here we can see the fundamental dilemma of globalizing. On the one hand, globalization is stimulated by production processes that are consistent throughout the organization to save costs; on the other hand, we find the obvious responses for sales and marketing people to adapt their products and services to the needs of local customers.

This dilemma hasn't vanished, despite the fact that two interesting global developments have occurred since the 1980s. Firstly a further increase of global integration, especially in the late 90s, occurred across cultural and company borders with the merger and acquisition wave. Secondly, and also in the 90s, there was a fundamental increase in the mobility of people. Within Europe this particularly came after the fall of the Berlin Wall, but there has also been an enormous influx of immigrant labor moving from (Northern) Africa to the European continent. In major cities like London, Paris, Amsterdam, or Berlin a significant part of the population do not have native-born parents.

There has also been a fundamental breakthrough of both mass media (aimed at particular groups, like MTV and CNN) and the Internet. This, obviously, has affected the internationalization of marketing. However it would be too easy to say that the markets have driven organizations to globalize. Globalization, even today, is still driven by increased global competition and simultaneous global restructuring processes. Patterns of consumption are simply difficult to globalize without any adaptation, due to national external factors such as legal, advertising, and distribution. However markets do appear, in some ways, to globalize as well – look at the converging patterns of fashion, consumerism, music, and education. For example a typical marketing organization such as Unilever rationalizes its number of brands and McDonald's continues to open new outlets outside the USA. But is there enough evidence to claim that the globalization of marketing is going hand-in-hand with the corresponding organizational processes of global integration (in spite of pressure groups who are against globalization at any cost)?

Research in the late 1970s and 80s has shown that there is considerable delay between new market penetration and the global consolidation of the infrastructure to support it. Hansen and Boddewyn (1975) and Picard, Boddewyn, and Soehl (1989) showed that between 1973 and 1989 there was a significant decrease in the degree of standardized marketing policies of American multinationals in Europe, in durable consumer goods. In non-durable consumer goods – except branding – there is an opposite trend. For a similar period, Ryan and Ratz (1987) observed a high level of standardization in the advertising world in terms of common themes across campaigns, their creative application, and the use they made of the media.

In contrast, Usunier (1997) is much more reserved about drawing the conclusion that, in the course of time, a global customer will emerge as a result of all the globalization processes. According to him global markets evolve more through globalization on the supply side. However, the demand side is much less willing to give up their own unique needs and wants. According to Clark (1987) the customer will never want to be a universal punter at the mercy of a global producer. Consumers buy a local brand and don't care if it is also offered elsewhere.

In our research at THT we have helped marketers elicit the dilemmas they face in their work and those that are faced by their organizations. Using face-to-face interviews as well as our web-based systems, we have accumulated over 6,000 basic dilemmas. Applying clustering and linguistic analysis techniques we quickly begin to see a number of fundamental dilemmas that are faced by organizations as they reach out to new markets. They are discussed in detail throughout the body of this book but can be summarized holistically, like this:

On the one hand...	On the other hand...
Should we sell what we can make (push)?	Or make what we can sell (pull)?
Do we strive for standard, global products?	Or do we try to sell unique products adapted to the needs and tastes of local markets?
Do we satisfy existing customer needs?	Or can we create new customer wants?
Do we sell to individuals?	Or do we sell to groups, thus creating fashion and trends for others to join in?
Do we sell functional benefits (it works)?	Or do we sell intangible benefits (status – look at "me")?
Is each transaction a unique, one-off sale?	Or is each sale part of a series in an ongoing relationship with a (long-term) customer?

And even more fundamentally,

On the one hand...	On the other hand...
Do we maintain a market orientation and always put the customer first?	Or do we satisfy our people and stakeholders?

In our parent book to this series, *Business Across Cultures*, we introduced some aspects of marketing across cultures. There is inevitably some overlap in order to make this more comprehensive and dedicated book on marketing readable without constant reference to the parent publication, and we have also drawn on some of the interviews in *21 Leaders for the 21st Century* (2001), which offer helpful and relevant insights.

We also need to avoid a list of "dos and don'ts." So, firstly, we will develop and explain our overall conceptual framework for categorizing value orientations. It is the differences across these orientations in different cultures that generates dilemmas. We can then extend our framework for reconciling these dilemmas to produce win–win solutions that transcend any particular culture or set of differences. Many of these dilemmas and their solutions will be illustrated with case studies taken from our research and consulting practice at THT. Again we see our role as providing a focus on a marketing knowledge framework *for* cultures, rather than one simply *of* cultures. We trust that our framework will offer practical help to marketers and strategists as they cope with an increasingly oligopolistic global marketplace.

Marketing professionals are becoming increasingly aware of the need to take account of culture when working in diverse markets. The issues of branding for different cultures and of how to develop a marketing strategy for the global market are current fundamental questions for us all. Our methodological framework based on the recognition, respect, and reconciliation of cultural differences offers an approach to addressing these challenges.

Initially we'll uncover some fundamental issues in marketing across cultures. Then we will use our seven dimensions model of culture to explore value systems and how these can help to explain cultural differences and the challenges they generate for marketers.

In later chapters we explore how dilemmas arise across the activities of marketing, including market research, branding, franchising, ethno-marketing, e-marketing, and strategic marketing planning. We'll give many examples of products and brands that have faced fundamental dilemmas when moving from local to international markets, and then on to global and finally fully transnational brands. We'll discuss how brands integrate the variety of value orientations into an integrated system of meaning. In Chapter 10 there are some exemplar cases for you to reflect on how well you have followed the thinking that pervades the whole book; you can check out your answers by going to the website

www.cultureforbusiness.com

that supports this book and offers some further interactive content.

CHAPTER 1

Marketing in a multicultural and changing world

Today's world is changing ever more rapidly. Four hundred years ago Nostradamus described events (Cen V, Quatrain 57) in which 9/11 can be recognized and, more specifically, the resurgence of fundamentalism (Cen IV, Quatrain 32). Whilst we are not concerned with such futurology or prediction, or with whatever views might be expressed as to whether the march of Islam is for better or worse, we are all going to have to live with it and the market changes that result. In addition, for the foreseeable future, terrorist threats are here to stay.

On the other hand, national economies have become increasingly deregulated and have opened up opportunities for international trade and competition. It has become the norm for organizations to compete for market share not only with their national competitors but also with international ones. Globalization has implications for stakeholders, workers, suppliers, customers, and local communities. Contemporary marketing is the link between this spread of production, transferability of finance, the mobility of labor, and the free flow of information across the borderless world. Technology is driving further profound changes as people on the other side of the globe can be reached in seconds, and for the cost of a local call.

In Anglo-Saxon economics, the traditional theory of consumer choice encompasses four elements about the buyer and the market:

- The buyer's marginal disposable income.
- The price at which the goods or services can be purchased.
- The values (tastes and preferences) of the consumer.
- The belief that consumers behave rationally and do the best for themselves.

No previous generations have had so many options for earning, buying, selling, and living as today. The axiomatic economic models, whereby the purchaser makes what appear to be consistent and logical buying decisions, are breaking down. They have to be replaced by models which explain how and why a new generation of buyers, with different and frequently changing value systems from changing cultures, think and act.

As a consequence, reality today is more complex as international trade becomes more and more part of daily life. Marginal incomes vary significantly across cultures and within cultures. Prices are not solely driven by market forces and elasticity of price – demand does not follow simple marginal analysis theory. Tastes and preferences are not only different in different cultures, but change rapidly as fads come and go. In many ways consumers are more discerning (complaining more frequently about poor service and their "rights") but are also "illogical," borrowing heavily on their credit cards although much less expensive sources of finance are available.

Since any country's imports are another country's exports, eventually they must be balanced and governments often intervene to achieve this by tariffs and barriers – or are required to do so by international monetary systems. Whilst balance-of-payments accounts may be balanced at settlement time, inequalities across the world are increasing. For example, in some countries a drought means that cars can't be washed, whereas in other places people may die and crops fail.

So now the British and Dutch drink French wine, Americans drive Japanese cars, and Russians eat American burgers and wheat. Nevertheless, we should recall that the basis for international trade is exchange. Uni-directional selling is not sustainable. Cultural and other international differences, such as the availability of labor and materials, lead to differences in costs and prices. Through international marketing effort and then trade, countries supply the world with commodities they can offer cheaply in exchange for other goods which are available cheaply elsewhere. Traditionally goods made by labor-intensive methods were likely to cost more relative to goods produced by capital-intensive methods in the west. However world trade has grown faster than world income, and many less-developed countries complain that industrialized countries are exploiting them by buying raw materials at low cost, then sending them back as finished goods at a much higher cost. Many industrialized countries are now exporting jobs to lower labor cost areas, as can be seen with the devlopoment of telephone call centers in India.

Customer loyalty can no longer be taken for granted in cultures where it has previously existed. In contrast it may be expressed in different ways in new destination markets, in a different culture, because of the different meaning that relationships play in the buyer-seller interface. But commercial success has to depend more on finding a new understanding of market dynamics than short-term, fleeting success through lucky accidents of matching or hitting a fashion trend.

Fed by the growing accessibility of information, money, and goods across borders, all of these changes present a constant series of challenges to marketers as well as governments. For most societies in the free world, the livelihoods, pensions, and future security of their citizens depends on the renewal, transformation, and survival of organizations, institutions, and relationships to prevent a "meltdown into collective confusion, insecurity and chaos" (Crainer, 1998). Leadership of these new organizations will require support to progress individual and social as well as corporate transformation. Future corporate success will only result from successful marketing identifying, creating, and satisfying customer needs so that the organization can deliver service and value to customers in this new environment.

CHANGING DEMOGRAPHICS

Marketers have always been concerned with changing demographics in order to profile customers and subgroups of customers. They are discovering how rapidly they need to rethink and reassess such groupings. We have to be concerned with:

- structural changes (in population, age distributions, fecundity/birth rates of different cultures),
- migrations – net of immigration and emigration (aculturalization, ethnicity, diversity, and the development of multicultural societies), and
- changes in beliefs and values held by different people (shifts, divergences, and convergence of cultural norms and values).

The total potential market is growing as the world population expands at an increasing rate although it should be noted that this growth is not uniform, and in some areas – including Europe – the population is actually declining (see Table 1.1).

The main growth continues to occur in the Far East, especially China and Korea, and in South America. Of course population growth does not imply a direct growth in market opportunity, especially because those countries with larger growth rates also tend to be those with lower GNP per capita. More importantly, population growth in these regions results in a larger low-cost labor force, which is why many US and European organizations operate in these countries.

However, even more dramatic are the changes in the structure of the population due to birth rates and life expectancy. These result

Table 1.1 Population data

Country or area	Population (000s)		
	2003	2025	2050
World	6,301,463	7,851,455	8,918,724
Africa	850,558	1,292,085	1,803,298
Asia	3,823,390	4,742,232	5,222,058
Europe	726,338	696,036	631,938
Latin America and the Caribbean	543,246	686,857	767,685
Northern America	325,698	394,312	447,931
Oceania	32,234	39,933	45,815

Source: United Nations Population Statistics and Forecasts, July 2003.

because of differences in fecundity (fertility, health of mothers, and survival rates) and other changes in society (women in more developed societies restricting pregnancies and/or choosing to delay the onset of childbearing) combined with longer life expectancy. In some countries, such as Bangladesh, Pakistan, and India, life expectancy will double over the course of less than a century (see Figure 1.1).

These changes have important consequences for marketers. In the west, age-generation profiling has become even more a part of the marketers' toolkit – witnessed by the growth in targeted services and goods to WOOPs ("well off older people"), DINKYs ("double income, no kids yet") and SWLAs ("single women living alone") replacing the older A1, A2, B, and C social class groupings.

Whilst migration has very little effect on overall population levels, it does contribute to changes in population structure. Immigrants usually come from different cultural backgrounds and offer and create different opportunities for marketers. Entirely new markets have

Figure 1.1 Changes in life expectancy. *Source:* United Nations Population Statistics and Forecasts, July 2003.

been identified and satisfied (like one for black adhesive plasters) for these immigrants as new customers. In addition immigrants

Smoking

As smoking declines in the west, tobacco companies have found an even larger and expanding group of new smokers in China. More cigarettes are smoked in China than anywhere else, with 1,643 billion consumed in 1998. Given that global consumption in 2000 was 5,500 billion, then one in every three cigarettes smoked is smoked in China.

"Tobacco companies are cranking out cigarettes at the rate of five and a half trillion a year," announced the World Health Organization, "nearly 1,000 cigarettes for every man, woman, and child on the planet."

Top five cigarette consumers:

1.   China: 1,643 billion

2.   US: 451 billion

3.   Japan: 328 billion

4.   Russia: 258 billion

5.   Indonesia: 215 billion

Source: US Federal Trade Commission Cigarette Report, 2003.

often become a new source of suppliers as they offer new, culturally-led products and services to the host community – such as ethnic food shops and restaurants.

THE MARKETERS' RESPONSE

At the very heart of marketing lies the product life curve, from which there is no escape. Eventually, over time, sales of any product or service decline, as it loses its appeal, the market becomes saturated, it becomes displaced by newer or cheaper replacement products, or simply as the original need it was satisfying no longer exists. Therefore the basic tool of the marketer is portfolio planning (Table 1.2).

At first sight, the new international markets are there to grab. But despite the claims of the free market protagonists, what constitutes a market economy differs across the world (Farnham, 1999). Thus marketers should not expect to transfer their own ethnocentric frameworks to other cultures directly without a methodology for dealing with the cultural differences (Table 1.3).

Table 1.2

		The changing market	
		Existing markets	*New markets*
	Existing products	Maintaining the sales of existing products to existing markets or established customers	Seeking new markets for existing products or services
The product range available for sale	*New products*	Developing new products for existing markets or established customers	Developing new products for new markets – either to satisfy existing demand or to create new demands

Table 1.3

System	Market	Regulation	Accountability	Labor	Value orientations
Anglo-Saxon/US	"Free"	The contract	Shareholder	Deregulated	Individualistic Achievement
Central European	Social	Public law	Stakeholders	Regulated	Social cohesion
Russian	Anarchic	Power	Managers–workers	Local	Diffuse
Japanese	Managed	Trust	Networks of organizations	Internal	Communitarianism
Chinese	Interpersonal	Trust	Families	Parochial	Paternalistic, Ascribed

In summary, there are many factors that combine to feed the growth of globalization. These include:

- An increasing number of countries opening up their markets, especially the Far East and China.
- The advancing reach of information technology and communications, including the Internet.
- Corporations seeking wider markets for their goods and services, cost reduction (or enhancements), and optimizing logistics.
- Support by the World Bank, OECD, GATT, and other agencies to enable world trade growth.

So how and why are corporations trying or learning to use these global differences in costs and material sources to manage their worldwide operations, achieve sustained growth, and survive against ever-increasing competition?

We refer, throughout this book and in others in the series, to how THT has made extensive use of web-based diagnostic tools in our research and services to our clients. In our portfolio of tools, we have developed the Globalization Readiness Assessment (GRA) tool. This web-based questionnaire has been subject to our usual analytical tests of reliability and validity, and has been completed by many thousands of respondents from a whole range of countries and types of industry. Respondents include our clients from our consultancy assignments, our own research and that of some of our affiliate PhD student projects.

Included in the GRA tool is the following question that seeks to identify the reasons for organizations to "go global": *What are the main motives for your organization to pursue an international strategy?*

(a)   Economies of scale: We go abroad to achieve scale advantages in the volume of transactions. We, and our customers, can profit from global economies of scale, where products and services are available everywhere around the world. In our business, competition takes on a worldwide stage instead of being limited to individual countries.

(b)   To prepare for global convergence: Traditional markets are highly affected by global convergence. Global convergence is the process in which countries develop more and more in the same direction and become more closely interrelated. This process is already far advanced and will continue in the future. As a result nation states will lose their relevance and it is therefore wise to anticipate, and even encourage, a "nationless" world.

(c)   Economies of scope and new markets: We go abroad to achieve increases in variety and scope, to broaden our range, and to discover new ways of reaching more customers via worldwide communication nets.

(d)   Lower transaction costs: We go abroad to achieve a critical mass to pay back our investments. These are increasing and any future financial success will largely depend on our ability to offset these costs in shorter periods of time.

(e)   Lower per unit costs: We go abroad for cheaper per unit costs, that is for the costs of each incremental unit of product or service. This is crucially dependent on the productivity of employees and the speed with which they learn.

(f)   Reputation of countries: We go abroad to establish and maintain a truly international reputation for our organization. In the past, countries used to have their own distinct characteristics; there were few international markets and strong pressures to respond to local needs. With borders disappearing these pressures will become weaker, while the need to be perceived as an international player, sensitive to needs of the international community, will become stronger.

While we found some variability in responses across respondents' functional disciplines, this was much less than might be expected; overall there is a considerable degree of consistency. Furthermore, option "d" (lower costs as the principal motive for global reach) was rated considerably lower than is normally indicated in the business management press.

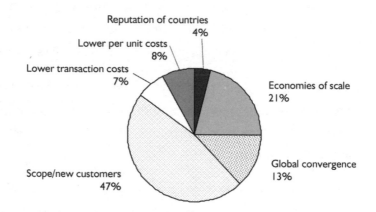

Figure 1.2 Motives for global reach

This clearly indicates the high priority that organizations place on the global marketing quest and, hence, the rationale for this book. Such motives for going abroad may be considered a wish list by many, so it is also constructive to look at how well prepared organizations are to meet these quests.

We therefore also asked the following question in our GRA tool. Respondents were asked to place their organization on a scale for each option. *For each of the following indicate on the scale how you think your organization is ready for the evolving global market place.*

Strategy development	In our company, senior management has created a sense of purpose in the organization, developed clear goals with associated measures, and created a corporate culture in which everyone understands the strategy and sees the connection between their work and the organization's goals, enabling effective international operations.
Performance measurement	In our company, individual and/or group performance measures have been defined clearly and linked to the organization's goals in such a way that it supports the development of an international mindset.
Organizational design	In our company, international roles and responsibilities, distribution of power, and authority facilitate internal operations so that the international customer finds it easy to do business with our organization and we find it easy to work with the international customer.
Knowledge management	The way that information and knowledge is generated in our company, converted from local knowledge to global knowledge and shared across cultural and regional borders, is highly effective. We learn from our cultural experiences around the globe.
Motivational energy	In our company, senior management has created a global working environment where everyone is motivated to engage with the internationalization process of the organization. Thus the potential energy of the organization benefits from the positive emotional states of employees, creating a global mindset.
External focus	Our organization has contingency plans to deal with global technological, political, regulatory, or economic changes that may evolve as different alternate business scenarios unfold across the world.
Strategic vision	In our organization we have a clear strategic vision with supporting basic values and processes according to which we integrate local needs within a global perspective.

Competitiveness	Across our organization, management monitors and anticipates the future direction of key global competitors while constantly innovating its products and/or services.

Answers and rankings based on the above were varied. In particular there were significant differences between responses from senior management and middle management. The former were generally much more bullish about their organization's readiness for the global market – presumably because middle management recognized that it would be their role to implement and deliver on targets. Here's a summary.

Organizational readiness	Mean response from senior management	Mean response from middle management
Strategy development	Well developed	Partly developed
Performance measurement	Needs more development	Over developed
Organizational design	Needs more development	Well developed
Knowledge management	Ongoing	Ongoing
Motivational energy	Well developed	Poorly developed
External focus	Needs more development	Satisfactory, but needs more development
Strategic Vision	Well developed	Poorly developed
Competitiveness	Well developed	Well developed

Source: clients of THT Consulting, 2000–2003.

The central thrust of this book is based on the analysis of the values of different cultures and the reconciliation of the dilemmas that these differences produce. But let's first note that fundamental marketing mistakes are too often still being made even at the most basic level of cultural differences.

Many of these arise simply from language, religion, and common courtesy. Established product names in one language may have different meanings in others. In advertisements, symbols or gestures in one culture (like the first finger and thumb) may have entirely opposite meanings in another. The color red, often meaning danger in western cultures, can send different messages about a product to Chinese audience, for whom red can represent success. Similarly, yellow as a color in marketing promotions may be offensive to Arabs when used in some contexts, yet convey freshness and summer in western cultures. Launches to promote new products, accompanied by buffet lunches, have been inappropriately scheduled during Ramadan in some parts of the Muslim world. The box on the following page gives some more examples of basic global marketing gaffes.

More important than these overt and more obvious aspects of culture are the differences that derive more subtly from the different meaning given by different cultures to apparently identical products or services.

We can more easily recognize explicit cultural differences by adopting an anti-ethnocentric approach, though we may not be aware of more implicit ones. Cultural due diligence is still absent from the management agenda and from many classic marketing models such as those of Porter. Most classical marketing theory has been based on single-culture research, especially the Anglo-American studies.

As explained in the introduction, it is our thesis that "culture" in today's marketplace is not simply a factor to be added in to the marketing equation, but a fundamental construct that pervades the whole of the marketing paradigm. As we noted there, this book is not a list of "dos and don'ts"; nor is it an ad hoc discussion of cases. We aim to offer a new conceptual framework that provides a way of thinking that can be generalized both across cultures and the spec-

Global gaffes

General Motors's promotion in Belgium for a car that had a "body by Fisher" turned out to have, in the Flemish translation, a "corpse by Fisher."

A Canadian importer of Turkish shirts destined for Quebec used a dictionary to help translate the label "Made in Turkey" into French. The final translation was "Fabrique en Dinde." True, dinde does mean turkey – the bird, not the country. That is Turquie.

KFC's "finger lickin' good" slogan was mistranslated in China as "eat your fingers off."

The Ford Pinto flopped when it was launched in Brazil. Mystified executives later learned that "pinto" is local slang for small genitals.

"Pepsi brings you back to life" was translated into Chinese as "Pepsi brings your ancestors back from the grave."

The lager brand Coors' slogan, "turn it loose," became "suffer from diarrhea" in Spanish.

trum of marketing activities, and that can be applied in a practical way.

Our new marketing paradigm is intended to provide a robust framework for the marketer and is based on the Three Rs: recognize, respect, and reconciliation. The first step is to recognize that there are cultural differences in marketing. Different views about "where the customer is coming from" aren't right or wrong; they are just different. It is easy to be judgmental about people and societies that give a different meaning to their world. The next step is to respect these differences and accept the customer's rights to interpret the world, and our products and marketing efforts, in the way they choose.

Many marketing professionals have told us that very often their clients don't know what they want and that they therefore need to create a market (push). Others, however, say that a marketing professional should thrive on the needs of clients and be able to listen carefully to them (pull). As soon as an organization becomes international it is faced even more with the imperative to reconcile needs and wants. Where internally oriented cultures, such as the US, might start with technology push in order to connect it to the needs of clients at a later stage, the Japanese might first "listen" to their clients' needs and be pulled by them in order to attach them to the developments of technology at a later stage. Because of these different views of the world, we have two seemingly opposing views of the contrasting cultures – those of the seller and buyer. The classical approach is to focus solely on customer satisfaction: "To make what we know we can sell." But we also have to consider our own corporate knowledge: "To try to sell what we know we can make." Thus, in our new approach, the task of the marketer is much more than simply abandoning their own strengths for the sake of customer satisfaction: It is to reconcile these seemingly opposing orientations.

The total reconciliation approach we offer requires the inclusion of stakeholders, customers, suppliers, employees, investors, and the community at large with a well-defined mission that is expressed through clear values and purpose. Thus tomorrow's organization is a business-led "charity" that promotes the reconciliation approach through research and continually refined enabling mechanisms. The role of employees must change from being only a human "resource" to being professionals who can find ways of applying their capacities to inspire these new sustainable organizations.

In the widest view, global marketing has to become the "acceptable face of capitalism," reconciling values associated with more materialistic cultures with those of "the simple life" ideology.

CHAPTER 2

Cultural differences in a marketing context: value dimensions

n this chapter we will establish our basic framework for explaining and categorizing cultural differences as a precursor for marketing across cultures. Later in the book we'll extend our discussion to include our new logic to reconcile marketing dilemmas.

MARKETING DILEMMAS DERIVING FROM CULTURAL DIFFERENCES: IDEOGRAPHIC AND NOMOTHETIC APPROACHES

All sciences, including psychology, tend to neglect this paramount fact of individuality. In daily life, on the other hand, we are in no danger of forgetting that individuality is the supreme mark of human nature. All during our waking life, and even in our dreams, we recognize and deal with people as separate, distinct, and unique individuals. (Allport, 1961)

Whatever the perspective undertaken by researchers into culture, many are unclear in indicating whether they are starting from an ideographic or nomothetic perspective – or even recognising that these two extremes exist. This is an important distinction, so let's explain further.

Allport describes how nomothetic is derived from the Greek word "nomothetikos," meaning the giving or enacting of laws. Ideographic, on the other hand, has its roots in the Greek "idio" meaning "one's own." The terms were established by Windelbrand (1904) who used them to differentiate between the approaches and aims of investigative disciplines. Kelly (1991) stated that "the (nomothetic approach) appears to be the study of *mankind*, while the (ideographic approach) is the study of *a man*." They can also be considered as the equivalents of the organization and the individual.

We'll consider both of these perspectives – both separately and together (or reconciled). The ideographic view is concerned with how consumers attribute meaning to the world around them and thus serves to help us understand buyers' cultural differences across national boundaries. In contrast we can use the nomothetic approach as a means of exploring cultural differences from the perspective of the marketing function, and thus examine what issues will be faced by leaders and managers as they seek to extend their markets to embrace new cultures and subcultures.

But even these are not separate, opposite perspectives. We must see how we can reconcile our approaches by developing a robust methodology, transcending individual customers, organizations, gender, age, and other variables.

Culture is about meaning. Advertisers bombard consumers with sensory stimuli – colors, music, smells, textures, and movements. These stimuli are intended to capture our attention and we then process them. This processing, and the interpretation we give to the stimuli, are dependent on our frames of reference or schema, and these frames of reference are different in different cultures. Putting it another way, a culture can be defined as a collective sharing the same frame of reference. Various marketing programs use techniques such as market research, consumer panels, focus groups, and taste panels in order to uncover these underlying frames of reference in order that a product or service can be offered to appeal to the wants and needs of the consumer. However the reverse is also true. Increasingly marketers seek to change the frames of reference and belief systems of potential customers through their promotion and advertisements. For example, greetings cards, male cosmetics, new jewelry (earrings for men and items for body piercing, perhaps) are all industries that have been created (or where societal changes are accelerated) by marketers. Marketers have sought to create or change the schema of consumers so they give a different meaning to these goods. If you don't send a greeting card to your father on Fathers' Day then you are somehow lacking. Men are still macho if they wear jewelry…

While we instantly recognise explicit cultural differences, as either consumer or corporation, we may not recognise the implicit ones, as we noted in the previous chapter. This explains, for example, inconsistencies between what consumers say and what they do. They may complain that the range of colors for the car model of their choice is limited, but actually tend to purchase only cars from a narrow range of colors – which are those that the manufacturer has already identified as those that sell. Even if other colors were available, the evidence suggests that consumers would be unlikely to choose them.

THT's research, evidence, and feedback from client groups has led us to develop and validate models and diagnostic instruments to reveal and measure these basic assumptions. They are based on the seven dimensions model of cultural differences that we have developed over the last fifteen years and are at the core of our frameworks for explaining and measuring cultural differences. The reconciliation framework has evolved from this.

Thus we can summarize that culture is about meaning, about what meaning is given to things, actions, and behaviors. Although an automobile is a means of transport, it has different meanings in different cultures. For some it is simply a means of getting to work, getting from A to B. In other cultures it is a sign of status and independence and in others it is a means of showing you belong to a group who have also chosen to purchase the same model. Hence the motive is different in different cultures even though the car might look similar from the outside – a box with wheels that you drive along the road.

We can begin to explore both the ideographic and nomothetic perspectives of the origins of meaning by using our seven dimensional model. This enables marketers to learn to recognise these cultural differences, to be prepared for them, and to check where and how they might exist and manifest themselves.

A TYPOLOGY FOR DILEMMAS OF MARKETING

In *Business Across Cultures* we presented the seven dimensions model of culture in some detail. As well as simply demonstrating cultural differences, this model enables us to characterize commonly occurring dilemmas from the tensions between the values from which they originate.

We can consider the dilemmas that arise across each of the following dimensions:

1.   Universalism–particularism. Do people tend to follow standardized rules or do they prefer a flexible approach to unique situations?

2.   Individualism–communitarianism. Does the culture foster individual performance and creativity or is the focus on the larger group, leading to cohesion and consensus?

3.   Specific–diffuse. What is the degree of involvement in personal relationships (high = diffuse, low = specific)? Does a specific business project come easily, out of which a more diffuse relationship may develop, or do people have to get to know their business partners before they can do any business with them?

4.   Neutral–affective. Are emotions controlled or do people display their emotions overtly?

5.   Achievement–ascription. Is status and power based on performance or is it more determined by the school people went to or their age, gender, and family background?

6.   Sequential–synchronic. Do people organize time in a sequential manner, doing one task at a time, or in parallel, keeping many things active at once?

7.   Internal–external control. Are people stimulated by their inner drives and sense of control or are they adaptive to external events that are beyond their control?

To show how this reconciliation can be achieved, let's look at examples of products and brands that have faced these dilemmas. By following the same reconciliation paradigm throughout this book, we can review a variety of basic marketing issues that are affected by culture, ranging from advertising to market research.

THE DILEMMA BETWEEN THE UNIVERSAL AND THE PARTICULAR

Universalist cultures tend to feel that general rules and obligations are a strong source of moral reference. People from these cultures tend to follow the rules and look for a single best way of dealing fairly with all cases. They assume that the standards they hold dear are the right ones and attempt to change the attitudes of others accordingly. Particularist societies are those where particular circumstances are much more important than any rules. Bonds of relationships (family, friends) are stronger than any abstract rules and responses may change according to circumstances and the people involved.

Thus some products for universalistic markets may need to begin by being homogenous and generic, but this does mean that the consumer will buy from any supplier as there is no difference between sources. Buying gasoline is an example – who you buy from matters little. At the other extreme, overparticularizing means small, highly differentiated markets with highly specialized products addressing each small segment – and with associated higher costs.

When a company has developed packaging and presentation of a brand to the point where it is instantly recognized, they are faced with the dilemma between keeping it the same (universal image) and having different versions (particularism) for different markets and over time. Packaging can look out of date very quickly as colors, logos, and fonts come in and out of fashion.

A consumer's capacity to detect or observe such differences is relative and the issue of when and how a difference is observed is relevant to many marketing situations. The stronger the original imagery, the greater the change required in order for that change to be noticed. Thus companies often update their packaging with small, incremental changes over time – so they stay fresh and modern, but don't lose the identity of the product through making noticeable changes or when the consumer is traveling overseas. Because consumers are subject to saturation of stimuli nowadays, with advertisements on every street corner, every web page, every radio or TV program, every page of every newspaper, organizations also need to consider how they can get their product or promotion noticed without irritating the consumer by overexposure and excessive bombardment.

Figure 2.1 shows the relative orientation of a number of countries on this dimension. This should help to link this cultural construct to the interpretations we have given in the examples of dilemmas (mani-

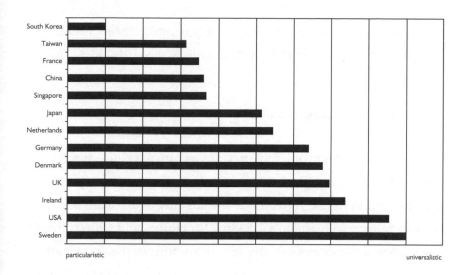

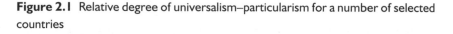

Figure 2.1 Relative degree of universalism–particularism for a number of selected countries

fested in marketing) that follow. The same format will apply with the other dimensions.

Chic tailoring

Christian Dior used to complain that American women attached less importance to small details of fit and finish than to general effect; they were more attracted by variety and change.

The survival of small firms, inefficient by American standards, is essential to the survival of the French idea of chic. The French conception of taste is not threatened by the popularity of jeans; they simply claim to cut jeans better than anyone else.

France is important to the world of fashion because it cultivates fine workmanship, beautiful materials, originality, and harmony. There is no evidence that the French as a whole appreciate these ideals more than other people. They have compromised themselves perhaps as much as other nations in accepting cheap imitations. French taste and French good taste are not necessarily the same.

Meeting or surpassing standards

Germans avoid compromizing on rules as much as they avoid compromising on quality. They spend money on good, reliable products, and they often define reliability in terms of a worst case scenario. Look at automobile ads in Germany. Brochures and videos briefly touch upon lifestyle issues, only to quickly turn to the "real stuff," a full report on all the environmental and safety standards that the new car meets. Ideally it does not just satisfy current legal standards but will also be able to meet the far stricter standards of the future. While you might dream of a fast race on the autobahn or a peaceful drive on the Romantische Straße, the ads will show you a series of detailed lab tests demonstrating all the different ways in which your new car could be smashed to pieces without any harm coming to the people inside.

Claims of exceptional performance may create suspicion

A Dutch insurance company found it difficult to convince German customers to buy their life insurance, even though their product had done exceptionally well in recent years. In their advertising campaign they stated that their customers' capital investment had grown as much as 20 percent annually. German customers were not convinced; such an exceptional increase in the price of shares could not be trusted to continue. To win over German customers, the Dutch company had to change their marketing strategy and promise a much lower return on investment.

Stressing Irish core values

Marketing strategies that work well in the US and UK are not always directly transferable to the Irish market. There are many cases of advertising campaigns that succeeded abroad but failed in Ireland because they conflicted with the strong universalist values held by most Irish people. The easygoing, informal nature of communication in Ireland can often camouflage deep-rooted core values. When these are crossed the Irish can react very negatively. It is important to be aware of the conservative, religious, local, and nationalist feelings that underpin many consumer reactions in Ireland. Today's Ireland may appear to be modern, forward looking, and in many ways very "Americanized," but campaigns that conflict with the Irish moral code of behavior are likely to provoke disapproval.

Certain Irish companies emphasize their Irishness and familiarity with Irish values as a means of competing with foreign companies operating in Ireland. For example, they might stress friendly service and the fact that they represent sound family values, saying that they've been a family-run business for the past fifty years or so. Another quality that is stressed is longevity; companies will state that they have no intention of leaving the country for more lucrative destinations when corporate tax incentives run out. The tendency of some multinationals to do this has left many people suspicious of their long-term commitment to Ireland. Some foreign-owned companies have now begun to market themselves in a similar manner, stressing the Irishness of their employees and products, and using Irish accents in their TV commercials.

Village life and inefficient retailing

Japanese social life and consumption patterns are much more particularistic than in most western nations. Tokyo, for example, is a collection of "villages," each with its shopping center. Because houses and refrigerators are small and fresh fish and vegetables are greatly prized, the Japanese shop daily. They go by bicycle or on foot, and shop in thousands of mostly small, mom and pop stores supplied by two tiers of wholesalers. Service is very personal and friendly, and the predilections of individual customers are well known.

Supermarkets and chain stores are hindered by the Large Scale Store Law and its application by local governments. Small shopkeepers are an important constituency and are protected. Quite a few used to work in companies that produce the goods they currently sell. They can exchange defective goods quickly, preventing unfavorable publicity for the company. But such a system is not without its costs. Supermarkets are fewer, standardization is less, and distribution costs are higher. Even successful foreign chains, like Kentucky Fried Chicken, employ twice as many people in Japan as they do in the States. The additional workers wrap the chicken carefully, bow, and smile. Japan spends on honorifics, people whose main task appears to be greeting and thanking customers.

The 24-hour economy has an impact on daily life in Japan. Convenience stores that are open late in the evening are now starting to boom.

Universal products

The Dutch universalistic orientation is expressed in their preference for universal products: a limited variety, available in large quantities, with a reasonable quality and a low price. The success of Hema department stores, clothing retail company C&A, the Dutch-based wholesaling company Makro, and the company brands of food retailer Albert Heijn can be attributed to this preference. The Swedish furniture retail company IKEA has been extremely successful in the Netherlands by using a strategy that appeals to this preference for the universal product.

This preference might seem to be in contradiction with Dutch individualism. Although the Dutch want to express their individualism in their buying habits, they don't do this by buying specialty products or famous brand names. They try to express their individualism by looking for what they consider to be creative variations and combinations of universal products.

Marketing for particular needs

Singaporeans are very particularistic about festive days. A festive day of any ethnic group is welcomed as a reason to celebrate and offer sales specials. Where, other than in Singapore, would you find a shop with a sign saying "Jesus is the reason for the season" to make people aware of the Christmas sales? Just before the Hindu Diwali festival, advertisements in the newspaper for cars, computers, and just about anything are labeled as "Diwali specials."

Singapore has always been a very diverse society in which the need for marketing to different ethnic groups has been taken for granted. Since the beginning of the last century, Chinese Singaporeans have distinguished between "Chinatown business," "ah so business" (Chinese business outside of Chinatown), and "ang moh companies" (western business). Because of rapid economic developments, different age groups in Singapore have very different consumer patterns as well, and it is extremely important to differentiate marketing for the different age groups.

Singaporean companies have a tradition of adapting to different market needs in a flexible way. A major Singaporean bank has this as its slogan for home loans: "The one thing we're very rigid about is flexibility."

Beauty products adapted to local circumstances

Marketing of products adapted to local circumstances can be very successful in Singapore. The founder of the Singaporean firm Coslab, selling therapeutic beauty products, found that he could not compete with the multinational American and European pharmaceutical companies who had dominated the global market for a long time. Instead he concentrated on developing products that cured tropical skin problems because there weren't many such products at the time. Since the type of rashes that occur in humid countries are markedly different from those in temperate climates, he was able to develop special products that were more effective in treating "tropical" acne, for example. He also developed new products to treat other skin problems particular to the tropics such as sensitive skin, pigmentation, dehydration, and uneven skin. He started a franchise for beauty salons using the products. There are now 200 outlets in Singapore and Malaysia selling his products.

Failure of Giant's particularistic logo policy

When Taiwanese bicycle manufacturer Giant started to globalize, it did not see the need for one universal logo in all its locations. Giant felt that there should be different logos for different locations so that every location would have a logo that would fit the local environment and reflect local creativity. However this particularistic policy did not work out well. Giant could not get equal effort and quality from all locations in the design of the logo and in the end they chose to go with a single standardized logo.

Mass manufacturing and mass market

For most of the twentieth century, America was the world's largest consumer market. Starting in the 1920s, the trend was to mass-market whatever machines could produce. America came to specialize in long manufacturing runs of simple products, cheaply produced, and widely advertised and distributed. It was the triumph of the universal product.

Nowadays customers are more demanding, and today markets are much more customer and niche oriented. As the advertising industry has expanded and evolved, it has also had an impact on the demand for more and more sophisticated and specialized products.

The global–local dichotomy

As we can observe in the above examples, the dominant dilemma in this dimension is the global–local dichotomy. This can be framed as: "Shall we have one standardized approach (identical product range and associated identical marketing support) or shall we go for a local approach (different products and local based marketing in each destination)? Are our customers best served by our becoming global and alike, or will they be more influenced by their particular national or local cultures?" (see Figure 2.1).

The dilemma is reconciled through transnational specialization: We continuously integrate best practice and satisfy customer needs by learning from the diversity of adopting, adapting, and combining the best.

Taiwan has suffered for some time from a reputation for low-end products and inconsistent quality. "Made in Taiwan" used to have the image of low price, low quality. The reputation for cloning led to an image of "me too" manufacturers, known for imitating designs

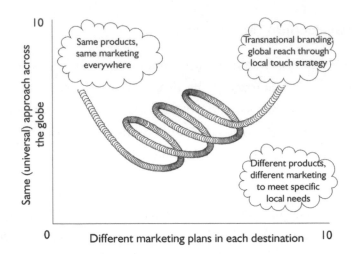

Figure 2.2 The global–local dilemma

and compromising quality to keep prices competitive. Acer Computers was one of the first Taiwanese manufacturers that managed to change the image of Made in Taiwan for the better. For some time, Acer was forced to use creative ways to avoid putting "Made in Taiwan" on its products because of the bad image. Then it started with its "global brand, local touch" strategy; it wanted to develop Acer as a global brand name that would also be associated with local assembly, local shareholders, local management, local identity, and local autonomy in marketing and distribution. "Me Too is Not My Style" was used as the title of a book by Acer's CEO. "Global brand, local touch" is a good example of the reconciliation of particularism and universalism in business strategy.

In the years of expansion Lego, the Danish toy company, wanted to improve their instruction booklets for the American market so that this would help increase sales. They wanted to be as successful as they were in Germany, which they took as their role model. Lego's research group had videotaped German kids playing with Lego. The children would carefully cut the sticker of the new box out, after which they started sorting the different elements and organizing them according to the colors in which they came. With the same extreme care they then took the instruction booklet and read it from cover to cover. Subsequently they built precise replicas of the models shown in the booklet. When the observers filmed American kids, the results were completely different. The majority of the American children took the box of building blocks and immediately started to tear it apart in great excitement. The pieces dropped on the floor, creating a mess from the start. Then they started to experiment without looking at the instructions; they didn't seem to care about them. Action was what they wanted, making their own things and following their own ideas, and their mothers praised them for their creativity and unique constructions. The German kids, on the contrary, were praised for following instructions. American children have some practical direction so they could learn by doing and by making errors, and seem to love a box of Lego because they see it as having infinite possibilities. In Germany, Lego is a means of learning how to follow instructions and perform tasks in a prescribed manner. The difference here is creativity by making unique combinations versus following universal instructions to reproduce pictures in the booklet.

Clotaire Rapaille eloquently showed that Lego found reconciliation in combining boxes for the international markets:

> Lego repositioned itself as a source of developing creativity and imagination. If they explained, however, that with one box of Lego there exist infinite possibilities, consumers would only buy one box, creating a loop. Lego needed to create a spiral, with possibilities for children to create more with two boxes than one, and still more with three than two. Instead of an instruction booklet, they needed a growth map, showing a

child's creativity growing from one box to the next.

(Rapaille, 2001)

This dilemma is illustrated in Figure 2.3.

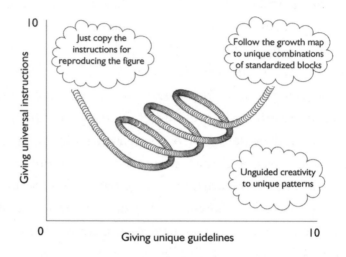

Figure 2.3 The universal–particular dilemma

THE DILEMMA BETWEEN INDIVIDUALISM AND COMMUNITARIANISM

The next of our dimensions covering how people relate to others concerns the conflict between what we want as individuals and the interests of the group to which we belong. Do we relate to others by discovering what each one of us individually wants and then trying to negotiate around the differences, or do we place ahead of this some shared concept of public and collective good? Everyone goes through these cycles, though people start from different points and think of them as ends or means. An individualist culture sees the individual as the end, and improvements to collective arrangements as the means of achieving it. A communitarian culture sees the group as its end, and improvements to individual capacities as the means to that end. But if the relationship is truly circular the decision to call one element an end and another a means is arbitrary.

This second dimension similarly gives rise to a number of key dilemmas. Is marketing concerned with satisfying individual customer needs and preferences, or is the focus on creating a trend or fashion that is adopted by a group? Individuals will then purchase to show that they have joined the group by following the shared trend. From the customer's perspective, do we relate to others by discovering what each one of us individually wants, or do we place ahead of this some shared concept which we can identify with and feel part of? Figure 2.4 shows the relative orientation of a number of countries along this dimension.

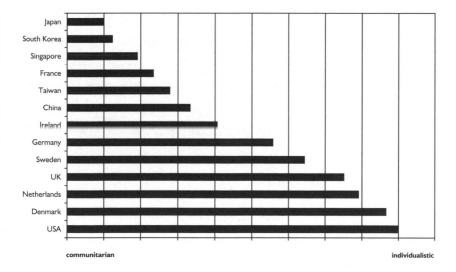

Figure 2.4 Relative degree of indivualism–communitarianism for a number of selected countries

Advertisements and commercials in China

The impact of the communitarian values of Chinese culture on the marketing of consumer goods is rather straightforward. Most goods are best positioned in a family or family-like collective environment. Family-like collectives frequently used in advertisements are colleagues, members of a sports team, or classmates at school. Within the collectives, the leading people are often given some special attention or a special role.

Celebrating the family in advertising

The communitarian orientation of the French reveals itself very clearly in some of its products and in the way they are advertised. Well known products are the Renault Espace (a family car) and family vacations organized by Club Méditerranée (better known as Club Med). After an initial rejection by the entire auto industry, Renault, the largest French manufacturer, showed persistence in the development and later very successful sales of the first compact family car. It was advertised as one that united families going on vacations. The enormous success of Club Med is also indicative of French communitarianism through family life. The whole business idea is to offer vacations for families, including grandparents, in a luxurious environment. This is very French indeed.

TV advertising in Germany

Until the early 1980s all television in Germany was public. It was financed by public television fees and advertisements were limited to short slots in the early evening. However after the introduction of private channels during the 80s, the amount of television advertising has increased quite significantly. Nonetheless, in comparison with other countries, it is still fairly limited; overall Germany is probably one of the countries with the least amount of TV advertising. Printed ads are much more common. In general, advertising expenditures in Germany are much lower than in most other countries. Compared to the United States, for example, the amount spent on advertising is significantly lower.

Comparative advertising

Comparative advertising, while common in some countries, is illegal in France. In the US this is a common practice; individualistic America has a tradition of overtly competing products. In contrast comparative advertising is seen as humiliating by the communitarian French. Under paragraph 1382 of the French civil code it is forbidden to compare products publicly, even in cases where there is only a slight bias or where the comparison is correct.

The public regulation of distribution

In marketing products on the German market, companies have to deal with a set of public regulations that may often seem rather restrictive. First, there is a law against unfair competition (Gesetz gegen den unlauteren Wettbewerb). This prohibits some of the more aggressive strategies to gain market entry and increase market share and sprang out of the strong tradition of cartels and "interest communities" that were active in Germany up until the Second World War. These groups were set up to hinder cutthroat competition with its potentially negative effect on the economy as a whole.

Although cartels and similar practices are now prohibited and tightly watched by the monopoly commission in Berlin, the notion that competition should not be too fierce and the push to avoid destabilizing effects on the economy are still rather strong and permeate public regulation. In general, public regulation is geared to pursuing public goals and not to fostering the free working of market forces. Planning restrictions are often used to channel behavior towards such goals. It may, for example, be rather difficult for a company to get a planning permit for a large out-of-town retail development as authorities are trying to protect shopping facilities in city centers. Retailers often have a tough time dealing with these kinds of constraints in Germany. After unification, the situation was different for a while in East Germany, and planning permits were generously granted. However, the situation there is now becoming more like that in the former West Germany.

Another frequently discussed restriction in Germany concerns the relatively short official shopping hours. Recently, these restrictions have been somewhat liberalized as a result of increased pressure.

"Uneconomic" levels of service in Japan

In Japanese business, good service can be taken to what westerners sometimes consider "uneconomic" levels. For example, a woman asks for a shade of lipstick that is out of stock in a drugstore. She is invited to sit down, offered tea perhaps, and a dispatch rider is sent from the wholesaler with the particular color she wants. Western economists would tell you that such high levels of service are not economically justified; the cost of delivery would lose the druggist at least 500 yen.

A communitarian system calculates on a different basis. What is the customer's continued loyal patronage worth? Might she not feel an obligation to that particular druggist and spend more money later? Communitarians ask what the relationship is worth, not the cost of the lipstick itself.

Self-sacrificing consumers

Consumers are subordinated to corporations in Japan. But is this a willing sacrifice? They wish to support Japanese business in its export drive by shoring up domestic sales and "buying Japanese."

Criticism of Japanese markets often assumes that Japanese consumers would want to buy foreign produce for a few yen less, given the choice, and that consumers think only of themselves. But is this so? So-called non-tariff barriers could be the result of concerted community choices, not the result of cheating or plotting against foreign imports. Certainly Japanese consumer organizations state that they willingly bear higher prices to sustain their nation. This is in part because they are not only buying a product, but are also buying the whole corporate contribution to society.

Communitarian yogurt

The main product of the Japanese company Yakult is a fermented yogurt drink that claims to have a positive effect on health. Yakult developed a unique delivery system for this product in Japan: house-to-house delivery by so-called Yakult ladies. These Yakult ladies are young women, dressed in a company uniform including a hat and gloves, who distribute the product in their own neighborhoods.

Yakult tried the Yakult lady system in the Netherlands when they first introduced the product there in 1994. However, being more individually oriented than the Japanese, the Dutch viewed unannounced visits to their homes as violations of their privacy. Another problem resulting from Dutch individualism was that it was difficult to find women who were willing to sell products in their own area. The fact that company uniforms are not very popular among the individualistic Dutch made it even more difficult to find women willing to take these jobs.

The problem was that the Japanese company was used to distribution systems based on personal contacts, loyalty, and communitarianism, while Dutch distribution systems are more impersonal and individualized. The Dutch see large scale supermarkets as efficient and practical and couldn't really see the advantage of the Yakult lady system. In the end, Yakult managed to reconcile its communitarian orientation with the individualism of the Dutch by redirecting its personalized marketing efforts to homes for the elderly and social gathering places such as train stations.

Commitment to Singapore

Commitment to Singapore and Asia in general is another communitarian theme that is frequently found in advertisements in Singapore. CMS Energy, an international company involved in a power plant project with a local Singaporean partner, placed an advertisement in Singaporean newspapers in order to show its commitment to Asia in general and to Singapore in particular. The advertisement emphasized that the company was committed to the people of Singapore and to bringing energy to Asia. The ad gave details about plants in other Asian countries. In addition, there was a personal presentation of the management team at the new Asian regional headquarters in Singapore. The presentation included pictures and information about their personal backgrounds and their Asian experience. It explicitly stated that one of the executive directors – who was from Singapore – had a wonderful wife and three delightful daughters born in Singapore and that he would bring Singaporean family values into the management team.

Distribution systems in South Korea

Retailing in Korea is still dominated by small shops. Distribution systems in Korea are quite complicated because they consist of networks with many chains based on close relationships. This distribution system is hard for a foreign company to enter. The most successful western companies in Korea have not tried to set up their own distribution networks, nor have they completely delegated distribution to local distributors. They are the ones that started an alliance with a local distributor and went out of their way to build a close relationship with that distributor. In Korea it is important to make sure that an alliance partner and the distribution and sales force feel that they are part of the company "community." To that end, some western companies offer training to their distributors' staff, give advice on marketing and promotion, and work closely with the distributors to get information about the retailers and the end customer.

Family restaurants in Seoul

Family-style restaurant chains such as TGI Friday's and Sizzler do very well in Seoul. Seoul has a strong tradition of restaurant business. There is a fairly large middle class of professionals in Korea who have a greater disposable income and are willing to spend this partly on entertainment. Family-style restaurant chains successfully cater to this market because they offer a night out for the whole family for a relatively low price. Many of these establishments are franchised to local Korean operators who are able to adapt the atmosphere to local expectations.

Family life in Taiwan

Demonstrating the values of family life and taking care of your family is a strong selling point in Taiwan. A company that sells pots and pans introduced a popular commercial starring two movie star lovers. In the commercial, the man was invited to a romantic candlelit dinner. The advertisement was reasonably popular, but based on feedback from the public the couple was replaced by a film star and his wife in the following season. The two come home and have an intimate dinner together as a happily married couple. Showing a warm and loving family life made the commercial more successful.

Alone means no friends

Advertisements for beer in Europe sometimes show someone enjoying a beer while alone. When the Taiwanese see an ad like this they think "That person is lonely. They have no friends." Advertisements for beer in Taiwan show lots of people, all having a good time together.

Shareholder sovereignty in the UK

Individualistic cultures disagree with communitarian ones about how much power individual shareholders should wield over the corporation they own. In Britain, shareholders have enormous power. The corporation is their property and they have the right to sell to the highest bidder. Senior managers often describe themselves as shareholder representatives working to ensure a high price per share and a good dividend. Many think that the purpose of a corporation is to make money for its shareholders. Shareholders can overturn management decisions or enforce their own decisions, and in the last few years shareholders have forced senior directors of some UK companies to resign.

Communitarian cultures, on the other hand, tend to encourage cross shareholding by banks, suppliers, subcontractors, and employees of the corporation. This effectively blocks hostile takeovers and gives banks and other institutional lenders veto power over would-be acquisitors. Changes of ownership are then friendly rather than hostile.

Marketing to individualists

Independence is encouraged in Britain and this has become more apparent in recent years. Demographic trends, such as fewer people getting married, single person households, and the increasing age profile of the population seem to be encouraging individuals to be self-reliant and independent.

Advertising in the UK often appeals to this self-reliant aspect of Britons, as shown in the text of a recent ad from the Prudential Assurance Company Limited:

> *It wasn't your style to burn your bra.*
> *Instead, you burnt the midnight oil building a career.*
> *What drove you on?*
> *It wasn't feminism, more individualism.*
> *Even with a loving partner you valued your independence and*
> *invested in your own pension.*
> *And look at you now.*
> *Shopkeeper turned potter and just turned sixty.*
> *We're proud to have helped.*

In the US, we can see similar effects. Although "self-reliance" cannot be translated easily into many languages, it has been eulogized in American literature by such writers as Ralph Waldo Emerson. Self-reliance is deeply ingrained in the average American from a very early age, and dependence is discouraged. Great emphasis is placed on personal growth and self-actualization.

Naturally, since independence and self-improvement are so deeply ingrained, advertising is often designed to appeal to this aspect of the culture. There is, for example, an advertisement that shows a man facing physical as well as mental challenges which ends by saying "Be all that you can be. Join the Army." Other well-known ads are the Marlboro commercials that show a cowboy on his horse, alone in the middle of the wilderness. The announcer invites the viewer to "come to Marlboro Country." The implied message is that in Marlboro Country, men are men and don't need anybody else. In more communitarian cultures, this type of advertising would probably not have much appeal, but in the US, it is quite effective.

THE DILEMMA BETWEEN SPECIFIC AND DIFFUSE

This dimension concerns the degree of involvement in relationships – the degree to which we engage others in specific areas of life and single levels of personality, or diffusely in multiple areas of our lives and at several levels at the same time.

Here we must determine what the customer's degree of involvement is. Do we see the customer as a punter, someone from whom we can make a fast buck, or is a customer the basis for an ongoing series of relationships over time?

In some cultures salespeople have to develop a relationship with potential customers before they can sell them anything. In France, for example, because the salesperson's relationship with the customer is personalized, that customer is more loyal to the salesperson than to the product. Consequently if the salesperson were to leave and to work for another company, customers would follow. In the US, in contrast, a salesperson's relationship with a customer is generally specific to their business dealings. Therefore anyone who has a convincing sales pitch will be an effective salesperson; because the US is a low context culture, the message is more important than the source of the communication. For this reason many American companies invest a lot of money in training. Sales training in the US generally emphasizes developing a strong sales pitch and dealing with the potential customer's considerations or objections.

This dimension can also be described as distinguishing between low and high context, which refers to the amount you must know about a culture or person before effective communication can take place. The context includes the amount of shared knowledge taken for granted by people when conversing, and the amount of reference to common ground. Figure 2.5 shows the relative orientation of a number of countries along this dimension.

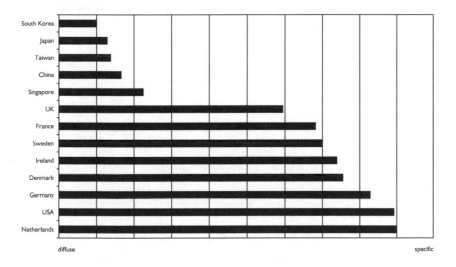

Figure 2.5 Relative degree of specific–diffuse orientation for a number of selected countries

Not what was said but the way it was said

In comparing American with Japanese responses to television commercials, research has found that Americans paid most attention to the specific message itself, to what was communicated about the product. Japanese viewers were far more interested in the way the presenter spoke and the sincerity of the communication. They were influenced more by the overall feeling they experienced when they saw the commercial, valuing the diffuse aspects of the message.

The role of the sales representative

Since relationships are specific in the Netherlands, the role of the sales representative is to establish good business relations with wholesalers and retailers. Provisional contracts, price policies, promotional materials, and advertising policies are all designed with a focus on building specific business relationships. Therefore if you expect a more diffuse type of business relationship in the Netherlands you may be disappointed. Nevertheless, if the Dutch can be convinced that financial gain is contingent upon establishing a more diffuse relationship, they will make an effort to do so.

Soft selling

High-context cultures like Japan, with a great amount of shared information, tend to practice the "soft sell." However, Americans and Europeans in Japan frequently complain that they do not know what commercials are actually selling; the appeal is so indirect that only a fully informed member of the culture understands the connotation.

High-context communication can only really be illustrated by an example familiar to Americans... One day a king was returning to his palace with his hunting party when he saw a huge pair of yellow hands extended on either side of the narrow pass. If he rode between them, would they suddenly close? So he tapped a page boy on the shoulder. "Go between those hands," he said. The boy passed safely, as did the whole hunting party, and the moral of the story is: "Let your pages do the walking through the Yellow Fingers." To understand such a message you must already be aware of the original slogan: "Let your fingers do the walking through the Yellow Pages."

Japanese communications are between insiders. Department stores have rear projection films of waves, clouds, and seashores; products are not mentioned. The mood of beauty is enough.

Implicit is better than explicit

Up front, "in-your-face" advertising does not work well in Ireland. The message or joke should not be immediately obvious. Irish consumers like to be entertained and kept guessing; they like to work out the message for themselves. A direct, forceful approach will not work as well as an indirect, understated, clever approach. Commercials work well when they appeal to the intelligence of the consumer to decipher the meaning but are not too obscure for people to figure out.

The Smirnoff vodka commercials are especially popular, as they cleverly combine humor, a sense of danger, surprise, excitement, and fantasy. There is always an innocuous scene, but the camera rolling in front of a clear Smirnoff bottle reveals an element of wildness or danger seen through it. For example, in one poster there is a flock of innocent-looking sheep, and in their midst, seen through the Smirnoff bottle, one of them is revealed as a wolf. Another Smirnoff poster shows a group of American warplanes flying in the sky with their noses painted to look like sharks. One plane, seen through the bottle, is seen to be really shark-like, as it has bitten the tail off the plane in front of it. A TV commercial shows a group of well-dressed people on a ship who, when seen through the Smirnoff bottle, turn out to be quite different: The smooth gentleman becomes a rough, sleazy-looking character, the prim lady becomes a vamp, and people who are running after each other become samurai warriors wielding meat cleavers. The commercials impress because they are techni-cally clever, incorporate black humor, and include an element of surprise.

Escalating reciprocity

Competitors in Japan and Southeast Asia are so formidable because they tend to develop relationships rather than simply develop them-selves. While American suppliers will rarely behave so as to lose money on a specific contract, Japanese suppliers will sacrifice sev-eral contracts to build up a diffuse relationship with a customer they believe to be important.

Given norms of reciprocity and obligation in Japan a supplier who overfulfills his contract – or in other words, does more than what is specified in it – can expect to see next month's order doubled or qua-drupled, in an attempt to repay his kindness. You are not expected to meet specifications, you are expected to surpass them; the more you do for your customer the more he will do for you, in a system of escalating reciprocity on both sides. Westerners then wonder why it is so hard to break into the Japanese market… It is hard to break into any relationship where A and B have "sacrificed" themselves to each other many times over.

Fantasy advertising

Research has shown that the French have a tendency to have their products surrounded by dreams and humor (both high context and diffuse) while the Germans and Americans have a strong tendency to show the specifics of the products by informative advertising. For example, in order to show the power of one its top cars (R9), Renault showed it driven through the country at great speed but without a driver. This highly imaginative advertisement had great appeal in

France, but failed in some countries where viewers wondered how the car could be driven without a driver and associated it with danger and craziness.

Developing strategies and implementing them

Americans are often stunned by elaborately argued and planned French strategies. The inspiration is positively Napoleonic, the details rich, and the coordination elegant. When risk is involved, planning and calculating tend to escalate until the conceptions are perfect. Yet the problem for any culture that starts with diffuse conceptualization is that the specific actions may be too late and not as well performed. We tend to be victims of our "logical" priorities, and French managers are no exception. Fast to deduce, they are slower to think inductively from specific results back to their formidable plans.

High-context advertising in France

French marketing is often highly context-dependent and holistic. Turn the television on, and you may not know what is being advertised even if you understand the words. As in most high-context cultures, advertising in France often involves a context that is meant to trigger associations among French viewers. Many French advertising campaigns are elaborate and attempt to create whole environments. For example, a complete Provençal village square was created in Harrods to sell French products; L'Oréal had portraits commissioned of "Les Dames de Beauté," beautiful ladies, mostly queens and royal mistresses, who inhabited châteaux on the Loire. The supposed complexion of each beauty was matched to an appropriate line of cosmetics.

Appealing to the general public

The history of western marketing theory has witnessed a development in which consumers have been dissected in ever smaller segments. A category like "young people" is meaningless in modern western marketing and even "female adolescents between 13 and 15" seems too broad to handle. Marketing is well on its way to personal marketing, in which each individual is a separate market segment. In China, however, where diffuseness and communitarianism converge, a good quality product is one that can be enjoyed by a large number – preferably all consumers. This is especially evident in advertisements for food and beverages. A very common set phrase in food advertisements is that the product is enjoyed by "men and women, old and young alike." TV commercials will substantiate that message by showing a typical extended family, consisting of three generations, all indulging in the food or drink that is being promoted.

Business and pleasure

"Business before pleasure" is a proverb that collides with Chinese diffuse values. Business can never be successful without a certain amount of pleasure. Business seminars are a good example of this. Seminars are a convenient way to introduce products in China, where traveling can be cumbersome and time consuming. However, Chinese expect a seminar to be a combination of business and a holiday. Seminars are usually held at resort-type places, and the organizers pay special attention to the quality of the meals. The social interaction during breakfast, lunch, and dinner is at least as important as that during the formal seminar sessions and the last day is usually kept open for social activities like sightseeing. For that reason, if a product is to be introduced in a seminar that would normally take two days, this should be extended to three days in China.

Another diffuse aspect of Chinese seminars is that after dinner, business and casual chatting are often intermingled. A good tip for companies that think of organizing seminars in China is to reserve a conference room for the evening as well.

Advertising to diffuse customers

This preference for intuition over reasoning can also be observed in the Japanese style of marketing. Their approach to the customer is diffuse. The Japanese take a holistic view of the customer as a person; they don't just see the consumer in the role of customer. Westerners are often amazed by how diffuse Japanese advertising messages are compared to the simple and clear information in western, specific advertising messages, as we've noted. Moreover many Japanese companies have company philosophies that are phrased in lyrical terms and reflect their diffuse orientation. Some examples are "Kyosei – working for the common good" (Canon); "For harmony and strength" (a bank); "The cycle of goodness" (YKK); "Spread joy through music" (Yamaha music). When they invest abroad, these companies find it difficult to explain their philosophies to non-Japanese, specific-oriented staff.

Singapore networks

Diffuse societies are often network societies, but Singapore is the ultimate network society. The networking culture gave Singapore a competitive advantage in Electronic Data Interchange (EDI). As an island nation with no natural resources, Singapore is dependent on trade. Singapore realized in the 1980s that new EDI technologies should be used to modernize the network. The implementation of the TradeNet concept was started in 1989. This is an electronic trade documentation system that has helped to cut the processing time on cargo shipments from one day to less than thirty minutes. It coordinates the flow of documentation. The Seaport Authority, the Airport Authority, the Trade Development Board, shipping agents, air cargo agents, customs, freight forwarders, and traders are all in one network. All parties involved can check documents, book facilities, and gain access to arrival and departure information.

Singapore adopts new technology at an incredibly fast rate because of its strong networking orientation. Other examples of such networks in Singapore are MediNet, LawNet (lawyers can access information and file documents with the court and different registries), and Asia Manufacturing Online (a display of the products of over 15,000 local and regional manufacturing companies).

The ultimate service concept

The most important thing in Singapore is to show that you care about the customer and want to develop a personal relationship. Advertisements in newspapers very often display photos of salespeople or real estate agents and state that they are "at your service with care." Restaurants advertise that they offer simple cuisine but luxurious and courteous service.

Singapore Airlines is the quintessential example of Singaporean ideas about diffuse customer relations. Singapore Airlines began as Malayan Airways Limited in 1937 when Singapore was still part of the Malayan Federation. It became Singapore Airlines in 1972 after the Singapore and Malaysian governments could not agree on the combined airline service. Singapore Airlines seems to have combined the personal service inherited from its Malaysian heritage and good financial planning from its Chinese Singaporean background. It was one of the first two airlines to offer free drinks, choice of meals, personal videos, and in-flight telephone service. It is seen as the benchmark in customer service with regard to cabin comfort and food.

Korean extras

The diffuse cultural orientation of Koreans makes their expectation of service different from that of most western countries. Koreans believe that a supplier should not profit from service. Even after the sale is completed, the needs of the customer should still be met. Trying to profit from service may damage a company's relationship with its customers. In Korea, the customer always expects to get something extra, in the form of discounts, free gifts, or free help in the event of problems. A supplier who charges for every service rendered is not appreciated. If fees for specific services are not explicitly mentioned in the contract, a Korean customer could well expect to get them for free.

Introducing new technology

One challenge many organizations face is how the introduction of a new technology will affect their relationships with their customers. The use of the Internet as a marketing tool will be discussed in much more detail in a later chapter. Let's now look at the introduction of the Automatic Teller Machine (ATM) and how it changes the relationship with the customer. One extreme view has been that the ATM would replace the main human-interfaced service of local bank branches. On the contrary is the viewpoint that bank managers held, believing that human trust was the essence of banking, and that this could never be replaced by machines. The human interface was necessary at all costs, in particular for elderly citizens.

Research shows that for many clients in diffuse societies, money serves as a sort of proof of social identity, and the bank is thus a place with which they retain very strong and intimate ties. For many, to some degree, the amount of money they possess lets them know how well they are doing in life in general. So, if the mission of a bank is to contribute to the development of diffuse identities, could the ATM perform that function? Or is banking becoming a specific commodity, along with everything else done by machines?

The dilemma can best be phrased like this: on the one hand, a bank needs to be a loving, caring, non-judgmental entity, a place where you can always have your basic needs fulfilled. On the other hand, it needs to be judgmental and ensure you pay back the loan you took out some years ago. Obviously the bank needs to reconcile these stereotypical "motherly" and "fatherly" aspects and have them feed into each other; both are necessary. Banks should offer "motherly" ATM services to all clients worldwide, not only to their own customers, but the "fatherly" bank could be more selective, respecting the ritual of signing documents in a personalized way, maybe even with imposing wood and leather in the offices to reinforce the effect. Spe-

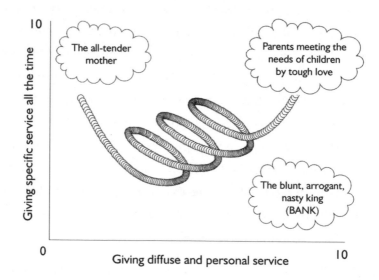

Figure 2.6 The specific–diffuse dilemma

cific technology does not replace diffuse human interaction. At its best, new technology results in more meaningful personal service. The reconciliation integrates high tech with high touch in tough love, and is illustrated in Figure 2.6. The success of ATMs internationally is the proof that it was well reconciled.

As we have noted before, marketing through reconciliation is therefore, once again, much more than compromise. We cannot stress this enough. It is the craft of trying to define specific areas in order to provide a more personal service to customers and thereby deepen the relationship.

THE DILEMMA BETWEEN NEUTRAL AND AFFECTIVE ORIENTATION

Reason and emotion both play a role in relationships between people. Which dominates will depend on whether we are affective – that is, display our emotions, in which case we will probably get an emotional response in return – or whether we are emotionally neutral in our approach. In the latter case we are still emotional, of course, but don't show it. What part does the display and role of emotion play, and/or is the display of emotion controlled? What shapes the purchasing decisions? Figure 2.7 shows the relative orientation of a number of countries on this dimension.

Peter Darke and his research team argue that it doesn't matter whether you're buying a new car or a new shade of lipstick (Darke et al., 2002). In all cases you are likely to consider both tangible factors (product features, price, etc.) as well as intangible qualities (such as how the product makes you feel). Their research demonstrates how affective (emotional) experience can be influential even when consumers are highly motivated and fully capable of making rational decisions on the basis of tangible features. Indeed, marketing

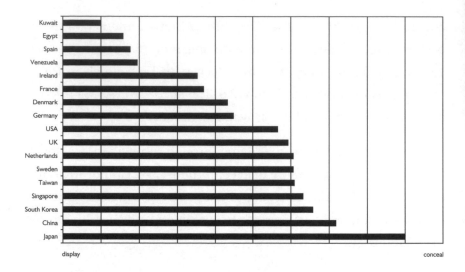

Figure 2.7 Relative degree to which a number of selected countries openly display emotions (affective = display, neutral =conceal)

research has shown the importance of affective cues (preferences based on feelings) and informational cues (preferences based on features) in the consumer decision making processes. It appears that affective cues have an impact on judgement primarily when consumers are less motivated to adopt a rational, analytic approach, especially when they perceive they have a diminished ability to judge products. Further, choices made with a high affective component are often perceived as impulse purchases which consumers ultimately regret. This is the familiar "buyer's remorse" syndrome. Affectivity also explains why many women enjoy "retail therapy" even to the point of window shopping with friends rather than making actual purchases.

Typically reason and emotion are linked or combined. When the customer expresses satisfaction (or dissatisfaction), they are trying to find confirmation in their thoughts and feelings – and trying to show they have the same response as others. This is embodied in the well-known theory of conspicuous consumption. Customers whose response is neutral are seeking an indirect response.

Advertising should appeal to emotion, but what few advertisers understand is that this sentimental dimension of advertising has a logic of its own. Most companies make the mistake of assuming that people purchase products and services for rational reasons, and so they give them several rational reasons to buy. These reasons emphasize specific features, benefits, quality, or guarantees. Some companies, however, know that the real reasons people buy a product or service aren't scientific or rational. They understand that emotion plays a big role in making purchasing decisions, and they tap into this emotion through symbols.

Take the age-old dilemma of increasing demand for wood products and the need for forest preservation. Both are desirable outcomes, even for environmentalists. Most people's notion of the forest is deeply imbued with sentiments of camping and hiking when they were children; when you cut down a tree you are killing it. So the Californian Forestry Association used ads saying: "This year we planted 2,400,230 new trees." But people didn't get the right emotion. Did they cut down more than they planted? They changed their ads by using a picture of a mother with a baby in her arms – simple, touching, and a universal symbol of nurturing and protecting. The text read: "For every baby born in California, we plant 100 trees." The new ad brought to the public's awareness the entire life cycle of the forest, which was the side of the industry that had been ignored in the past.

Jingles

One marketing technique that has been exploited in the US is the use of jingles or songs. The songs tend to be short and upbeat (Americans love enthusiasm), and they repeat the same chorus several times, making them easy to remember. In his sixteen tips on television advertising, David Ogilvy, founder of the Ogilvy & Mather ad agency, says, "If you do not have much to say [about a product], put it in a song, but make sure audiences can understand the words of your jingle." Although this form of advertising is sometimes viewed by non-Americans as silly, it is often the "silly" commercials that most stick in people's minds. They get the viewers' attention, and they remember the name of the product. Consequently this type of advertising can be quite effective in the US.

Humor

Since the expression of positive emotions is encouraged in the US, many companies use humor to sell their products to an American audience. For example, a popular TV commercial for deodorant showed a head shot of an old woman saying "Grandpa says I need Ban roll-on for what ails me, but I don't feel sick." Next you hear the voice of the announcer saying "Maybe Grandpa does," and then you see Grandma with a shocked look on her face. It is very possible that this commercial would not be at all well received in other parts of the world because humor is culturally determined. Moreover, in some cultures, it would be considered inappropriate to joke about your product and/or to make fun of an old person. However Americans really liked it because it appealed to their sense of humor; for that reason, this commercial was very effective in selling its product to American consumers.

We might compare this with Carlsberg Humor. The British are relatively neutral, meaning that they like advertisements with understated humor. One particular Carlsberg (Danish beer brewer) advertisement is an example of this.

A Danish couple are shown receiving therapy. The wife says that she can't stand her husband any more, she despises him. The therapist asks how long this has been going on. The wife replies "since he started his new job." The therapist then asks what he does. The husband says that he's a long-distance lorry driver, delivering all over the world. The therapist asks what he delivers and the man looks at the floor, too embarrassed to answer. The wife turns on the husband and says angrily "tell her." The husband then admits he delivers Carlsberg Export. On hearing this, the therapist (a woman) leaps across the room and attacks him. The punchline, heard as a voice-over, says "Carlsberg – the Danes hate to see it leave as much as we like to see it arrive."

Humor is an integral and valued part of the Irish communication style and, as such, it is generally successful in marketing products to an Irish audience. However, humor is notoriously difficult to transfer across cultures, so care should be taken to match the Irish style. An example of successful humor is a Guinness TV commercial where a comic actor dances in a crazy way to a catchy tune while drinking Guinness. The implicit message seems to be "I'm mad and fun, and I don't care what people think." It appeals to many Irish people's image of themselves or how they would like to be: individuals who express themselves in a funny, offbeat manner, with a happy-go-lucky, "devil-may-care" attitude.

Pop songs and artists

The use of popular songs associated with a product is often used in the UK. This is often more effective than using a jingle, which might be found irritating even though memorable. The songs tend to work better if they are linked with the product in some way. For example, Cadbury's launched a new hot chocolate drink. Their ad features supermodels on the catwalk. Everything starts to collapse and they fall in heaps, tearing their dresses. A singer begins to sing "when things go wrong, I'll be there for you" – well known in the UK as being by the soul band Hot Chocolate. He stands out as the one calm feature amidst chaos, dressed in a suit of Cadbury's signature purple, holding out a steaming cup of hot chocolate to the distressed models.

It isn't just the musical association that might be missed outside of the UK. It might not be appropriate in some countries to show models apparently being humiliated in this way, with their clothing in a state of disarray.

Presentation styles

Presentation styles in Taiwan are subdued. The Taiwanese are used to sales representatives who are not very expressive. Therefore using a lot of hand gestures and body movement may be less effective when presenting to the Taiwanese. They may be suspicious of sales-people who are overtly enthusiastic or who spend a lot of time talking about the tremendous superiority of their product. Talking "too much" is often associated with not knowing much, or to use a Chinese saying, "You have more saliva than tea."

In contrast, the neutral orientation of the Dutch is reflected in their presentation style. Don't expect a Dutch salesperson or team to give a passionate presentation about their product. Presentations tend to be sober and low key, but at the same time informal and friendly. This style may be misinterpreted by people from other cultures. For example, since the Dutch are not inclined to show tremendous enthusiasm, Americans can misinterpret this to mean that Dutch presenters don't really believe in their products. Germans tend to interpret the Dutch informal presentation style as unprofessional;

the Dutch tendency to use self-mockery may be seen by Germans as a lack of self-confidence.

Friendly service in South Korea

Personnel in the service industry in Korea work hard, but given the neutral orientation of Koreans towards those who are not within their circle of intimates, it is difficult to get them to make a serious effort to be friendly to strangers. Expatriates in Korea sometimes perceive this as a lack of customer service. They also complain about unfriendly government officials. However once you get to know people in Korea, or have an intermediate contact person who knows them, service will be much more friendly. The lack of friendly customer service to those without contacts may lead to opportunities for those western companies that are especially good at delivering high-level customer service.

Creating an overall feeling tone

Rather than displaying overt emotion to sell a product, the Japanese will strive to create an overall "feeling tone" in an advertisement. This approach is especially popular when advertising traditional Japanese products, such as tea or miso shiru (soup). For example, the tranquility of old traditional Japan requires little display of human emotion to get a message across. A recent ad for tea begins with four people in samurai costumes on a gondola-style boat. They are drinking the tea while slowly moving through the water as if they are in a dream. Then one calmly says "Lunch is just about over. We'd better return to the office." There are weak grunts of agreement. This hits a chord with the Japanese because they understand the feelings and atmosphere even though there are no strong changes in facial expression.

Ads that caused offence

What is considered funny in one culture can be misunderstood in another, interpreted at best as silly and at worst as offensive, with both reactions being contrary to the desired effect. For example, an Irish banking group recently introduced an advertising campaign portraying naked men with fig leaves and bibles. This ad had been successful in the UK. In Ireland, however, it caused much offence and there were so many complaints by the clergy in offices around the country that it had to be withdrawn. What was seen as a joke in the UK was considered bad taste in Ireland, where both nudity and religion are sensitive issues.

Another advertisement that bombed was a Benetton commercial, showing a new-born baby still attached to its umbilical cord. The "shock value" marketing approach of this image did not work and resulted in more offence than appreciation from the Irish public.

Sales promotion

In promoting their products, Germans may often appear to be less enthusiastic than their counterparts from more affective cultures. Rather than trying to create a positive emotion in their customers, German salespeople prefer to emphasize the "objective" character- istics of the product and often use complex, pseudo-technical terminology to describe the product's advantages. When a new product is launched, it is therefore often more important to convince one's own salespeople of the benefits of the product rather than appealing to their emotions.

Cheering and publicly celebrating individual star performers in the sales team is also rather unpopular. The recognition of such achieve- ments is often done in a very neutral way that excludes hype or dramatic effects.

Verbalizing emotions

A remarkable way of neutralizing the expression of emotions is to describe them in words, rather than showing them through gestures, facial expressions, and tone of voice. Just saying "I'm happy" without the nonverbal display of the emotion may strike affective people as unbelievable. For more neutral people like the Chinese, however, it is common to verbalize the emotion without a trace of the other signs of happiness. This can be observed in Chinese commercials. A person or a group of people will tell you, completely straight faced, how happy they are with a certain product. They will then continue by explaining why they are so happy. Just being happy is not enough to convince the reader or viewer; there has to be a reason as well.

German advertising rarely intends to be funny. Jokes are very rare and advertisements avoid making the product or its manufacturer look ridiculous at all costs. Slapstick or silly rhymes and jingles are therefore rather unpopular. Seriousness and a neutral, stereotypical happiness rule supreme. For more intangible products, advertisers usually choose the conservative setting of a happy family or loving couple whose perfect world is maintained by having the advertised product. For more technical products, on the other hand, advertisements clearly focus on the "objective" product features.

Endorsements by authorities in China

One way in which neutrality towards displaying emotions is reflected in Chinese advertising is the frequent use of experts rather than enthusiastic users of the product being advertised. A common western way of advertising pharmaceuticals – for example, let's take an antacid – is to first show a person suffering from heartburn, followed by a shot of the same person after taking the antacid. The expression on the face of the sufferer leaves no doubt about the effectiveness of the drug. While such techniques are also used in China, pharmaceuticals are most frequently endorsed by a person wearing a long white coat (a doctor). Even when a happy patient is shown, the doctor will also be there confirming that the product is approved by experts. In a similar way, candy may be recommended by happy children, but a parent, doctor, or kindergarten nurse will also be there to add that the product is good for the child's health, does not harm the teeth, etc.

Reconciling affective and neutral cultures

Overly affective (expressive) or neutral cultures have problems in relating with each other. The neutral person is easily accused of being stone cold and having no heart; the affective person is seen as way out of control and inconsistent. When such cultures meet it is essential for international managers to recognize the differences, and to refrain from making any judgments based on emotions – or

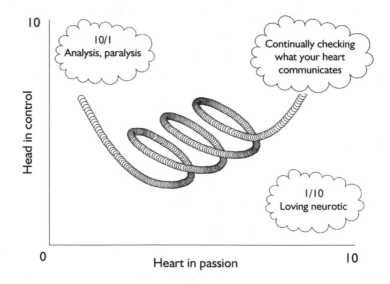

Figure 2.8 The emotional–neutral dilemma

the apparent lack of them. This aspect of culture is quite clearly seen in the amount of emotionality people can stand across cultures.

Let's look at one example of reconciling passion and control, which we have mentioned in previous books, but which is clearly relevant here.

Club Med's prodigious growth had overstrained its traditional management structure. It had become intoxicated by its self-celebrations, week after week, and was not keeping track of costs or logistics. The company's downward spiral had begun and chronic under-investment made it worse. It was not competent in the more neutral hard side of the business (travel, finance, logistics, etc.) Resorts were not profit centers and several had lost money without anyone realizing. Opening was often too early in the season or not early enough. Moreover, hospitality had simply been increased with no awareness of diminishing returns; the food and wine expenditure had escalated too far. When it is about esprit, ambience, and all the affective and diffuse aspects of life – leave it to Club Med. This was also their under-sponsored strength. At this point CEO Philippe Bourguignon was very aware that he had to reconcile these neutral and affective necessities. He helped Club Med to refine the art of placing immaterial experiences above the bits and pieces of the material world, while insuring that the bits and pieces paid off.

The wholeness of experience with its *esprit* is vital. But taken too far, (as Club Med had in the early 1990s), the personalized and unique vacation was driven to the point of destruction. It had become a vendor of incomparable experiences but couldn't survive in a more cost-conscious world. But the opposite, more neutral approach, where elements are standardized into a reliable, high volume and therefore affordable holiday, would risk abandoning Club Med's founding values.

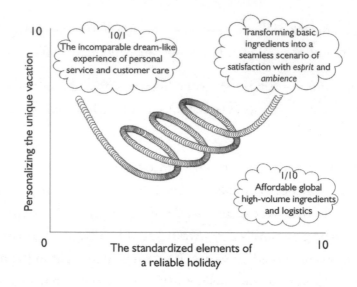

Figure 2.9 The global ingredients of a personal dream

With ever-advancing living standards, the separate elements of luxury and good living are available to more and more people. What is often missing and is more elusive is the integration of these elements into a diffuse and affective sense of satisfaction, a *savoir vivre*. Bourguignon no longer manages villages, but a shared spirit, a seamless scenario of satisfactions, an *ambience* or atmosphere, like Planet Hollywood or the Hard Rock Cafés, augmented by food and wine. The dilemma is shown in Figure 2.9.

CHAPTER 3

Cultural differences in a marketing context: further value dimensions

T he previous chapter covered the first four of our seven dimensions. Now let's look at the remaining three.

THE DILEMMA BETWEEN ACHIEVEMENT AND ASCRIPTION

All societies give certain people higher status than others, showing that unusual attention should be focused upon them and their activities. Some cultures accord status on the basis of personal achievements whereas others ascribe status by virtue of gender, age, class, education, etc. The first we call achieved status and the second, ascribed status. While achieved status refers to what you do or to what you have done, ascribed status refers to who you are. Achievement-oriented cultures market their products and services on the basis of their performance. Do customers want functional products that achieve a utilitarian purpose or are they buying status?

In achievement-oriented cultures, the emphasis is on performance, reliability, and functionality. In ascribed-status cultures, such as those in Asia, status is ascribed to products that naturally evoke admiration from others, such as high technology and jewelry. You can tell the time from a $1 digital watch just as well as you can with a $10,000 Rolex. But the latter is a symbolic representation of status, not only a watch. This status is less concerned with the functional capabilities of the product. Motives for acquiring ascribed status by making purchases vary across cultures.

Of course the same product, such as a Mercedes, is sold in different countries. But in Germany you will be selling reliable, quality German engineering that will get you to work down the autobahn quickly and safely; in India, with exactly the same product, you

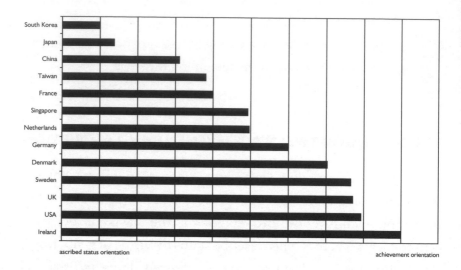

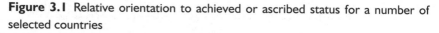

Figure 3.1 Relative orientation to achieved or ascribed status for a number of selected countries

would be selling status. Figure 3.1 shows the relative orientation of a number of countries along this dimension.

Use of experts in advertising in China

We looked briefly at endorsements by authorities in China in the previous chapter. Let's consider it again here. Acknowledged authorities are used by manufacturers all over the world, but their power of persuasion goes virtually unquestioned in China. The influence of ascribed status in Chinese culture is most conspicuous in the use of authorities and experts in marketing campaigns.

The influence of experts has increased considerably in the course of economic reforms. The bulk of Chinese R&D and product development is conducted in a network of research institutes. In addition to the large national institutes, there are also research centers established by provincial or municipal governments. As a part of the reforms, the research institutes now also have to provide at least part of their income. One of the ways for them to generate income is to help manufacturers improve their production processes or to develop their inventions into marketable products. An easy way for Chinese researchers to make some extra money is to assist manufacturers in promoting products. Many write articles about the products that appear in prominent publications; others promote the products at seminars, etc. Those who enjoy national fame may even be featured in television commercials.

Status is not only ascribed to people, but also to buildings, locations, etc. It would be an impossible task to make an exhaustive list of Chinese products that use the Great Wall as their brand name. There are Great Wall cigars, Great Wall wines, Great Wall computers, and Great Wall canned foods. Famous foreign locations, like the Egyptian pyramids, are also popular as brand names in China. In a similar fashion, status is ascribed to a famous brand. This is a trait of Chinese culture that has regularly forced western companies to litigate against Chinese imitators of their brand-name-with-identical-logo packaging. One of the brands suffering most from this "honor" is Coca-Cola. Several colas have emerged and disappeared in China after Coca-Cola's booming success in the country. The most interesting domestic cola product was Shaolin Cola, named for the famous Shaolin temple, the cradle of Shaolin kung fu.

Celebrity endorsements

In the US, a popular way of marketing new products is through celebrity endorsements. In Ireland this is much more rare, and one can count on one hand the number of celebrities advertising products on TV.

This is partly due to the fact that the Irish do not like to be told what to think or buy by people who may see themselves as superior. They tend to be cynical about the motives of the celebrities involved and there is a general mistrust of the rich and social elite. For example, if a successful Irish millionaire recommended driving a certain type of car, the typical reaction would be "It's fine for him…" This reaction reflects the mistrust as to where someone's money came from that is common among the Irish. They treat celebrities differently than Americans do. In fact the Irish refuse to give status openly to stars and are just as likely to react with cynicism as with enthusiasm to the suggestion that they want to be like them.

One exception to this attitude toward celebrities is the Irish attitude toward sports heroes, especially those they can identify with on a personal level. Advertising that has used well-known Irish athletes has had a lot of success in Ireland. Michelle Smith-DeBruin's success in winning three gold medals for swimming in the Atlanta Olympics in 1996 was followed by her brief appearance in a shampoo commercial and in another aimed at encouraging people to speak the Irish language. She inspired a very positive reaction, as an ordinary person who had managed to achieve her dream through her own hard work and, in doing so, had brought success to Ireland. People felt they could connect with her ordinary background and fly with her heroic success.

Sports sponsorship also proved to be a valuable marketing strategy for the auto manufacturers Opel, when they took a risk in sponsoring the Irish soccer team for the World Cup in 1990. In the end the team's success far outstripped everyone's expectations, and soccer's consequent rise in popularity resulted in excellent free advertising for Opel.

In most countries, marketers often reach their targeted consumers by using models in commercials who look like their targets. However since status is ascribed to Caucasians in Japan, they are often used to sell products.

There are three categories of Caucasians used in marketing in Japan. The first is the Caucasian Hollywood star. Jodie Foster has successfully promoted coffee and Harrison Ford, Kirin Beer; Leonardo DiCaprio advertises credit cards and autos. The second category is the stereotypical Caucasian blond who represents ultimate beauty. These models advertise clothes and many other products. The last category is the slightly Japanese-looking Caucasian, who represents ultimate Japanese beauty. These models often promote products such as cosmetics, which the consumers feel need to be made specifically for the Japanese.

Japanese-looking Caucasians are also often used in ads for Japanese banks. Sakura Bank uses a Caucasian model with slightly Japanese features in traditional Japanese settings; they want to attract women since they control household finances. Depending on the product and target, Caucasian models are very effective in sending a message to the consumer.

Koreans are very easily influenced by people with high status, such as experts, gurus, and celebrities, so many companies use such people in marketing campaigns. They can be used for advertisements but also for other forms of publicity. Health experts are frequently used to promote food or body care products. Companies are eager to associate the name of a management guru with their company. The use of local Korean celebrities in advertisements has proven to be very effective. Samsung used Kim Won-june, a 19-year-old local singer, to promote its teen clothing line, Count Down. Count Down is now extremely popular and Kim Won-june became a national celebrity.

Using celebrities to promote products can also be very successful in Taiwan. Sports celebrities, pop music celebrities, local celebrities, movie celebrities can all be effective. The most important thing is that they symbolize the lifestyle that viewers aspire to.

Although celebrity endorsement is used in the UK, it tends to be rather different than that used in the US. Achievement is admired, but the British tend not to take their heroes too seriously. They may gently make fun of them or show them in a situation where they are laughing at themselves. Examples of this are the advertisements for Walker's crisps (potato chips). Gary Lineker, a well-known soccer player respected for his integrity, is shown adopting a variety of effective but silly disguises in order to cheat other people out of their crisps. The implication is that you'd better watch out, these crisps are so good that anybody might be waiting to steal them. In a recent promotion, empty crisp bags could be exchanged for free books for your local school. The advertisement shows a school headmistress collecting full packets of crisps from children and one boy asks "But why do they have to be full bags, Miss?" "They just do!" she replies. The next shot shows the headmistress taking the crisps into her room, where her double is tied up and struggling. The headmistress with the crisps tears off a mask to reveal Gary Lineker – triumphant in getting the crisps yet again. Some cultures would find it inappropriate to show children being exploited in this way. Some would also find it inappropriate to make fun of a national hero like this.

There are many uses of celebrity endorsements in the US. For example, Michael Jordan has a whole line of Nike athletic wear. The idea, of course, is that if you wear the same shoes as Michael Jordan, you will be able to jump as high as he can on the basketball court. This type of marketing is particularly effective if you are appealing to younger consumers; they are more likely to tell their mothers that they want Wheaties (an athlete-endorsed breakfast cereal) if they have seen Michael Jordan eating them for breakfast on TV. Young Americans are often easily convinced that if they wear the same clothes or eat the same foods, they will be able to achieve the same level of greatness.

Measurable results

Many UK companies, like American ones, test their products to show how well they perform. Advertisements then use the results of the test. For instance, a major cat food manufacturer states: "Of those who expressed a preference, nine out of ten cat owners said their cats preferred [our brand]." This emphasis on measurable results is common in the UK and seems to be effective. It is also used when marketing services. Individuals applying for work are also encouraged to quantify their achievements on their curriculum vitae (résumés). Sometimes these achievements are stated in an individualistic way, as if other people were not involved in their accomplishments.

Senior–junior relationships

The importance of age and experience in relationships cannot be overstated. In ascribed-status cultures, status is ascribed to anyone who is older or who has entered a university or company before someone else. It is accepted that the older person is wiser and always deserves respect. In the university and company settings, there are even special words to describe this relationship. The Japanese consider people who enter before them to be *senpai* and all those after them to be *koohai*. The decisions made by *senpai* are respected and adhered to by koohai even if there is strong disagreement. In addition the Japanese are expected to learn from their *senpai* and are therefore not promoted above them.

A recent advertisement for eye-drops shows a young worker squinting at the computer screen and rubbing his eyes. An older-looking man offers him eye-drops with an "I know what he needs" look on his face. In the last shot the younger man smiles, and the older man puts his arm around the younger man's shoulder. The older man has passed on his knowledge to the younger worker. A marketer could ruin the image of a product if it is promoted in a way that indicates disrespect for an older person or senpai.

Corporate image

Building a strong corporate image is an important marketing tool. The status and prestige of a company influences the buying decisions of customers. Koreans tend to be very brand loyal, and brand image is extremely important. Sony, IBM, Motorola, Samsung, Calvin Klein, and Gucci are examples of strong corporate brand images. The image of quality is often more important in terms of influencing buying decisions than the price of the product. The press can help tremendously in building a good corporate image in Korea. It is a good idea for top managers to establish some informal contacts with journalists and to involve the press in PR campaigns. Sponsoring big events and being visible at them as a company is also very effective.

Cook like a professional chef

In countries that place high value on achievement, advertising often involves some kind of endorsement. The implication is that if you buy a product you will be as good as the high-achieving person who is endorsing it. For example, an advertisement for pans in a recent woman's magazine in the UK read: "Designed by professionals, used by the UK's top professional chefs such as [two top chefs named] and now exclusively available to you. Cook like a professional chef for just four instalments of £49.99. Impress your friends with this completely new 11-piece range of professional stainless steel cookware as used by BBC's Food and Drink and the Carlton Food Network."

Reconciling achievement and ascription

A French project does not get underway solely because it is self-sustaining and will ultimately generate income, but because it is felt to be important for the hegemony of the firm. Typically French firms can easily develop large and complex projects if their top management feels they are important – regardless of the return on investment. This could be referred to as the TGV syndrome (TGV stands for Train à Grande Vitesse, the "train with great speed" developed by SNCF, the French railway company, as a matter of national priority). The TGV is an interesting example because everyone agrees that the result has been worthwhile. However, for the people involved in the project, building the thing – whatever the cost – was far more important than creating a self-sustaining activity. As it so happens, the TGV is now also profitable in commercial terms, but financial profit was not its first objective or priority. *Investment à fond perdue*, along these lines, is typical of French culture.

In practice, most French projects need a patron to get off the ground. The project will continue, as long as le patron, the boss, is happy; which means as long as the boss feels the project is necessary. Again, to the British or Americans, this can sound like disguised nepotism, but it is in fact the symptom of a truly different way of operating. The relationship between superior and subordinate is closer to feudalism; you have my blessing to do whatever you want, and I have your support if I need it.

Both the TGV and the supersonic airliner Concorde have incurred substantial financial losses and, by British or American standards, may not be regarded as fine achievements but as commercial failures. Yet the French admire state of the art technology and ascribe status to it. Furthermore, since accountability is difficult to define in terms of specific results, no one seems to have looked closely at the financial figures. An entire project might cost far more than can be paid back in thirty years, and it is often unclear whether the original investment will ever be recouped.

All great projects of this kind have a patron in the government and represent brilliant engineering, a work of art and science. They are supported by a relationship of trust (*confiance*), or rather mutual confidence between the sponsor and the executor. This relationship is mostly established based on ascribed competence, which is measured in terms of Grande École background, previous post, and general opinion rather than demonstrable results.

What is it worth to France to invest so heavily in infrastructure and be Europe's major transportation hub? Does the payoff include

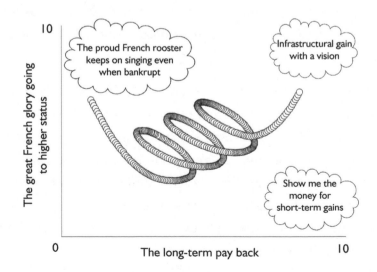

Figure 3.2 From "catastrophe" to "gloire"

less automobile congestion, faster trunk roads, cheaper exports, involved investments, fuel saving, and national reputation? The truth is that the payback from better infrastructure is almost incalculably large and isn't well represented by ticket sales, but by what the alternatives would cost. After all is said and done, even the Concorde, losing as it did $40 a minute whilst flying, may well have advanced aeronautics and, in that sense, was worthwhile (Figure 3.2).

THE DILEMMA BETWEEN INTERNAL AND EXTERNAL CONTROL

The sixth dimension of culture in our model concerns the meaning people assign to their natural environment. Does a culture try to control or dominate nature, or submit to it?

Before the fifteenth century in Europe, nature was seen as an organism. People believed that nature – the environment – determined what human beings needed to do, that nature controlled them, rather than the reverse. With the Renaissance this organic view became mechanistic. Leonardo da Vinci depicted nature as a machine; if you can do that, then you begin to realize that pushing in one place causes a reaction in another. And so the idea that nature could be controlled developed. This is a mechanistic view, that the environment is something out there that we can control.

In cultures in which an organic view of nature dominates individuals appear to direct their actions outwards, toward others. Their focus is on the environment rather than themselves. This is known as external control. Those people who have a mechanistic view of nature have, in addition to the belief that man can dominate the environment, a tendency to take themselves as the point of departure for determining any course of action. This is known as internal

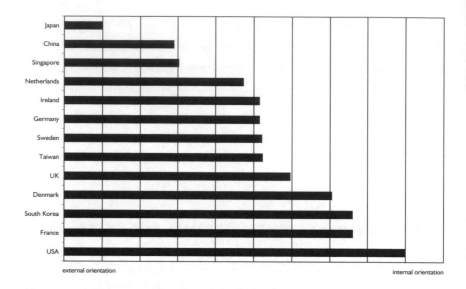

external orientation   internal orientation

Figure 3.3 Relative degree of internal–external control for a number of selected countries

control, and Figure 3.3 shows the relative orientation of a number of countries on this dimension.

The main issue with this dilemma is to connect the internally controlled culture of technology push (selling what we can make) with the externally controlled world of market pull (making what we can sell). Here's an example.

Renault planned to have one of its models "speak" to its customers. The company hired THT to find out how the car was supposed to speak to its driver. Should it say "You need to put gas in the car soon" in a feminine voice or in a masculine voice? Should a matter-of-fact tone or a cautionary one be used? The answer Renault got was unexpected: Drivers didn't want the car to speak to them at all. They didn't want to be "outsmarted" by a car; the driver was supposed to be the intelligent one, the one in control. Rather than having the car tell them when the gas was low, the drivers wanted direct, simple access to the information when they needed it. A digital gauge did not meet this need because drivers found the information hard to read and process quickly. They preferred having a simple, visual representation of how much gas they had left in the tank. This finding was confirmed in research conducted by Volvo. According to them: "The instruments on the interior of a Volvo are designed ergonomically. They appeal to the eye; they also have analog dials, not digital displays. Research has convinced us that drivers feel more comfortable with familiar analog dials than with digital readouts." Both Volvo and Renault have discovered the correct way to communicate fuel status to customers: through a visual gauge.

In earlier publications we have suggested that the most important tension facing marketers is the dilemma between this orientation to the internal or the external world. This antagonism becomes even clearer if your organization offers its products or services in an international context. It is quite obvious this orientation on control, or locus of control, is culturally determined. And obviously the solution lies in the connection of this antagonism.

In research at THT we have asked over 60,000 business people to chose from the following propositions:

(a)   *What happens to me is my own doing.*

(b)   *I often feel I cannot take control of the things that happen in my life.*

Let's look at the results across nationalities. Respectively 88% of Israelis, 86% of Norwegians, 82% of Americans and, yes, 76% of the French chose answer "a." On the other extreme – the externally controlled, who take the outside world as their point of departure – we find 67% of Venezuelans and 61% of the Chinese saying that answer "b" applied more to them than answer "a." (The relative orientations shown in Figure 3.3 are based on our internal–external dimension scale, which is computed from a whole series of questions similar to the above.)

Undervaluing these cultural orientations is liable to cause problems in selling products in cultures which marketers do not understand. Let's look at one example.

Americans seem to want everything to be under their control: their lives, their children, their partners, their bodies, their bank accounts, even international politics. The French company Danone, itself also "in control," has seen what results from underestimating this orientation. Their very expensive ads launching their French cheese in the US had absolutely no impact on buying behavior. In their campaign Danone emphasized the delicious smell and sensuousness of the cheese by showing female fingers caressing and pinching it. In France this is routine, determining the maturity of the cheese and used to see if there is some "life" in it. Cheese is allowed to mature outside of the refrigerator, often until it is runny. Conversely for most Americans cheese is associated mainly with the cheeseburger and is wrapped in plastic and kept in the refrigerator. Cheese is only edible if it is pasteurized and very "dead." Danone's ad appeared distasteful, and that was terrible for sales. Eventually Danone launched a campaign where the same cheese was recommended as being good straight from the refrigerator, was seen as well-packed, and was checked in detail.

But is marketing not by its very nature simply the anticipation of the customer's needs and wishes? The customer is king, after all. Not at all! To focus exclusively on customers at the cost of your own values is very dysfunctional. Staff in organizations such as Ritz-Carlton Hotels have understood this. Instead of "Sorry, that is impossible," they will say "I'll see what I can do for you." They have been trained never to say "no," but never to respond with an unconditional "yes" either.

Fons stayed at the Ritz-Carlton in Naples, Florida. His family arrived late at the beach and noticed that all the recliners were occupied. Fons talked to the hotel's beach guard, who said that this was quite normal at that time of the day. "But we've just arrived from the Netherlands where there is little sun," was Fons' immediate response, "and we'd really like to be able to sit outside." The staff member said that no other chairs were available, but asked them just to wait. Five minutes later he returned, together with two colleagues and the luxurious chairs from the hall of the hotel. These were taken to the beach and Fons' family were able to sit in an excellent place close to the sea.

But we cannot draw the conclusion that the employees had been brainwashed by the saying that "the customer always comes first." The obvious conclusion from that point of view is that the staff automatically come second. It concerns the reconciliation of two orientations that are both incorporated in a relationship of high quality. On the one hand, there are the demands of the customer; they pay for service. On the other hand, there is care for the staff; people give a large part of their life to the organization. As an organization you can demand nothing if you fail to look after your people well, and that applies to your customers too. Ritz-Carlton speaks of tough love: "where ladies and gentlemen serve ladies and gentlemen." Quality relationships are both demanding and caring. The more you give for your people and customers, the more demanding you become. If, on the one hand of the dilemma, too much care predominates without reciprocal demands, both customer and employee will go. And if you demand no care the result will be the same. The "customer as king" idea has produced a number of spoilt customers, resulting in a situation where employees do not want to satisfy their demands. In an ideal situation, a customer needs to be looked after well, but in such a way that you can demand some things in return. In this way internal and external orientations are united.

Customer orientation in China and the US

In a cultural environment where a lot of attention is given to outside forces, companies are very interested in finding out what customers want. Manufacturers do their best to make or develop products that fulfill consumer needs. With the recent economic reforms, Chinese companies have been made responsible for their own profit or loss, and this has made them even more consumer oriented. For example, many Chinese manufacturers now conduct R&D activities in close cooperation with customers. Western manufacturers who wish to sell on the Chinese market will also need to be attentive to the needs of consumers and be willing to adapt their products and services to the Chinese market.

The strong Chinese belief in stories plays a significant role in marketing. In China, the company that is the first to introduce a certain product is usually the most successful. One of the main reasons behind this is that such a company can literally construct the market by creating stories or rumors beneficial to its products. These stories are as readily believed by Chinese consumers as facts, especially when the stories have an academic element to them, and they will be used as benchmarks to compare other products. Companies entering the Chinese market later, even with better products, will find it extremely difficult to counter these stories.

The usual practice in America is deviance-correcting feedback. You have an inner-directed purpose. You start to implement it. You get feedback that you are not quite on target. You take corrective action and persevere in your chosen direction.

The outer-directed Japanese proceed differently. They produce a variety of outputs in the expectation that some will be more acceptable than others; hence all deviate from each other. The customers tell you which deviation they prefer and the result is deviance-amplifying feedback, or what Maruyama called "the Second Cybernetic Revolution" (Maruyama, 1963). It is as if you were sailing for America, but chanced on Bermuda and decided to live there instead. Deviance amplification puts emphasis on luck, serendipity, and happenstance.

French hard sell versus meetings of the mind

Hard sell – the direct sales approach of convincing potential clients on the spot – is rare in France. You risk insulting the treasured rationality of French people by forcing them to draw "your" conclusion, not their own. It is best to provide information that clearly points to the conclusion you wish to draw without drawing it yourself. A lack of respect for others' intelligence can cost you dear. "Les Americains sont des grands enfants," or Americans are big children, has been a common saying for a few decades. Don't, for example and as a generalization, remind French people of their childhoods; discipline was strict and (by American standards) humiliation was common, so underestimating intelligence and reducing adults to the status of children is far more perilous than overestimating it.

French audiences like indirectness, especially subtle plays on words. Volvo won a French advertising contest with the picture of a small girl strapped safely in a rear seat, and the caption "Always take care of the future. Especially when the future is behind you." The importance of such humor is that it requires the meeting of minds. It shows a more abstract mindset compared to a pragmatic, down-to-earth, Anglo-American approach.

French culture is full of exclusive clubs, secret joys, private pleasures, and recherché, carefully selected goods. You are never really "in," and if you are accepted in one selected circle, you will be excluded from others. The clash of values between one circle and another is a treasured vein of French humor, as in *La Cage aux Folles*, an internationally successful movie about gay transvestites who accidentally meet moral crusaders.

The Germanic focus on quality

If you want to sell your products in Germany, don't only rely on competing on price. Germans focus on quality even if it means paying more. Many Germans are willing to spend more in exchange for reliability, and there is a general tendency to mistrust the cheaper product.

German companies expect to sell on the basis of quality, as well as on delivery performance and after-sales service. All these aspects imply confidence in the product and the supplier. Moreover, you can control quality and delivery performance of your product, but you can never control your competitors' prices.

Marketing Irishness

An effective food marketing strategy has been to include already popular products as ingredients in creating a new product. For example, a few years ago a whole range of unusual Irish mustards, including ingredients such as Irish whiskey, Guinness, and Irish honey, successfully entered the market. This marketing approach of linking a new product to the reputation of an already successful one reflects the combination of internal and external locus of control that is characteristic of the Irish. It also reflects the Irish synchronous orientation to time, where the life cycle of products does not just include birth, growth, maturity, and death but is a reproductive cycle. Products A and B can "give birth" to product C.

It has often been noted that what the Irish are best at exporting is themselves. This not only refers to emigration, but to "Irishness" in any form. They have been quick to recognise the potential market for Irish goods among foreigners. There are only approximately 3.9 million people living in the Irish Republic itself (a further 1.7 million live in Northern Ireland), but the number of tourists visiting the Republic each year is far greater. If one includes all Irish emigrants and people who identify themselves as being of Irish origin worldwide, then the Irish number about 90 million. This means that there is an extremely large market for specialist products that are associated with being Irish.

One of the things that most people immediately think of when they think of Ireland is the typical Irish pub. For many years Irish pubs have enjoyed success abroad, and the recently formed Irish Pub Company has introduced "traditional" Irish pubs into many major cities around the world. It seems an ironic twist at a time when many of Dublin's traditional pubs are being replaced by more modern (and now smoke-free) European-style bars.

Kaizen: the art of refinement

Japan's major inroads into western markets have come less from products that the culture has originated and more from products that the culture has refined. For example, Ampex, a US Corporation, manufactured the first video recorders, used largely by the TV industry to record programs. It was the Victor Company of Japan and Sony who developed and refined the video recorder for consumer use, much as Canon produced the "home copier" with the changeable drum after Xerox pioneered the office machines.

Refinement and development should not be underestimated. Billions of dollars of investment were needed to get the price of video recorders down to a few hundred dollars and the tape width from an inch to half an inch. It helps to be outer-directed, because this cultural tendency focuses on what customers want. It makes Japanese products user-friendly and perfectly customized. It is in the continuous improvement of products that Japanese companies excel.

Trendy and unconventional

Singapore's external orientation leads to the national pastime of "shopping, shopping, shopping." Orchard Road is still a shopper's paradise. Singaporeans always want to be up on the newest trend and it does not matter what that latest trend is. It may be the hottest Japanese designer of the moment, rollerblading, surfing the Web and downloading music, but Singaporeans are up on it.

Singaporean youth culture especially values things that are unconventional. Many companies make use of that fact in their marketing campaigns; they know that if they can present their product as unconventional, it will sell.

The modest approach

A modest approach can be more effective than boasting about the achievements of a product. Volkswagen had a full-page advertisement in Singaporean newspapers in which they mentioned a test done by an auto magazine. In very small print, the ad said that tests had been done comparing the Volkswagen Passat with the BMW 3-series and the Mercedes C-class: "Result – clear victory for the

Passat." In much bigger letters above the advertisement it said "Far be it for us to blow our trumpet."

Korea: buying the latest thing

Koreans like to have the latest thing and tend to buy the newest design or model available on the market. When it comes to trends, they are willing to accept western influence. "Made in the US" or "Made in Italy" can give a product a competitive advantage. American fast food companies such as McDonald's, Kentucky Fried Chicken, and Pizza Hut do very well in Korea. The most successful foreign companies are the ones that manage to combine the image of a foreign brand with some degree of adaptation to local circumstances and preferences.

From copying to innovation and improvement

When the Taiwanese department store Chung Yo started a joint venture with the Japanese Matsuya in 1990, one of Chung Yo's primary goals was to adopt the customer service concept from Japan so as to be a level above the Taiwanese competition. The Japanese did not believe they would be able to do that. However, within a few years Chung Yo was able to show that they had copied and improved the concept of "leaving a deep impression in the heart of the customer."

The Taiwanese shoe industry is a good example of the sequence from copying to learning to innovating that Taiwan has gone through over the past few decades. Taiwan started as a manufacturer of cheap shoes. There are some 5,000, mainly small, companies producing shoes in Taiwan. Nowadays most of the cheap "Made in Taiwan" shoes are actually made in mainland China, where wages are typically only 10 percent of the wages in Taiwan. The fashionable and more expensive (sport) shoes are still made in

Taiwan. As in other industries, this manufacturing is mainly OEM (original equipment manufacturing) for international brands like Nike, Reebok, and Clarks. OEM is characterized by low margins and low risk; the marketing and stock-holding risks are taken by the customer.

The Taiwanese industry entered a third stage at the end of the 1990s; they moved to ODM (original design manufacturing) and OBM (original brand manufacturing). The Taiwanese Footwear Manufacturers' Association coordinates the collection of knowledge from Italian and British shoe manufacturers and designers. Taiwan has an R&D institute for shoe design and manufacturing and sends students abroad to learn the newest technology.

The Taiwanese government actively stimulates innovation through the Taiwan Innovalue Program, which advertises in international publications to show the added value Taiwanese manufacturers give to their products through innovations. The program tries to convey the message that Taiwanese entrepreneurs are strong in "creative imitation." In fact they sometimes understand what an innovation represents better than those who created it, and they are able to use innovations in a creative way for a commercial purpose.

To invent something, to be its author and originator, is associated with high status in an internally-referenced culture like the US; to refine and develop something that was invented elsewhere is less prestigious. Hence, many products that were invented by Americans have been refined and sold by the Japanese, who are more external in their orientation. For the Japanese, the process of refinement has very high cultural prestige and is considered an art in itself. By reconciling the internal and the external approaches, you can get the best of both worlds – a new technology that has been perfected and modified to offer maximum customer satisfaction.

UK loyalty cards

A relatively recent development in the UK is the issuing of loyalty cards to customers in order to encourage them to shop regularly in a particular store. These were initiated by an oil company offering "points" which could be collected when buying gas and then spent in Argos, an unrelated store; previously points and coupons from gas stations could only be exchanged for a limited range of goods like glasses, soup bowls, and model cars. Giving points for Argos was, for many people, just like giving them money. The element of choice appealed to their internal locus of control. Also, for those people driving company cars and doing high mileage, whose gas was paid for by their employer, this was effectively an added bonus. The garages and gas stations in these schemes were able to demonstrate a significant increase in customer loyalty. Loyalty card schemes are now offered by many retailers.

Recently, however, there has been some over-saturation of these cards which has resulted in "choice fatigue." As with any oligopolistic marketplace, an initiative like this works in the short term to provide differentiation, but only until competitors copy the idea – to the point where it then becomes an irritant for the consumer. There are also signs of a more "political" reaction to them, particularly among younger consumers who often see them as a form of privacy invasion.

DILEMMAS ARISING BECAUSE OF DIFFERENT MEANINGS GIVEN TO TIME

People need to coordinate their business activities and so they require some kind of shared expectations about time. In the same way that different cultures have different assumptions about how people relate to the world, they also approach time differently. These dilemmas are about the relative meaning and thereby the impor-tance that cultures give to a number of apects of time. These include how they give meanings to the long versus short term and the past, present, and future. How we think of time has its consequences. Especially important is whether our view of time is sequential – a series of passing events succeeding each other – or whether it is syn-chronic, with past, present, and future all interrelated. In the synchronic view ideas about the future and memories of the past both shape present action. Are you driven by the clock, arriving at the office at 9.00 a.m. because that is the start of the working day, or do you arrive in sufficient time for the first significant event, the first meeting?

When we look at how people organize time across cultures we can see a wide variety of differences. Graphically the two differences can best be explained as shown in Figure 3.4.

Do we view time as sequential or synchronic? Is it based on short-term or long-term interests? And, finally, do we predominantly focus on the future, the present, or the past? These are three basic elements of time that are seen differently through different cultural lenses.

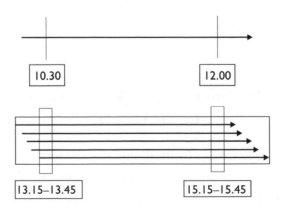

Figure 3.4 Time orientation – sequential/synchronic

With sequential cultures, time is an objective measure of passing increments. The faster you can act and get to the market, the more effective will be your competitiveness. In contrast, synchronous cultures like doing things "just in time," so that present ideas converge on the future. The more synchronous your timing, the more competitive you will be.

In THT's research we have found evidence that cultures have quite different time horizons. On the one hand we know cultures that run from quarter to quarter. Here you can see salespeople dating their sales with the next week's date – because they have already achieved their sales targets for the current period and so this sale can be counted towards the next period's target. Others seem to plan a lot further ahead. They are very effective in reaching far-end goals at the cost of short-term flexibility. Rapaille (2001) has termed the first, short-term, approach "animal time" and the second one "founding time." The American code for time, for example, is an animal one that emphasizes short-termism and the immediate present: just do it, instant gratification, shareholder value, "greed," and the like. Mainland China's approach to possible reunification with the Republic of China (Taiwan) is long-term, over several future generations.

Short-termism

Short-termism is the expression used to describe the pressure by money markets for profits now, in the short term. Every corporation has to balance the harvesting of profits for present use with the need to reinvest earnings back into the business for the long term. Wall Street puts a lot of emphasis on the short term and on ROI (Return on Investment). Equity capital is generally more short term than debt capital. America uses relatively more equity capital while cultures like Germany, Japan, Korea, and Singapore use relatively more debt capital. American financial analysts try to reduce long-term propositions to the short term.

Birth, growth, and maturity of products

American managers tend to see products as going through the same life cycle as people. Hence products are born, go through a phase of rapid growth, then mature, and finally die.

Mature products, like ripe corn, should be harvested before they die. Such products are sometimes called "cash cows." They should be milked for everything they are worth before they near the end of their useful life. What is missing from the metaphor is the reproductive cycle. Products of almost any age can generate new products if they are well cared for. As we saw earlier in this chapter, when we looked at marketing Irishness, Products A and B can "give birth" to Product C. This reproductive metaphor is less common in the US because it requires a synchronous approach to time, and Americans are sequential in their approach. American managers are quick to plan for the death of Product A because it makes room for Product B. This is what is referred to as planned obsolescence.

Time to market

The "time to market" is the period of time taken from the start of the development of a product until it is offered to customers in the marketplace. A variation is "time to break even," or how long it takes to earn enough money to cover expenses. Generally speaking, American managers seek to make this time lapse shorter and shorter. A window of opportunity can close in your face if you are as much as a few weeks late. Even if you are punctual, a competitor may get there faster. For customized goods, the interval between a customer specifying what is wanted and delivery of that product must be as short as possible.

In sequential cultures, most attempts to decrease time to market, or time to break even are based on pushing people and events to move faster. This is the consequence of thinking sequentially. Push equals linear acceleration, going faster. The problem with push strategies is that there is only so much energy available. When A is pushed, B and C become neglected and, moreover, too many different projects all pushed individually end in gridlock.

Pull strategies are popular in Japan. The Japanese start by "thinking backwards" from a future rendezvous with the customer to the pattern of current activities needed to make that rendezvous happen. All the necessary resources are pulled towards that rendezvous so as to synchronize at the customer's site, precisely when needed, or "just in time." Note that these do not arrive too early or too late. If the customer gets behind schedule the rendezvous is rescheduled with extra time used for quality improvements or for another customer. If the supplier gets behind schedule resources are added so that the promised rendezvous is kept. Those who use pull strategies tend to put their focus on long-term effectiveness.

Fast and slow

Because of the monetary value placed on time in the US, companies that have a product that will save people time usually emphasize this feature. One example was a television commercial for Macintosh computers. A snail appears, slowly crawling across the screen. On top of its shell is a Pentium chip. The voiceover narrates a few simple sentences about how slow the Pentium chip is compared to the latest Macintosh chip. Time is considered so valuable in the US that anything that will save people time generally sells. Consequently this is often a feature exploited in advertising.

Life in Taipei is fast paced. Therefore people really enjoy the new communication media; advanced information technology is readily available. Consumers can be reached relatively easily via the Internet, and e-commerce has had a rapid start. The Taiwanese tend to accept new developments in marketing rapidly. The convenience store concept was accepted within a very short time and there was also a very rapid acceptance of supermarkets. In three years supermarkets went from serving 5 percent of the population to serving 50 percent.

In addition, the Taiwanese sometimes seem to work hard mainly to be able to buy the newest things and the latest model of anything and everything. Many worry about these signs of materialism. Possessing newer and better things seems to have become the main goal in life and, these days, progress is synonymous with earning money. The big question associated with the introduction of the two-day weekend in Taiwan is whether the longer weekend will not merely generate more commercial opportunities for the leisure industry.

When relationships are more important than speed

Customer service is an important marketing strategy in Ireland, but efficiency must not entail sacrificing the human relationship. Most Irish people would prefer to wait longer in a queue for friendly service than to be served more quickly but in an impersonal manner. Personal contact is very important for Irish consumers. For that reason doing business in banks and post offices, for example, is generally a pleasant experience in in Ireland in that one is greeted with friendly service. Marketing strategies, which aim to save the consumer time by ruling out the personal touch, have had limited success so far. For example, shopping by mail-order catalog is currently being aggressively pushed at Irish consumers but, despite the busy nature of most people's lives, it has failed to catch on as yet.

If the relationship is to last, then what's the hurry? The French know that it takes time to invest in an enduring relationship. You have to show respect for the client or supplier. You give them time by waiting for them to join you; you do not then use that time in a way that makes you unavailable, should they enter the room. A "readiness to synchronize" must be shown.

She attended to the customer behind me

"I was buying a book at Orly Airport, and the woman at the cash register took my credit card, wrapped my book and then calmly attended to the person behind me in the line. 'Hey,' I said, 'why don't you finish serving me?' She looked at me disdainfully and pointed a polished fingernail at the credit card authorization machine. Sure enough, it had not yet okayed my card, but did so a few seconds later. I signed. I still think she should deal with one person at a time." The origin of the speaker's objection lies in sequential assumptions. Given the delay necessitated by credit card checking, it actually saved time in this instance for the assistant to attend to the person behind and allow the transactions overlap.

"I went into a French travel agency because I needed to get my tickets back to New York changed," said an American manager. "The woman behind the counter amazed me by the number of things she was doing at one time. Another woman had brought in her baby for the agent to admire. She was speaking on the telephone, examining my ticket, checking seat availability, making 'coochy-coo' noises at the baby and talking to the baby's mother, all at the same time. I decided to check my ticket carefully in case she had made mistakes, but she hadn't! 'Next please!' she said, to get me out of the way."

Members of synchronous cultures develop the capacity to "parallel process" their mental activities and are sometimes amazingly adept. This ability is rare among men in sequential cultures. Remember the wisecrack about President Ford: "He has trouble chewing gum and walking at the same time."

While personal service is not always good in France, it is certainly involved. One foreign diner was told "Vous mangez mal, madame," – you eat badly, madame – by her waiter because she had salmon both as an appetizer and as a main dish. She was furious.

In good barbershops, a hairdresser who shares your interest can sometimes attend to you. The mingling of hairdressing with interesting conversation is seen as more important than strict sequence, and you may have to wait a few minutes for the right conversation…

The 24-hour economy

Singapore's time orientation is synchronic. Singaporeans like it when there is always something to do. Singapore is rapidly becoming a 24-hour economy. There are 24-hour food courts, the Singapore port is open 24 hours a day, 365 days a year, and there are 24-hour medical clinics.

Korean companies take a very synchronic approach to marketing. In their efforts to win global market share quickly, Korean companies tend to start several marketing efforts at the same time. Daewoo expresses this attitude in the slogan: "It's a big world, and there's a lot to be done." Park Gun Woo, director of Daewoo Motors Benelux explained his marketing strategy at the Seoul launch of the Korean sales operation in March 2000 by saying "I choose for speed." His goal in the Netherlands was winning market share rapidly, and he did this by spending a large budget on making the name Daewoo known. He accomplished this by sponsoring a Dutch soccer league team, for example, and by giving away 200 cars to people who would act as test drivers. He was later cited in the Dutch national press as saying that working extremely hard, seven days a week, and expecting others in the company to do the same was "part of the deal" in his company.

In Taiwan shops are open long hours every day of the week. Shopping is a social activity to meet friends, to go with the whole family, to eat, or to go to the cinema. Shopping malls that include recreational facilities are preferred. Theme parks that combine different activities such as Leofoo Village are also quite successful. This is a big amusement park just South of Taipei City, containing a zoo and a safari park, Wild West sections, and an Arabian Kingdom.

For routine activities, such as weekly grocery shopping, British people, like their American counterparts, prefer fast, efficient service. They expect that if lines build up at supermarket checkouts, more cashiers will appear to open other tills and reduce the lines. They are likely to get angry if someone "jumps the line" by moving in ahead of them. Some supermarkets have a "10 items only" lane and if someone goes through with more items they are likely to be reprimanded for doing so. These two examples are probably a combination of the value placed on time and the universalist preoccupation with rules.

History and advertising in China

The Chinese reverence for companies with long histories is reflected in the marketplace. As awareness of the power of the consumer is growing, more and more Chinese organizations are conducting market research to find out about consumer preferences. In most sectors, the fame of the brand is indicated as the single most important factor that influences Chinese consumers. A three-year-old IBM computer would be preferred to a brand new clone, even by buyers who are familiar with the speed of development of computer technology.

Reconciling sequential and synchronic

It is striking how well effective leaders can plan sequentially but also have a strongly developed competence to stimulate parallel processes. We all know "just in time" management as the process in which processes are synchronized to speed up the sequence. Furthermore an effective international marketing campaign will also integrate short and long term and past, present, and future.

Let's look at an example. The Heineken tradition is great but at the same time the seeds for decay are in it. For over a hundred years Heineken has appealed to people's taste. Historically the company's reputation has been maintained at great cost. Recently, however, many special beers have entered the market jeopardizing the established names in the trade. Heineken's approach to innovation was cautious. The company had to maintain the consistency of Heineken's attraction; they had to change to remain consistent. One way of innovating in a way that's not dangerous is to clear a space for a totally new approach, which is separate from existing success and will not endanger it.

Heineken's dilemma was the tension between tradition and stability, and the elusive nature of its success. The company very cleverly embarked on two forms of innovation, which are relatively safe. Process innovation searches for better and newer means of creating the same result and reserving a "safe area for creation." Product innovation allows new drink products to be invented from scratch, without involving Heineken's premium product in these experiments. Heineken's reconciliation of this dilemma is shown in Figure 3.5.

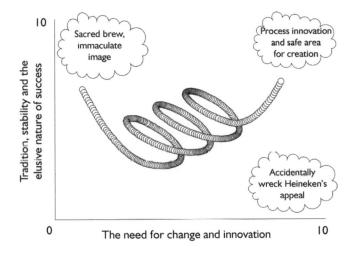

Figure 3.5 Don't mess with success

In conclusion, our new marketing paradigm requires a mindset that reconciles the continuing dilemmas that can arise from all of the cultural dimensions we have looked at in both here and in Chapter 2. Today's successful marketing is the result of linking learning effort across each dimension with the contrasting orientations and viewpoints.

CHAPTER 4

Marketing research across cultures

I n this chapter we'll consider both the methodological and practical issues in undertaking marketing and market research across cultures. Some further details of our research methods and techniques are also given in the Appendix.

Market research should be distinguished from marketing research. The former is mainly concerned with the task of quantifying the size and nature of markets and buyer behavior whereas the latter is broader and encompasses all aspects of the company's marketing activities.

THE MEASUREMENT OF MEANING

The predominant methodologies that appear in the extant literature on market research are rarely equipped to go beyond any "first order" interpretation, i.e., interpretations of the dominant culture of the researcher. Much of what cross-cultural scholars have suggested in the last 30 years has been consistently ignored. Furthermore, the dominant school of thought derives from psychology. In an attempt to be "scientific," the main conclusions seek to claim universal psychological motivations explaining the behavior of consumers despite the fact that cultures are particular (Callebout et al., 2000; 2003).

All research outcomes are dependent on the methodological stance taken and this is no less so than in international market research. While the physical scientist alone defines a set of variables to be observed, in social sciences in general and in market research in particular, the observational field usually starts with the subject's preselected and preinterpreted cultural meanings. As Cicourel so profoundly says: "The social scientist must attend to the meaning structures employed by the actors of the scene he [sic] wishes to observe and describe, while simultaneously translating such meaning structures into constructs consistent with his theoretical interests" (Cicourel, 1964).

Therefore precise measurement of social action, so fundamental in international market research, rests on the study of the problem of meaning and begins with reference to the commonsense world of everyday life: "Measurement presupposes a banded network of shared meanings, i.e., a theory of culture" (ibid.).

In fact the main criticism to be made of market research is that it is often methodologically flawed, even in domestic markets. It is frequently too simplistic, looking for easy answers. Rarely is there any real ontological quest for the truth in spite of the millions of dollars spent as a result of the data gathered. Even at the basic level, there is a fundamental methodological tenet that market researchers can never know the questions that should really be asked in their surveys. Most just make them up; if you knew what questions to ask, you wouldn't need to conduct the survey in the first place. When extended to international market activity, the methodological problems become even worse.

Kant, in *The Critique of Pure Reason* (1781), examined the bases of human knowledge and created an individual epistemology. Like earlier philosophers, Kant differentiated modes of thinking into analytic and synthetic propositions. An analytic proposition is one in which the predicate is contained in the subject so that the truth is self-evident. But he pointed out that synthetic propositions are those that cannot be arrived at by pure analysis and can only result from experience of the world. Thereby objects of themselves have no existence, and space and time exist only as part of the mind, as "intuitions" by which perceptions are measured and judged. More narrowly, within metaphysics, idealism is the view that all consumer products are mind-dependent and can have no existence apart from a mind that is conscious of them. Metaphysical realism has traditionally led to epistemological skepticism, the doctrine that knowledge of reality is impossible, and has thereby provided an important motivation for theories of idealism, which contend that reality is mind-dependent and that true knowledge of reality is gained by relying upon a spiritual or conscious source. This may seem very theoretical, but again it reinforces our thesis that culture is a system of shared meaning. Market research must understand the system of meaning in the culture in which it is collecting and interpreting data.

Primary market research usually involves:

- Survey research: typically to judge reaction to a proposed product, awareness of brand name, or to assess attitudes.
- Observation: has the advantage of no interaction with the subject. This could involve observing whether people turn left or right when they enter a store or leave a car park – so as to help with positioning and location planning.
- Experimentation: This can involve tasting panels, or test marketing, or special promotions and discounts for limited periods.

In any survey research or in some experimentation, the observer is part of the field of action. As such, the observer and the instruments used to measure a group of actors' set of shared meaning, act as a "grid" or "filter" for the definition of certain forms of data. The world of the observable is not simply out there to be described and measured, but the observer and the measurement system can influence what is out there.

Ideally we sould seek a situation in which measurement is entirely free from error, a situation, however, which cannot be achieved

(Campbell, 1928). If we only accepted "true measures," those free from error, market research would be impossible to conduct: "If the chance of error alone were the sole basis for evaluating methods of inference, then we would never reach any decision, but merely keep increasing the sample size indefinitely" (Churchman, 1948).

We can distinguish between three major sources of error that can frequently occur in international market research.

- One is related to the sampling procedure both within and between cultures.

- A second source of error is inherent to the measuring instruments used for the collection of data. It focuses in particular on the validity and reliability of instruments used in international market research. This source of error can be minimized through the design of the questionnaires and via the administration of validating interviews.

- A third source of error accompanies the administration of the measurement instrument. It manifests from the fact that the responses of the subjects under investigation are influenced by the way the study is presented to them in terms of its purpose and possible consequences.

Sampling errors

One of the problems with cross-cultural market research is sampling. The sampling method and criteria for selection depends largely on the type of research that is being conducted (Campbell and Stanley, 1966; Berry, 1980). Two main strategies are recognized as satisfying the requirements that are intrinsic to the complex procedure of comparing market characteristics in two or more nations or cultures.

The first uses samples that are broad and representative of the culture involved (Smelser, 1976). In this case different social levels of the culture are represented and different characteristics of people are included, such as age, sex, education, occupation, etc. According to this "broad sample strategy" (Roberts, 1977), as many variables as possible are to be taken into account, because otherwise cultural influences cannot be singled out from other determinants. This type of comparison is often used in public opinion polls which, on the basis of representative samples of natural populations, try to randomize out the subcultural differences.

In international market research, one can also choose a second matching strategy. This is based on the use of narrow samples, in which information is drawn from similar subcultures in different countries. Samples are matched which are intended to be functionally equivalent (Hofstede, 1980). In other words they resemble one another sufficiently well for purposes of analysis – with respect to certain definitional criteria. The logic behind this "method of controlled comparison" is that selecting cases that resemble one another In significant respects can control for potential sources of variation (Walton, 1973).

To maximize the functional equivalence, one needs to include only a few specific types of functions in the narrow sample, e.g., professional staff or housewives. This type of matching allows one to observe the effect of the type of function on the differences found in the various other dimensions between the participating cultures (Smelser, 1976). It is, however, very important that in the sampling procedures attention is given to the fact that the specific functions and positions of the group involved is analyzed in the context of the larger society in which they operate. Too many easy assumptions have been made about the comparability of functionally equivalent samples; for example, the role and status of working women is quite different in different cultures. This might have a significant influence on the conclusions drawn from the results of inquiry. Note that in some cultures, the matching sample may not even exist. How could we compare the reasons for buying certain things expressed by senior female managers in the west with the reasons given by senior female managers in the United Arab Emirates? The equivalent role just is not there.

Research instruments in international market research

Even national market research itself has many complexities. It is all aimed at reading the mind of the (prospective) client: a difficult job that increases dramatically when you try to go beyond national boundaries. Since the simultaneous launch of products and services is becoming increasingly popular, market research across cultures is becoming more frequent. And cross-cultural differences in this type of research cause similar dilemmas to the ones a researcher is facing in general cross-cultural research. Most dilemmas occur in the area of validity and reliability of the instruments in use – ranging from interviews to questionnaires. In-depth, unstructured, interactionist interviews may give results that are valid (that is, closer to the truth for the individual interviewee) but not reliable; that is to say that the next interviewee will be likely to provide a different range of insights. Survey questionnaires may produce results that are consistent (i.e., reliable) but that are not necessarily true. Thus, as considered below, the researcher is also faced with a fundamental dilemma – to reconcile truth with generalizability.

Cross-cultural validity

Validity has generally been defined as the quality that indicates the degree to which an instrument measures the construct under investigation (Bohrnstedt, 1970). To achieve this you first need to develop an insight into the cross-cultural environment before being able to formulate the objectives of research. For example, multi-local research raises some quite different challenges from global market research. In the former you should focus on deciphering the local particularities of the product in the mind of the local user, while in a global environment the focus is much more on finding similarities in users and products. The objective of the research also changes dramatically, whether you want to find out what kind of advertising campaign needs to be launched or what kind of features the product should offer. Obviously the complexity increases significantly once cultural boundaries are crossed in all areas of validity, in particular when socio-cultural and psychological factors influence the attitude of a particular group.

We can distinguish four levels of cross-cultural validity (Douglas and Craig, 1983):

- construct validity
- content validity
- sample validity, and
- instrument validity

Let's examine the first two in some detail.

Construct validity

This first type of validity, according to the American Psychological Association, "is evaluated by investigating what qualities a test measures, that is, by determining the degree to which certain explanatory concepts or constructs account for performance on the test." It validates the theory underlying the instruments constructed. In fact what is needed are several independent measures of one concept, one construct. In international market research construct validity becomes of utmost importance, in particular when it concerns the validity of *concepts*: The comparison of concepts is crucial in cross-cultural market research. Even if you try to measure and quantify basic concepts such as friendliness, cleanliness, sex appeal, and (dis)satisfaction, you can observe quite different ways in which they are expressed in behavior and experienced by the individual or group.

It is, for example, well known that complaints about a product or service express a feeling of dissatisfaction in almost all cultures. But in some cultures a complaint is only given in the context of a relationship that needs improvement. In other words, the producer gets another chance. The logic is one where you write down clearly what went wrong so that the next time you'll get better service. In other cultures, on the contrary, a complaint is like a farewell letter, something along the lines of: "Let me tell you why I will never buy your products or services again."

Another area of validity is the one around *function*. The equivalence of function is very much overestimated in global market research. According to Frijda and Jahoda (1966) you cannot compare any measurement when similar activities or products play different functions in different societies. Quite often similar functions are assumed across cultures in international research by monocultural research teams. The function of an automobile is quite different across cultures. In some it is purely a mode of transportation while in others status plays a dominant role or it is seen as a vehicle to tour around in. A watch is either predominantly an instrument used to read time, a collector's item, or a fashionable attribute.

Another construct validity check is whether *measurement* equiva-

Different constructs of quality

Most American companies have adopted the Japanese attitude of doing things right the first time. However while Americans pay lip service to the Japanese concept of first-time perfection or zero defects, experience shows that they actually don't want to do it right the first time. Rather there is an attitude based on "no pain, no gain" – you have to learn from your mistakes.

In the auto industry, for example, General Motors found out that selling "perfect" cars with no mistakes decreased the appreciation of their customers significantly. Big jumps in GM's image were made when the small number of mistakes were treated adequately and quickly: "What a great company. When you have a little problem with your car they pick it up, replace it with a new one and the next evening it is brought back. Fixed." The message is clear; the people who had a problem with their cars had a chance to experience how much GM cared.

In a study within AT&T it was revealed that the phrase "total quality control" appealed to Japanese workers, but was deadly for the Americans. None of the managers was interested, so they were asked what they were doing wrong. The program was redesigned, giving managers tasks to do, and they were videotaped failing these tasks. The people who came in talking about "doing it right the first time" and "zero defects" failed again and again, but then learned from their mistakes.

In America "zero defects" means perfection. For the Japanese perfection is attainable; for the Americans, only God can accomplish perfection. The three words "total quality control" represent the most negative combination possible to the American unconscious. So when AT&T stopped copying the Japanese and starting seeking quality the American way – through trial and error – success was imminent. The training program was devised around quality and started with planned failure. Whereas the Japanese would give managers a rule book to study in order to achieve perfection, AT&T developed a process in which initial failure was built in, so the mangers could learn through trial and error to create quality that they would then view as a personal accomplishment.

Companies should not purposefully make products with defects so that they can show customers they care, but they do need to consider another attribute in addition to the quality of the products or service: the quality of the relationship between the product and the customer.

Source: Adapted from Rapaille (2001).

lence has been attained. The very popular Likert scale, for example, gives quite good discrimination within a culture when you score 23% very good, 17% good, 11% moderate, 42% bad and 7% very bad. In France and Germany people tend to score less extreme on scales (Pras and Angelmar, 1978), which could partly be related to differences in the meaning of translated words. In general, however, there is also evidence that in certain cultures, the extremes (very good or very bad) are used only in highly exceptional cases. Research has also shown that US Americans have a tendency to score significantly more positively than their European counterparts. This viewpoint is confirmed in the analysis of THT's workshop reviews over the past 20 years. The confirmation holds true to both monocultural and international sets of participants attending similar workshops. Although the use of scales is notorious across cultures, it can still be applied in line with the pretested instruments available in the past. The problems frequently arise because there are different interpretations of what "strongly (dis)agree" means, for example, or how respondents seem to be repelled or attracted by the word "undecided."

One way to avoid the problems of differences across cultural scale interpretations is to use forced-choice questionnaires. The standardized questions of a fixed-choice questionnaire can furthermore be designed to incorporate the language and cultural meanings inherent in the respondents' perspectives on daily life and in the questioner's own perspective. By using this type of questionnaire you aim at providing solution types of responses in the different cultural settings related to the "inner" attitudinal states of the (group of) people. In fact, such a use of standardized questions with fixed-choice answers, as Cicourel remarks, provides an empirical solution to the problem of meaning by simply avoiding it. The claim that the "inner" states or "meaning structures" somewhat correspond with the actual response patterns can thus be supported by empirical evidence.

From the outset, however, one needs to realize the limitations of any device which is used to measure meaning in market research, including the forced-choice questionnaire. Note that the "forced" character of the responses restricts the possibility that people's perception and interpretation of the items will be problematic and which, by a static conception of role-taking, does not eliminate the problem of situational definition.

An advantage of this type of survey is that it leads itself to translation into numerical representations. Not many more alternatives are open to overcome these limitations than to minimize the number of possible errors of the measurements of meaning. Any type of questionnaire, however, is an instrument with which the observer communicates with the observed. One other important step, therefore, is the careful analysis of the use of language as the symbolic representation of meaning structures.

Language

Many of the instruments developed for researching the market are in English. The dominance of the Anglo-Saxon world in business and marketing makes problems of translation notorious.

The medium of language acts as a "grid" for defining and letting certain forms of information through to the observer. The error that is caused by this "filter," however, can be reduced. In the process of measuring meaning in international market research it is important that both questions and responses need to reflect the respondents' daily world and be couched in the everyday language that they are familiar with. The evoked answers should not be altered by the particular relevance structures under investigation. Therefore, in the construction of a questionnaire you need to take it as fundamental to use commonsense terms as used in everyday life. These might be quite different in different cultures. Obviously in the case of international research, with questions being presented in a variety of cultural settings, the use of this type of everyday language is even more important.

Standard questions administered in different cultural settings might run the risk of being interpreted differently by virtue of linguistic difference (Evin and Bower, 1952). The use of language, however, is not only important in the process of translation. It starts to be important in the design of the original instruments. Is the language carrying the meaning it purports to carry? Is it stated in such a way that it does not allow for various interpretations in different cultures? Does it express situations which might provoke defensive responsiveness?

There are a variety of ways in which major problems of misinterpretation can be avoided. In particular, in high-context cultures the use of short questions or reactions to a word or concept can be very unreliable. The use of stories is a good way of communicating with the respondents, because people tend to think in stories. Bateson (1980) states the case for the primacy of representatives:

> There's a story which I have used before and shall use again: a man wanted to know about mind, not in nature, but in his private large computer. He asked it "Do you compute that you will ever think like a human being?" The machine then set to work to analyze its own computational habits. Finally, the machine printed its answer on a piece of paper, as such machines do. The man ran to get the answer and found, neatly typed, the words: THAT REMINDS ME OF A STORY. A story is a little knot or complex of that species of connectedness which we call relevance. Surely the computer was right. This is indeed how people think.

In the formulation of stories abstract words need to be consistently moved to concrete areas. In doing so the difficulty of achieving equivalent meanings diminishes. In addition, in the design of alternative life situations, it is advised to use those situations that are similarly basic and significant to the potential samples you want to investigate. In doing so the likelihood that a forthcoming translation of it from one language to another will result in a serious alternation of the intended meaning is lessened (Hofstede, 1980). You also need to find samples where the subjects under investigation perform similar activities – thereby sharing common problem areas – which decreases the complexity of the process of achieving this format.

When stories are gathered through questionnaires or through interviews many techniques are available to analyze the meaning of things said. There is software available (words in context) that can sort the essential meanings of what people were trying to say. This software looks at the combination of words and counts the number of words that arise. Obviously lots of extra effort still needs to be put into getting the meaning you want to examine. A multicultural set of analysers can do wonders, in particular by discussing the differences in findings.

Translation

Once these aspects of language are taken into account in your formulations, careful attention needs to be paid to the translation of the questionnaire. Translation problems are notorious. The object of translation – being an important source of error – is to achieve equivalence of meaning, resulting in equivalent interpretations across cultures. A careful translation, followed by a "back-translation" or synchronized by a "parallel translation" does not necessarily dispose of all difficulties (Duijker and Rokkan, 1954). Even between European languages, literal equivalence may result in different connotations, sometimes to the extent of rendering scale items meaningless (Frijda and Jahoda, 1969; Mayer, 1978). Therefore the purpose of translation is to achieve equivalence of concepts and not words. In some cases, however, the utilization of different items of similar intent cannot be avoided, which in turn entails complications when it comes to interpretation. But in types of cross-cultural market research an intuitive judgement is often worth more than an objective standardization (Satori, 1970).

Emic and etic

In the comparative study of societies two approaches are commonly used: the "unique approach" or nomothetic type of study, and the "comparative approach" or ideographic type of study (Frijda and Jahoda, 1969). The choice between the nomothetic or ideographic study approach needs to be made carefully because its specific mode of explanation, its mode of organizing variables, and the research techniques employed needs to best fit the subject matter.

Since Sapir looked at the different types of cross-cultural research in 1932, the discussion around the uniqueness of cultures has not disappeared. On the one hand, there is the "emic" approach, which believes that any culture has an attitude and behavior that is unique to the group. On the other hand is the "etic" approach, focusing on the search for universal attitudes and behaviors across cultures. Special attention, therefore, needs to be paid to finding concepts that are not so peculiar to a single culture or group of cultures that no instance of the concept can be found in other cultures. The comparability of concepts is improved by simultaneously making them more abstract and inclusive.

In this process of climbing and descending the ladder of abstraction, we face a continuous struggle between the "culture-boundedness" of system-specific categories and the "contentlessness" of system-inclusive categories.

So, in addition, in order to achieve the maximum possible equivalence of concepts translators must be as familiar with the context of the material to be translated as they are with the languages concerned. Despite these precautions many unexpected problems may still arise and translations often need to be anthropological rather than literal.

Before presenting any translation to the participating subjects of the research, versions need to be checked by in-culture people or, even better, by professional local researchers. The various versions of all instruments need to be checked on whether all items are conceptually equivalent and well-adapted to the cultures under survey. Back translations may be used, as also may stories and "thick descriptions" rather than short statements, which are more sensitive to a translation of meaning.

Content validity

This type of validity refers to the degree to which the instrument being used represents the concept about which generalizations are to be made. The first step that needs to be made in market research is to optimize the content validity of the instruments by searching the international literature carefully in order to determine how various authors have used the concept (Bohrnstedt, 1970). In this procedure special attention needs to be paid to capturing the various shades of meaning of the concepts under investigation. Series of items need to be constructed, which include each of the substrata of the domain of content, a procedure that the literature refers to as "sampling from a domain of content" (Blalok, 1964). Instruments that measure multidimensional concepts need to be constructed in such a way that those items tap into the subtleties of meaning within each of its dimensions. This exercise is an intellectual version of cluster analysis, as used in statistics.

A final check on validity could be attained by conducting validating interviews using a pair of interviewers from different cultural backgrounds. This needs to be done in order to capture as many shades of meaning as possible.

CROSS-CULTURAL RELIABILITY

While the validity of an instrument reflects the correlations between measures of the same construct when the measures are maximally independent, its reliability concerns the degree of agreement among maximally similar methods. In attitude measurement there are several techniques for evaluating the reliability of a measure. They can be split into three major classes: measures of stability, measures of equivalence, and a measure of discriminant reliability. The first aspect is the measure of stability, or "test–retest" reliability. In order to overcome the limitations of measures of stability, such as the problems of "reactivity," measures of equivalence have turned to become a more and more valid alternative. Discriminant reliability refers to the use of scale scores to distinguish between two or more existing groups in a population.

For the purposes of international market research we need to take the application which gives information about the ability of the instrument to distinguish between two or more groups. This test of the discriminatory power of the instrument under investigation is especially important in cross-cultural research, the validity of which stands or falls by the differences found between the cultures involved.

Problem areas in cross-cultural market data collection

Many scholars have pointed to the difficulties of cross-cultural data gathering, presenting important sources of error in the measurement of meaning (Berrien, 1967; Berry, 1980). However, in international market research there are ways to minimize sources of error that are specifically related to data-gathering in cross-cultural environments. Increasingly you need to become aware of the humble attitude needed.

First effects can be taken to reduce errors in the administration of the questionnaire. In some cultures the use of questionnaires for market research is familiar and laws protect people from the abuse of data gathered in this type of research. In others it is a unique event and, quite frequently, anonymity is questioned at every step. Some developed societies, such as Germany, often question the purpose of research in order to make certain that data and results are used properly. This is even amplified when questionnaires are done orally through, for example, the telephone. Some cultures don't need to know the person on the line; others, however, want to know the individual to whom they are revealing their intimate thoughts about a product.

In the use of a questionnaire the assumption is made that people are individuals with a clear attitude and opinion about a certain product or situation. When THT were doing research in Japan we found that subjects wanted to have a discussion about the question before answering it. Obviously there are individual opinions in Japan, but these are formed after a collective discussion.

In general, clarity about the reasons and purpose of research helps significantly in most cultures. People appreciate getting a better insight into the why and how of the research. Some cultures, however, insist on getting feedback, while others see it as a duty to give their opinions and feedback is not asked for or may even be rejected.

Defensive responsiveness

The defensiveness of respondents is a roadblock across the path of

virtually all research programs that use either the interview or questionnaire technique. It is not at all unusual to encounter defensive
evasiveness relative to some types of questions in groups of respondents or by individuals. For example, inquiries about sexual
relations or religious beliefs might be accepted and answered fully
in one culture, whereas in another they would be considered so
threateningly intrusive that the very asking of them could disrupt
the interviewer–interviewee relationship. Generally, in any survey
research where the investigators become actively involved in generating data, they are, in principle, able to control certain sources of
error. This can be done by informing the participants about:

- The purpose of the research. For what organization is it being
  carried out and what will be done with the end results?
- The role of the investigator. Which organization is the investigator working for and what are the codes of integrity that
  apply?
- The role of the participant. Subjects need to feel secure, for
  example, about their anonymity and privacy, and about the
  anonymity of their answers.

Questionnaires can be designed in ways that reduce the possibility
of their creating some forms of defensive responsiveness. First of all,
in sections which introduce a specific set of questions, interviewers
can remind the subjects of the fact that there are no right or wrong
and no good or bad answers. Secondly, the section on subjects' personal data can be kept for the end of the questionnaire, or even done
separately.

The content of the questions needs to be chosen with the utmost
care. As Guthrie observed, generalized questions referring to a
wide range of similar concrete patterns are a far better means of
minimizing the effects of defensiveness than are particularized

questions (Guthrie, 1971). Even more precautions can be taken without reducing the degree to which one measures meaning. Kluckhohn and Strodtbeck (1961) suggested avoiding questions in areas of behavior where defensiveness might be expected. Third-person phrasing can be used in the written presentation of problematic life situations in order to attain a situation in which interviewees are invited to give their opinions about statements made by third parties. This reduces the possibility of personal identification, which might lead in certain cultures to various forms of defensive responsiveness.

Despite all precautions market researchers will still retain areas where defensive responsiveness might occur in some cultures. It may furthermore be helpful to construct questionnaires where the commonsense content of the messages is such that interpretation is quite invariable to the interpreter (Drever, 1974).

Ethnocentrism

The very idea of cross-cultural market research, we are afraid, reflects most probably a western, universalistic value position. In a dictionary of psychology, ethnocentrism is defined as an "exaggerated tendency to think the characteristics of one's own group or race superior to those of other groups or races." To avoid ethnocentrism in data collection, you should develop instruments for cross-cultural use cross culturally. A way of culturally decentering the data collection methods is to work in multicultural market research teams.

Data analysis

One of the objects of analyses of data coming from market research instruments is to gather essential meaning in the buying behavior of those people researched. In the endeavor of gathering meaning there are basically two ways in which, out of a complex mass of information, one can find underlying relationships: by reflection and by computation. In the design of research instruments reflection on qualitative relationships needs to precede computation.

A process of computation of a quantitative nature follows this reflection on qualitative relationships. The quantitative account includes all that is contained in the corresponding qualitative one, and as such both are necessary, not antithetical or alternative: "Quantities are of qualities, and a measured quality has just the magnitude expressed in its measure… [it is] not a matter of ontology" (Kaplan, 1963).

Statistical analysis of the data

We need to analyze the problematic methodological issues that underlie the type of data treatment applied to the meaning of human behavior. In this type of market research some characteristics of the obtained data need to be analyzed, such as the levels of analysis, within-culture regularities, and the level of measurement.

Level of analysis

In market research data are often collected from individual responses on questionnaires. These data come from individuals within a specific culture, within a specific society. Before analysis, the data needs to be transformed into societal or cultural data through a process of calculation, either from mean values of variables for each location or, in the case of dichotomous variables, from percentages. What we observe here is the existence of two possible levels of analysis: the individual or ideographic level and the societal or nomothetic level, as mentioned in Chapter 2.

Correlation analysis of market data, in which we study the relationship between the meaning of a product and the behavioral orientations of its potential buyers, leaves the following choice (Hofstede, 1980):

- a global correlation between all individuals regardless of the society they are in;
- a number of within-society correlations, one for each society, between those individuals belonging to that society, and
- a between-society correlation, or ecological correlation, based on the mean scores of the variables for each society.

In taking the first alternative of a global correlation between individual scores we disregard the culture from which the individuals are drawn. This aims to explain the variance in the individual scores of the various value orientations. In itself this procedure is quite valuable, but it does no more than analyze the relationship between the individual's "personality" in terms of the individual set of value orientations and conception of the product. It does not reflect on the relationship between the group's set of value orientations, nor its (shared) conception of the product. We should resist the temptation to generalize the findings that result from this procedure to the cultural or ecological level, because in that case we would be trapped in an "individualistic" fallacy or what Hofstede has termed the "reserve ecological fallacy," that is, the "construction of ecological indices from variables correlated at the individual level" (ibid.). It involves inferring relations at higher levels of generality on the basis of observed relations recorded at lower levels (Scheuch, 1966; Smelser, 1976). This type of fallacy is the result of the false assumption that cultures can be treated as individuals, while in fact they cannot: "Cultures are not individuals: they are wholes, and their internal logic cannot be understood in the terms used for personality dynamics of individuals. Ecologic differs from individual logic" (ibid.).

A second alternative statistical treatment that refers to an analysis that results in a number of within-society correlations, one for each society, between those individuals belonging to that society, is of interest from a cultural point of view, but is not to be confused with ecological correlations. A confusion between these two types of correlations is known as the "cultural or ecological fallacy" (Alker, 1966). It is the fallacy "which involves the inference of correlations at the level of individual persons on the basis of correlation among aggregated attributes" (Smelser, 1976). The results of the validity and reliability tests of the questionnaires within and between cultures, therefore, are only applicable for that specific purpose and should not be allowed to be translated into ecological conclusions. For attaining ecological correlations a third alternative statistical treatment has to be executed.

This third alternative, which is referred to as a between-society correlational or ecological analysis, is the major statistical instrument for the treatment of cultural data and thus for international market research. It concerns the relationship of culture and market behaviors that is assumed to occur on the ecological level.

The variables that concern the conception of the product or service on the one hand, and the variables that concern the organization of meaning or culture on the other, are similar to what Lazarsfeld and Menzel referred to as "structural properties" of social units – those properties "which are obtained by performing some or all of the others" (Lazarsfeld and Menzel, 1961). Reference is made to regularities in the meaning a population assigns to a product and to behavioral orientations. It is in the sharing of meaning that we transcend from the individual to the ecological level.

In order to be able to establish ecological indices from collected data of individuals from a society both the conception of products and the various value-orientations are shared by its members. This information can only be achieved by a within-culture analysis.

Within-culture analysis

The analysis of data obtained from the individuals in each specific location gives one the necessary information on which one can determine whether the individuals share – to a certain significant extent – the meaning assigned to the product or service on the one hand, and to value orientations on the other. It refers to "intra-cultural regularities."

Level of measurement

The application of certain statistical techniques not only depends on the nature of the research questions that they are designed to answer, but also on the nature of the data to which they may be applied. The nature of the data determines, to a large extent, the appropriate statistic and the appropriate interpretation of the results. The most basic information in this context of the level of measurement of each of the variables is the data set.

The specific characteristics of measurement in the social sciences are one of the basics on which rests the choice for particular statistical tests out of the numerous correlational analyses that are available. In the scoring or measurement of social variables the social scientist, like the physical scientist, assigns numbers to observations in such a way that the numbers are amenable to analysis by manipulation according to certain rules. The operations that are allowed on a given set of scores are dependent on the level of measurement achieved.

In view of the fact that most instruments used for international market research are aimed at performing ordinal-level measurements – the specific country scores can ultimately be ordered in ranks only – we are committed to the use of available non-parametric statistics. Studies using statistical methods for determining the relationship between quantified variables across cultures are called halogeistic ones. The method we use for this purpose at THT is partial correlational analysis (Robinson, 1950).

UNDERTAKING MARKET RESEARCH WITH ETHNIC MINORITIES

It has been argued that problems have arisen in marketing because a substantial amount of ethnic minority research is conducted with reference to social science theories developed during the 1960s and 70s, when racial and ethnic populations were dramatically different in terms of their numbers, education, income, values, and lifestyles (Williams, 1995). However researchers have more recently identified the need to consider the issue of how to conduct research on ethnicity that overcomes these limitations. The focus of research outputs resulting from this change are geared towards research methods per se rather than helping market researchers involved in marketing to ethnic groups (see, for example, Stanfield, 1993; Stanfield and Dennis, 1993).

Social class has been a method of differentiating buyers among the white population but is more complex when we try to apply this to ethnic minorities, where discrimination in the labor market can often lead to people from those minorities working in lower-level occupations than might be predicted on the basis of their qualifications (Brown, 1992; Phizacklea and Miles 1992; Sly, 1994). Level of educational attainment may provide a better indicator than social class, but Indian, Black African, and Chinese individuals are more likely to have higher educational qualifications than the white population, though they are still more likely to be unemployed (Sills and Desai, 1996).

Qualitative market research with ethnic minorities can also prove problematic. Sills and Desai (1996) describe how difficulties can arise quite simply from language differences or from the use of idioms (in a non-English first language population), let alone from how people participate differently in focus groups or respond to interviews. Some ethnic groups tend not to participate in group discussions at all, for example, or often bring their families.

Many organizations are poorly placed to meet the needs of the ethnic minority market, resulting in the operation of "colorblind" marketing strategies but couched in terms of equality of opportunity for all. Law (1997) suggests that this response is fairly common within organizations and shows that they are not taking the ethnicity issue seriously.

We have sought to explain and demonstrate how our logic extends to a new thinking for international marketing. The constant theme of having to reconcile dilemmas is paramount. Part of the problem is that many professionals will have to unlearn what they have held dear for many years. As world markets have become an oligopoly, the classical approach has been to identify and exaggerate differences. In the past, differentiation was thought to be king. But evidence from our research at THT shows that to achieve true international success, differences should be celebrated and then integrated. As trading in the global village becomes the norm, market planning that can accommodate cross culture becomes mandatory. The approach described here will be an essential component of the marketer's toolkit to trans-nationalization.

We have sought to explore methods and techniques that range from how empirical data can be gathered as a basis for decision making, through market research in general, through to international research in particular. Let's conclude with a serious plea that researchers and practioners alike need to be humble in the measurement of meaning. Otherwise statistics becomes an instrument that closes a scientific system which needs as much openness as possible. In market research we have to go beyond a scientific inquiry into an appreciative inquiry.

Many problems will be encountered in market research Many are very similar to the problems encountered by doing any multicultural research. We should all try to eliminate client versus vendor thinking when dealing with marketing research. These two are not adversaries; both should be working toward the success of the business. The real client is the customer who buys your product.

CHAPTER 5

Branding across cultures

Major brands are under pressure. Kashani asserts that "if they are to survive, a new approach to building brands is needed" (Kashani, 1999). And, we would add, this is even more the case when seeking to transfer a brand identify across cultures.

Branding is about creating and maintaining perceived customer value. It is much more than putting a name on a package, displaying a logo or icon, or paying a movie star a large fee to wave your product in the air. Ideally we should think of a product with better value as being better made, coming with better customer service, and achieving higher performance. Through branding, the manufacturer promises to deliver these positive benefits.

Globalization contributes significantly to the commoditization of any product, as new sources of competitive supply emerge, competitors seek out lower labor costs, or exploit alternative technologies. Branding is also intended to combat this trend by seeking to maintain exclusivity, differentiation, or other forms of uniqueness. In addition we should also give credit to many major brands as indeed being the best products available. Many positive brand reputations are often justified, with high-quality products resulting from contin uous improvement because manufacturers need to keep their branded products ahead.

CULTURES AS PRODUCT ENDORSERS

Solomon, Bamossy and Askegaard (1999) have asked whether we take care to distinguish between Australian or Chilean wine, take pride in Greek feta cheese, go to some length to convince guests that they will like authentic Italian grappa. If we do, then we are like most consumers, who sometimes pay attention to the influence of a product's country of origin and use this when evaluating and choosing products.

At the cognitive level, there are many products where the issue of country of origin adds little or nothing to the buying decision. We may not care, for instance, if a cheap, functional ballpoint pen comes from Taiwan, Hong Kong, or an Eastern European country, because the simple technology is culturally transparent. Any country can make a ballpoint pen. In contrast we would prefer to buy Armani clothes made in Italy rather than the Philippines. A strong brand name can compensate for a country with a weak manufacturing image. Honda has even shipped cars that were assembled in the US back to Japan, so strong is the Japanese belief in the quality of the American-made Honda!

Country of origin tells the consumer something about the product. It is clear that the "made in…" label is important to many consumers. The reaction to this by manufacturers can sometimes be exaggerated; Peter bought an expensive necktie in Italy recently, to discover that the label said that the tie was indeed "made in Italy." But printed on the label were also the words "label made in Taiwan"… As Solomon et al. state, with the rise of patriotism, regionalism, and ethnic identity around the world, multinational regions and individual countries, as well as sponsored export agencies, will continue to promote the positive associations of their countries.

THE MEANING OF BRANDS ACROSS CULTURES

Brands, products, and services are complex systems of meaning. Different issues about different meanings that are given to these facets pervade a variety of cultural dimensions at the same time. In this section we'll combine a variety of dimensions that, in their very unique combination, become an archetype.

Marketing is frequently defined as structured knowledge that we apply to bring goods or services from the producer to the user. Brands are thereby the bridges that link products with users. Products are not the same as brands, although sometimes users may experience them as such. Brands are also simply names; they form a language.

Brands are obviously very closely related to values. Values represented in brands are not "added" but integrated, since all values are differences that rarely add up. Hence all values are dilemmas. Good branding resolves dilemmas by offering consumer solutions.

The smart use of brands seems to have been very lucrative for companies in the last few years. If we observe teenagers' buying patterns, then it is easy to see that the brand is frequently more important than the objective characteristics it represents. Subjective perception is therefore worth quite a lot of money. Interestingly most basic research shows that immigrants and their children buy branded clothing even more frequently than locals. Some research concludes that they are attracted to branded clothing in order to build a bridge between the traditional culture of their parents and the culture in which they must live. Nevertheless, what attracts people to a brand?

There are a many ways to position a brand. Censydiam, a leading market research agency, shows one of the better analyses on their website. Every year they publish their longitudinal study of the positioning of car marques. They use a 2 × 2 matrix, where one axis shows the degree to which emotions are expressed, and the other the degree of social integration (see Figure 5.1). It is splendid to see how the producers of these brands confirm their cultural preference.

The majority of the French and Italian brands are represented on the

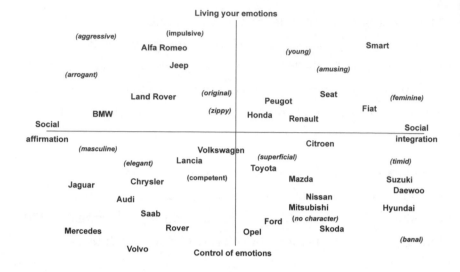

Figure 5.1 Perceptual mapping of car marques

expressive side. On the emotionally more neutral side are British, Swedish, and Japanese cars, with Opel and Ford. It won't astonish anybody that on the side of social differentiation Alfa Romeo, BMW, Jaguar, Mercedes, and Audi occupy the field, whereas on the social integration side Fiat, Suzuki, Nissan, and Daewoo dominate the game. But most interesting is that the international top sellers – Peugeot, Volkswagen, Renault, and Toyota – are all near the cross point of the two axes. Is that because an average or compromising score is rewarding? Is it because they occupy a large playing field of which this score only reflects the average? Or is there something more at play here, something that a 2 × 2 a matrix cannot express well?

THE CHALLENGE FOR BRANDS

Most successful brands pose a problem, dilemma, or anomaly and go on to claim that their product can resolve that dilemma. The more familiar the situation is and the more it engages cultural archetypes or mental programs, the quicker consumers will understand and bring their cultural ideas to bear on the issue. For example, young children and babies are popular symbols of innocence, trusting their caregivers to look after them. Any danger to a child evokes an immediate protective response from witnesses. There would be screams from the street, for instance, were a child to be seen hanging out of a high window anywhere in the world.

It is striking that many successful brands all refer to a tension between two values, and that they credibly claim that their product can reconcile these dilemmas effectively. Let's look at some examples.

When Apple introduced the rainbow apple with a bite out of it as a logo in 1977, it was a clear reference to Eve's apple, the fruit of the tree of knowledge of good and evil. On the one side it referred to the attractiveness of the enormous knowledge and possibilities that the user was given, and on the other it referred to the ability of the user to be able to serve a computer and deal with enormous complexity.

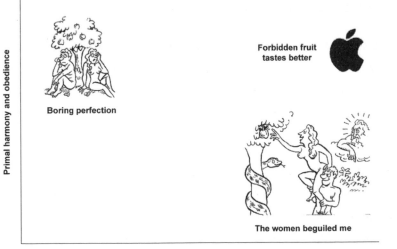

Figure 5.2 Apple: knowing is disobedience

The reconciliation that Apple could offer was that it was possible to do both playfully. This is shown in Figure 5.2.

For a long time MasterCard stood as a model for finding an assessment between the satisfaction of material with spiritual matters, and the social and emotional meanings giving sense to all of this. Their tag line was "There are some things money can't buy."

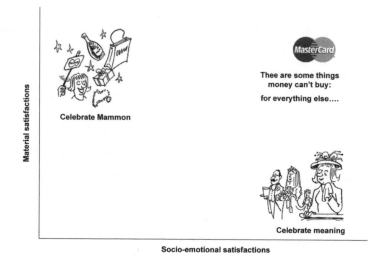

Figure 5.3 Credit cards and meaningful lives

Starbuck was the name Herman Melville gave to his first mate in *Moby Dick*; no one remembers that today as they sip their cappuccinos. Starbucks' coffee can be seen as a reconciliation between the familiar safety of port and adventure on the wild sea of exotic coffees.

The HSBC bank approaches THT's own field. Their humoristic "The World's Local Bank" ad campaign shows – in a particularly consistent manner – all kinds of differences between cultures. The consistent pattern is that one organization (the HSBC Bank, of course) can help you in a multiplicity of cultural misunderstandings.

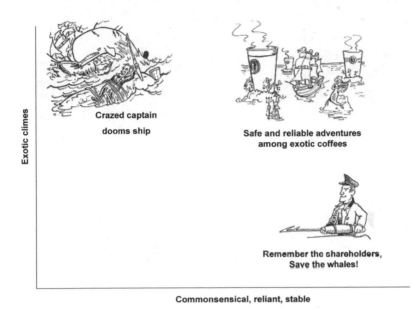

Figure 5.4 Starbucks – safe and exciting exploration

In a prizewinning campaign, which we have already referred to briefly, Volvo has attempted to reconcile speed and security by showing a child in the back of a car accompanied with the copy:

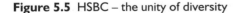

Figure 5.5 HSBC – the unity of diversity

Figure 5.6 Volvo – dangerous road hogs and safe children

"Always take care of the future. Especially when the future is behind you."

Obviously positioning brands on mutually excluding orientations in a 2 × 2 matrix has proven its usefulness, at least as a starting point for analysis. For example, it is striking that the axes can not only be interpreted differently but also expressed differently across several cultures. In the UK, for instance, Stella Artois – a high-status brand – is considered a socially differentiated symbol, whereas in Belgium it is on every street corner, because you can always find a bar with Stella conspicuously displayed. Saab is seen as a mundane family car in Sweden, whereas in the US it is a sign of the fact that you have succeeded in life. Moreover some brands succeed in reconciling seemingly contrary values internationally. Renault has successfully created a quite specific image, applying the slogan of "Créateur d'Automobiles" to a complete range of models. Volkswagen tries to unite youthful dynamics with reliability. Possibly a third dimension is necessary to explain their success, particularly in the way in which they try to reconcile contrary values.

MARKET BELIEFS ABOUT BRANDS

Consumers develop beliefs about companies and their products in the context of their own value systems. Thus some shoppers will go to a "large" store because they believe that there will be more choice as the store is physically large, whereas in reality a small, maybe specialist shop may have a wider range of particular products to select from.

Marketers think that some of these beliefs are fixed and therefore ought to be shared by all cultures. For example, Goldberg et al. (1990) identified that consumers tend to believe that:

- Brands are all the same.
- Generic products are just the same products as brands, but are sold with different labels at a lower price. Quality is the same, except in the case of "seconds."
- The best brands are those with the highest sales. (This produces positive feedback, because the more a marketer can establish a brand the more it will sell because it is selling well…)
- When in doubt, a local or national brand, rather than international one, is a safe purchase.
- Consumers can't save money in stores that always have sales.
- Stores that are just open offer lower prices.
- A good brand or product will sell itself and doesn't need to be pushed constantly. The harder the advertising push/sell, the more the consumer associates this with lower quality.

- When you buy heavily advertised brands, you are paying for the label and not the quality of the product.
- Products from larger companies are cheaper than those from smaller companies – because they can pass on economies of scale to the purchaser.
- Synthetic goods are lower in quality than those made of natural materials.
- New products should be avoided until the price falls from the initial premium and any problems are sorted out.

On this basis, marketers are faced with a series of dilemmas when transmuting their brands across cultures. Do they assume consumers are universalistic and will always follow these beliefs, or do they particularize, perhaps because it is late on the day before a birthday and they must buy a gift before the shops close?

Such basic beliefs by consumers are said to derive from the principle of cognitive consistency, which means that they value harmony in their thoughts and feelings and are motivated to maintain it. This explains why we may hear people saying something like this: "I know I wouldn't like Guinness, which is why I've never tried it."

Consumers can recall constructs from memory more easily if the words used in brand names are composed of words from their more frequently used vocabulary. It is then easier for them to remember these brand names due to the higher levels of awareness the names already have and because of what they evoke. Younger people will often have a different vocabulary from their parent's generation, and that immediately induces some market segmentation.

A second choice is to develop a name that at least sounds like a familiar one or uses similar phonemes to those in the consumers' mother tongue. The name "Coca-Cola" scores well on this model in

China. The almost identical words mean "tastes good and makes you happy" and the Chinese have also given it a nickname of "ke-le," meaning enjoyable, which is easy to remember. Not surprisingly those brand names in China with a western flavor have a higher level of awareness with the younger generation than they do with potential consumers in the urban middle class or those in rural areas. Conversely "Chinese-sounding" brand names have a higher level of awareness among the latter categories of consumers, because they look and sound more familiar.

In 2001, Dong and Helms gave these examples of translations of brand names for Chinese markets:

Translation type	Original	Pronunciation	New meaning	Model	Target market segment
Free	Apple Computers	ping-guo dian-nao	same	neutral	All
Literal	Microsoft	wei-ruan	No meaning	neutral	All
Created meaning	Ford	fu-te	Happy and special	neutral	New rich entrepreneurs, corporate customers
Modified meaning	Head and Shoulders	hai-fei-si	Sea with flying silky hair	Western	All
Modified meaning	Oil of Olay	yu-lan-you	Oil of orchard flower	Chinese	All
Literal, but meaning lost	Kraft	ka-tu	No meaning	Western	Younger generation, urban middle class
Literal, but meaning lost	BMW	bao-ms	Precious horse	Chinese	Rich entrepreneurs

Companies can no longer hide behind the carefully manipulated image of their product brands. Even giants like P&G and Unilever have learned that they must explain themselves to global consumers more effectively. Consumers are more demanding than ever before and competitors are ruthless. Therefore those companies that can reconcile brand names from their original parentage with the cultures of the new markets using these creative translations have to work a lot less hard in communication by heavy advertising. Brand name translation is so much more than simply avoiding any embarrassing faux pas.

But what is important behind this model is that attitudes and meaning are formed in a context and are therefore different in different cultures. For this reason, the consumer tends to infer hidden dimensions in the product or service from tangible or observable attributes. This is why we are keen to tidy the garden, put flowers on the table, and make the bathroom smell nice when we are trying to sell a house, hoping prospective buyers won't notice the terrible traffic noise outside. Carefully washing and polishing a car that hasn't been serviced or maintained for ages is similar.

The key to moving brands across cultures is therefore to reconcile the original attributes that helped establish the brand in the first place with new associations relevant to the value orientations of the new market. Thus in a culture that has a long time horizon and a propensity for the past in terms of the way they give meaning to "time," consumers will form an association between the quality of a brand and the length of time the manufacturer has been in business. In cultures with more of a future orientation, they will tend to form a positive association with new variations of an established brand. In other words, purchasers tend to see what they are looking for. But for the brand managers, this is a major challenge: to try to influence these basic beliefs. The dilemma is between the changes required for the new market versus keeping the original brand image.

It is interesting that the categorization of products has strategic significance here. How a product is grouped determines its competition and what criteria prospective purchasers will apply. When trying to estimate the market share of Heineken beer, do we include only other premium beers, or lager, or all beers, or even soft drinks? What is the group of alternatives from which the consumer is making a choice? The concern for the international brand manager is to discover that the brand they are responsible for is not in the same "category" as it is in the original, successful home market. People from low-context cultures tend to see smaller categories – they are more specific about their range of choices. They want a lager beer, so what choice is available to them at the point of purchase? Those from diffuse cultures see the need for a drink as part of a meal or social setting and as an element in the whole scene. They may not start from the perspective of wanting a beer, but wanting something that is complimentary to and reinforces the total situation.

This is easy to misjudge. Pepsi A.M. was an attempt to position this brand as a coffee replacement with consumers who would normally start the day with a cup of coffee. It was so successful that consumers wouldn't drink it at any other time, so the product failed to broaden its market.

Today's brand manager needs a conceptual framework to help navigate this minefield. Macrae and Unclex (1997) propose "brand chartering." They break the problems down to three steps, which we translate into our "language" as the dilemmas that derive from:

- creating and communicating the brand,
- managing the brand system and organization, and
- directing and structuring the brand.

The first process involves eliciting the dilemmas that arise from how certain products can be branded so that they offer value to consumers and customers in a profitable business model. This means understanding issues of meaning from the essence, identity, and heritage of the brand. The basic dilemma is between the meaning communicated by the brand owner and the meaning given by the potential buyer. Differentiating what you have to offer is becoming increasingly difficult as markets become ever more oligopolistic. Many markets – such as that for small family cars – are perceived as converging in attributes by consumers. Being different costs a fortune and requires full risk assessment. Smaller players have an advantage as they can offer distinctiveness.

The second process is also a dilemma. On the one hand we need local adaptations, but we have to retain consistency in the operational management of the brand. How does the international supermarket chain Tesco maintain its commitment to both food and clothing when it has branches in disparate locations? More checkouts may be required in some areas where customers want fast service. In others, such as Eastern Europe, this type of "new" shopping in plentiful stores is a social experience, and talking to your neighbor at the (relatively few) checkouts is part of the pleasure – not the pain – of that experience.

Finally, in structuring the brand, marketers face the dilemma of how far to push the marketing of the end product as the brand. Renault is recognized as a corporate brand, whereas the Clio is advertised as a distinct brand within the portfolio of vehicles. What is the appropriate architecture? And by architecture we can question at the strategy, organizing, and operational levels.

We can also usefully consider the notion of brand archetypes, which we discussed in *Business Across Cultures* in more detail. The aim is to

Pears' Soap

Pears' Soap was one of the longest running brands in marketing history and was named after a London hairdresser, Andrew Pears, who patented the translucent soap bar. The famous "Bubbles" marketing campaign featured a small boy and established Pears as part of everyday life across both sides of the Atlantic.

As Haig recounts (2003), in recent years the mass-produced block of soap has been replaced by liquid products such as shower gels, body washes, and liquid soap. "In pursuit of cleanliness, the soap bar has been deemed unhygienic," Madelaine Bunting wrote in the *Guardian* (October 2001). It is especially seen as such in the US.

In addition, the Pears brand was built on advertising and when such support was taken away, the brand identity lost its meaning and became irrelevant. Brands built on advertising need advertising to sustain them.

The market share fell to only 3 percent and Unilever announced that it was to discontinue the brand in February 2000. The shift to liquid soap products was obviously a factor in the decline of Pears but Unilever held on to their "Dove" soap. This still sells exceptionally well because it is highly differentiated – it is bought not for cleanliness being next to godliness, but for keeping skin soft and beautiful.

develop a perceptual map of how value systems translate into consumer needs, and thereby define characteristics of brand products or brand services that meet these needs. By linking this thinking to our

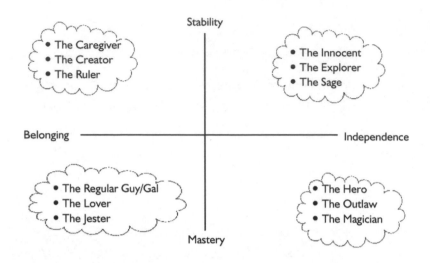

Figure 5.7 Brand archetypes

seven dimension model – described in Chapters 2 and 3 – we can construct a number of typologies by combining the dimensions. For example, if we combine individualism on one axis with challenge and stability on the other, we find a number of archetypes that are shown in Figure 5.7

Each metaphor gives us the origin of the dilemmas that brand managers face. The metaphors in the first category of independents (top right) are the Innocent, the Explorer, and the Sage. All three archetypes in this category are individualistic in nature. The Innocent is universalistic, internally oriented, ascriptive, and past oriented; typical examples are Coke and McDonald's. The introduction of "New Coke" showed what happens if you deviate from the archetype. This was developed with a somewhat sweeter taste to compete more directly with Pepsi; it didn't work. Coca-Cola had to return to classic Coke, as being "the Real Thing."

Successful products also exist in an opposite set of archetypes (shown bottom left for this example). This trio give the customer the impression of "belonging." They all share a communitarian orientation. For instance, the Lover types are often present in cosmetics, fashion, and travel organizations, and refer to sex appeal and beauty. They share an affective, diffuse, and external orientation. Latin brands – such as Yves St Laurent, Diesel, Gucci, and Ferrari – are leading the pack.

In order to be successful internationally with any particular brand marketers need to reconcile contradictions between the archetypes to a higher level. The reconciliation of opposite systems of meaning, or archetypes of brands, achieves success by making them less sensitive to differing cultural interpretations. The aim should be to create an integrated brand.

CHAPTER 6

Franchising across cultures

I n recent decades there has been considerable interest in the internationalization of brands from both practitioners and academics alike. A well-documented body of knowledge now exists covering such themes as the motives or reasons for international expansion, the extent and direction of international activities, flows of know-how, and individual company experience (Quinn and Doherty, 2000). However, we would argue that most of this literature is limited to mainly reflective analysis of success and failures without the development of any robust conceptual framework for informing future practice. We'll therefore extend our dilemma analysis model to franchising as a means of channel integration.

FRANCHISING AS A DISTRIBUTION CHANNEL

The term "franchising" can describe a wide variety of business activities, but the contemporary franchise system commonly in use is referred to as business format franchising. Franchising involves a company with a proven business format (the franchisor) selling the rights for someone else (the franchisee) to use the modus operandum or brand name that has already been established. The franchisee pays license fees or a share of profits for these rights. They may also agree to make purchases of the finished goods (or raw materials) from the franchisor and benefit from the share in bulk buying or the economies of scale in manufacture. The franchisor often undertakes continued advertising support of the brand, although this may have the intent of seeking more franchisees as well as supporting sales for existing franchisees. The advantage is perceived by the franchisee as a low start-up risk by entering a business formula with proven success and exploiting an established corporate name. Training and other support may be offered by the franchisor. Thus franchisees are able to operate their own businesses to exactly the same standards and format as the other units in the franchised chain (Grant, 1985). Franchising grew rapidly in the 1980s in domestic markets, especially for service-based industries such as carpet cleaning, fast food, car hire, and double-glazing.

Franchising also provides companies with a mode of entry to international markets. This approach to internationalization is initially attractive as it provides a means to assess (albeit in an inter-subjective way) anticipated profits versus perceived risk more readily. In order to minimize perceived risk, many organizations have opted for the franchising of their brand. This is based on the premise that the brand will transfer across national borders whilst retaining its associated image for consumers. One of the problems associated with transferring image-based values developed in the country of origin to foreign markets can be addressed by posing the question "Does a brand mean the same to a group of customers in the country where the brand was established as to customers in the new target country?" (Brown and Burt, 1992).

At THT we have worked with BAA (originally British Airports Authority). In their earlier stages of growth they chose to develop airport terminals, with associated extensive retail property development, in countries that were similar to their UK origins in terms of culture. Clearly, companies try to minimize business risk through gaining experience of like markets by organic growth or acquisition rather than higher-risk markets that may be targeted by franchising or joint ventures (Moore et al., 2000). Most of the evidence from the literature tends to support the view that initial markets for franchising are chosen because of their geographical or cultural proximity to the domestic market.

START-UP COSTS

From a business perspective, international franchising appears to offer lower risk than other means of entering overseas markets, because fewer up-front investments are necessary. With increasing political turmoil and the ever-accumulating balance of payment deficit of the Bush administration, franchising looks like an attractive option for any American business wanting to move abroad. Despite these propositions, US franchise systems have been slow and hesitant to expand internationally though they are well established in domestic markets. Many reasons may account for this but it is likely that while there were ample growth opportunities at home the imperative to go elsewhere was lacking. Additionally many companies lacked international experience, had limited financial resources, and assessed the risks of operating in foreign markets as being too high (Eroglu, 1992).

The assertive view is that franchising is a bold and imaginative concept and offers perhaps the fastest, most proven technique to introduce commercial methods of distributing goods and services, creating jobs, and encouraging entrepreneurship in countries starved for decades of most of these features of society that are taken for granted in the west. One cannot but be struck by how often franchising, with its familiar components and easily understood principles, serves as a sort of bridge between widely varying cultures, sometimes even where there are ancient rivalries. United by the shared goal of bringing developing countries into the mainstream of the world economy, franchising can be seen as a tool to use in reaching that goal. And this recognition is a powerful incentive to set aside language, cultural, and historic barriers (Zeidman, 1993).

POLITICAL RISKS

In the immediate aftermath of the 9/11 attacks, symbols of America became targets all over the world. As the most recognized American icons, franchises were high on the hit list of those protesting against the bombing campaign in Afghanistan and later the war in Iraq. The franchised operations were a representation of the American Way. In Karachi, crowds chanting "Death to America" made their way through the streets of Pakistan's largest city and, when turned away at the US consulate, headed straight for one of the 18 Kentucky Fried Chicken units and set it alight. In Indonesia, home of the world's largest Muslim population, three KFCs were looted. Similar actions and boycotts of American products spread well beyond Muslim countries, too.

Consider the widespread problems faced by McDonald's – a pipe bomb in Istanbul; a bombing in Xian, China; a revelation the following July that militants arrested for a bomb attack on the US consulate in Karachi had also been planning to bomb McDonald's; a bombing of a franchised unit in a suburb of Beirut; another blown up in Moscow in October, 2002; one torched in Riyadh, Saudi Arabia the following month; three people killed at a McDonald's at an eastern Indonesian town on the occasion of the breaking of the Ramadan fast. Indeed, since 1990, franchises have been bombed or burned by various groups in France, Belgium, Mexico, Britain, Chile, Serbia, Colombia, South Africa, Turkey, and Greece. The most recent attack to the date of writing, following the beginning of the Iraq war, wounded five in a suburban store in Beirut. Such actions were unlikely to have been considered at the risk assessment planning stage when franchising in these countries was being evaluated.

DILEMMAS OF FRANCHISING

Franchising that seeks to minimize risks and optimize profits is faced with a number of tensions that need to be reconciled. Again we can see the importance of the global versus local brand image, control versus independency, and, finally, focused versus broad brands.

Franchising dilemma 1: global versus local brand image

For many franchisers, the solution has long been obvious: just fade into the landscape. KFC is as good an illustration as one can find. In Japan it sells tempura crispy strips, in Northern England it stresses gravy and potatoes, in Thailand it offers fresh rice with soy or sweet chilli sauce, in Holland it makes a potato and onion croquette, in France it sells pastries alongside the chicken, and in China the chicken gets spicier the further inland you travel.

McDonald's also continues to adapt. There is a meat-free McNistisima menu for the fasting Greek Orthodox in Cyprus, a McRye burger in Finland, a McNifirca burger in Argentina, a kosher McDonald's in Israel, and a McKroket in the Netherlands. Consider the latest fast-food sensation in Kuwait City: the McArabia, an "Islamized" product on Arabic flat bread and served in a restaurant described by the local marketing director, without a trace of irony, as "the mother of all stores."

When is your pizza hot?

"I like my pizza when it is hot," declared Dr Hashem H. Al-Refaei, one of our Arab PhD students at THT.

A western Pizza Hut manager thought that this could (only) mean that he liked it either when it was just out of the oven or when it was spicy. But a Pizza Hut manager from the UAE understood the subtlety of localized meaning. Hashem had meant "I like a pizza when the *weather* is hot."

This localized adjustment to a menu is a visible manifestation of a more profound strategy: "multi-localism" – what we might call "democratizing globalization," so that people everywhere feel some stake in how it impacts on their lives. Has McDonald's packaged itself to be a "multi-local" company by insisting on a high degree of local ownership, or is it just a dictat from HQ insisting on local menus? Poland has emerged as one of the largest regional suppliers of meat, potatoes, and bread for McDonald's in central Europe. The company is gradually moving from local sourcing of its raw materials to regional and now to global sourcing; every sesame seed on every McDonald's bun in the world comes from Mexico. Friedman asserts that "people will only take so much of 'globalization,' to the extent that companies with a US origin will only be successful through being multi-local, by integrating around the globe economically, without people feeling that they are being culturally assaulted" (Friedman, 2000).

The Friedman thesis ("No two countries that both have a McDonald's have ever fought a war against each other") is obviously no longer technically accurate, but the underlying construct still deserves attention. What Friedman fails to recognize is that globalization does not have to be an all-or-nothing proposition. Let's not forget the economic and social benefits that franchising can offer countries: much needed foreign investment, products that are in demand, entrepreneurial opportunities, the combination of local and regional sourcing, and the culture of customer service and reliable operations, which indigenous operations will surely emulate.

The point is that the franchise system has become far more than just a familiar brand name in these countries; its effects extend well beyond those enjoyed by franchisees and their customers. But being a local brand everywhere is not enough. Information needs to feed back into the main centralized system to generate a truly transnational approach.

Lets see how McDonald's has reconciled this first basic dilemma of franchising its core brand.

Reconciling centralized commonalities with local, decentralized variations

This dilemma that McDonald's demonstrates so clearly is the increasing variance in local tastes and supplies, especially in economies recently rocked by currency crises and economic turbulence. Not only is food flavored differently in different places but supplies can also fluctuate in price, so that substituting domestic rice for imported potatoes is not just preferred by customers but may also be cheaper.

As McDonald's brands expand internationally it becomes increasingly important for indigenous managers to make decisions based on local knowledge. It may be a relatively "small" matter, like adding garlic or soy sauce, but this makes all the difference in satisfying local palates and would be difficult, if not impossible, to identify or dictate from HQ. McDonald's may also mean different things in different lands; a quick, family meal for travelers on a US interstate, an unusual guarantee of quality in Moscow, the cheapest source of protein in Cairo, the least expensive air-conditioned restaurant in Dubai, etc.

Those in the field know things that HQ in Chicago cannot, unless it is well informed – and even then such feedback may lose the subtlety of localized meaning. There is no way that McDonald's HQ can know everything about local tastes in every one of its foreign outlets. Such information is not "hard" but "soft." It's something local managers know because they live in the country and it is largely a question of subjectivity.

In many places, food is highly spiced. Historically this was to disguise the fact that it was not fresh; spices were used as preservatives in the days before refrigeration and gave meat a longer shelf life, especially in hot countries. Even where meat is refrigerated and in perfect condition, the taste for different spices lingers and has now become a culinary art and a local delicacy. As the dilemma in Figure 6.1 indicates, the centralized control needs to be interwoven with the variations of local taste and supply.

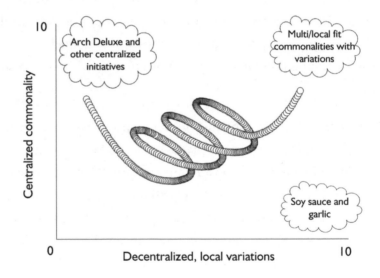

Figure 6.1 Centralized commonalities versus decentralized variances

On the vertical axis is the McDonald's centralized, global system headquartered in Chicago and symbolising the American Way. On the horizontal axis is the decentralized, diverse, localized variations in taste and custom, of which soy sauce and garlic are examples, deliberately chosen as variations unlikely to be widely generalized throughout the system, since these preferences might be seen as a trifle exotic.

Note that both centralized initiatives like Arch Deluxe and decentralized exotica like soy sauce and garlic contribute little to McDonald's profitability – in terms of the cost of provision and the selling price of products dressed with them. What does work is multi-localism, that is, multiple fits into a variety of markets. These may all be based on beef and buns, thereby achieving vast economies of scale. Yet local flavorings and fixings may assure customer acceptability – not only in terms of acceptable taste, but also in terms of local symbolism with which the customer can identify. In short the product is in some respects common and in some respects variant, and this combination assures wider acceptability – and more profits for McDonald's – than would otherwise be the case through sustained and increased sales.

But there is a second issue of equal or greater importance. McDonald's is also in search of new product ideas and these may originate anywhere. The company has become deservedly famous by promulgating and spreading universal rules for global fast food outlets. When you discover some effective rules for satisfying customers it is best to operationalize these quickly, before your competitors do so, and achieve scale advantages. (In Boston Consulting parlance this is the "experience effect.") But all rules inevitably run into more and more exceptions, or particular preferences, that the rules have not anticipated. This does not only happen in foreign cultures, although exceptions are more likely and numerous there. It also happens in diverse regions of the US, so that the Egg McMuffin, the McFlurry, etc., originated in particular regions, while new salad dressings were discovered in France.

McDonald's has now made as much money as it can from the "old rules" of hygiene, consistency, economy, and mass marketing. Too many of its competitors are doing the same thing and it is now facing an oligopolistic challenge as a result of its success. All "universal" rules eventually encounter the limits of their universe, beyond which profits fall away quickly. "Hamburgerizing" the world is likely to prove unpopular, especially where American traditions of bland food are perceived to be imposed on spice-using countries.

All universal systems of effective rules and brands need to be renewed. How does this happen? By creating new rules that not only account for traditional customers, but the new, exceptional customers with different preferences who were in danger of going to competitors.

We have to grasp that any particular exception, when it first arises, can become part of a revised rule. Those "fussy" customers in Kyoto, Japan who want something different could be helping to create a new rule for the future. Within perhaps a year, McDonald's could be supplying sushi in all cultures with fish-eating diets.

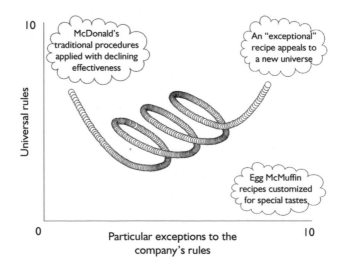

Figure 6.2 McDonald's reconciliation

The way in which McDonald's has reconciled universalism versus particularism, or rules versus exceptions, is shown in Figure 6.2.

Thus activities might be decentralized but the information about the activities is centralized. Mass customization has become the credo of the reconciliation between standardized and universal products and customized and particular adaptations.

But McDonald's is going beyond the theme that "all business is local." The company's executives have said that they are responding to concerns of too much localization. McDonalds is in tune with its decentralized foreign operations where it actively experiments; from there it takes the best local practices and tries to use them in other areas of the world. It then globalizes the best local practices. The result is a transnational organization in which exceptions and rules modify the existing principles.

This evolution is thrown into sharp relief in times of international violence. Consider how McDonald's tries to keep the locals happy in hotbeds of anti-Americanism.

- In France, advertisements featuring cowboys who boast that McDonald's franchises refuse to import American beef "to guarantee maximum hygienic conditions."

- In Serbia, handing out free burgers at rallies and adding a Serbian nationalist cap to the golden arches icon under the slogan "McDonald's is yours."

- In Indonesia, installing large photos of franchise owners making the hadj to Mecca, the staff wearing appropriate clothing on Fridays, and new TV commercials emphasizing local ownership.

- In Saudi Arabia, a Ramadan promotion by the Saudi franchise includes a 30-cent contribution for every Big Mac to the Red

Crescent and to the hospital in Gaza for treatment of Palestinian causalities.

The approach has worked in absorbing and surviving conflicts in the past. But in today's supercharged terrorist atmosphere, will it be effective in the face of the unprecedented scale of the current assault on "Americanism"?

Franchising dilemma 2: control versus independent brand image

In addition to the fast food restaurant business, a diverse range of retail companies have also become aware of the advantages for international expansion that the franchise model may bring. This approach has been adopted not only by niche retailers, for example Benetton, Body Shop, and Yves Rocher, but also other retailers such as Casino (France), GIB (Belgium), and UK stores Marks & Spencer and BHS. Of course this has not been the only mode of expansion for these organizations; they have employed other strategies in parallel with franchising.

Franchising theory is based on the concept of the principal–agent relationship where one party (the principal) delegates work to another (the agent) who performs the work on a day-to-day basis. In the standard theory of the firm, under the divorce of ownership from control, shareholders represent the principals in the relationship and management the agents. In the context of the principal–agent relationship, agency theory highlights the importance of the information transfer process and associated monitoring costs. This information problem arises in the principal–agent relationship because agents, being in day-to-day control of a company, have detailed knowledge of its operations. The principals have neither access to this knowledge, nor, in many cases, the ability to interpret the information, even if access was perfect. Quinn and Doherty contend that the franchisor–franchisee relationship parallels the principal–agent relationship, thus allowing agency theory to provide insights into international retail franchise activity (Quinn and Doherty, 2000).

One of the fundamental aspects of agency theory is information asymmetry. For example it can occur where differing levels of economic development exist between foreign and domestic markets, where there are differences in retail regulation with regard to employment law, planning regulations, and opening hours, and where the internationalizing firm's ability to assess the risk of the foreign venture is limited due to these complexities. As such, the franchisee (the agent) has much more detailed knowledge of operations in the foreign market than the franchisor (principal).

Other examples arise where cultural practices of both consumers and management differ between the home and host countries, where human resource management practices differ, and where the degree to which domestic managers would be exported to run and better monitor the foreign operation varies.

Given the geographical and cultural distance factors, it may be proposed that supporting and maintaining an international franchise network is considered particularly difficult, and that subsequently the cost of providing franchise support is usually higher in an international as opposed to a domestic setting. In an international franchise network, it may be more feasible to use coercive sources of power.

Agency theory, on the other hand, suggests that the control and power base should rest with the franchisor. This is due to the risk of opportunism and moral hazard as a result of the existence of the significant amounts of intangible assets and the potentially high information asymmetry problem that is characteristic of the retail sector in particular. Of the types of franchise agreements that can be chosen, master/area franchising and joint venture franchising offer the retailer the greater amount of control and power. Coupled with the appropriate type of franchise agreement should be a stringently enforced franchise contract to protect the sector-specific intangible assets. However standards may be difficult to maintain in practice.

When the question of international expansion arises, a company should begin by assessing their strengths and weaknesses to determine their preparedness for it. Whether the franchisor completes the assessment or uses outside resources, evaluation should include:

- competitive capabilities in the domestic market,
- motivation for going international,
- commitment of owners and top management to international expansion,
- product readiness for foreign markets,
- skill, knowledge, and resources to expand, and
- experience and training.

This assessment is only a beginning and there is much more to consider before a sound decision can be reached.

Though the domestic system may use a long and well-established support infrastructure that allows reasonable and effective control to manage the system, the cost involved to build the same degree of infrastructure internationally is often exorbitant. By choosing exclusive area development as a format for international expansion, a territory of sufficient scale is awarded so that the franchisee's economic model can fund a professional infrastructure to self-support the business. The franchisee can factor in functional areas such as training, marketing, and purchasing. Using this method, the franchisor provides direct and indirect guidance and support to local professionals.

Thus this type of franchising supports two important tenets of successful international expansion: "Think local–act local," and "build franchisee self-sufficiency." Both tenets lead to high degrees of efficiency and effectiveness for both the franchisee and franchisor. Area development also benefits the franchisor by usually not discounting fees or royalties. The dilemma is illustrated in Figure 6.3.

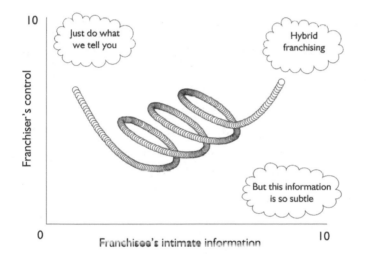

Figure 6.3 The franchisee–franchisor dilemma

Hybrid subfranchising combines the desirable traits of master franchising with key elements of exclusive area development. It awards a large territory to a master franchisee who must first operate a minimum number of outlets and maintain a minimum percent of all operated shops. Additionally, subfranchising activity is limited to exclusive area subdevelopers. The rights for subfranchising are awarded jointly by the franchisor and master franchisee. Subfranchisees are granted exclusive territory with a shop development requirement that exceeds a set minimum. Many of the negatives associated with master franchising are avoided using this method (Evankovich, 2003).

Franchising dilemma 3: exclusivity versus broad brand diffusion

The last dilemma that we will consider has to do with the reconciliation of the need to extend the range of high-status products with the need to keep the scarcity that comes with a high-status brand. Let's start with a case study.

The internationalization of a fashion designer's brand

V-Star is a fashion designer brand that was formally founded in 1986 by its main designer George Vallows. His first set of products was "catwalked" in Milan, New York, and Paris with rave reviews. Although many of his initial products had denim as the major fabric, Vallows extended his portfolio in the early 1990s to evening dress for both sexes, and even to designer bath fashions. After his success in the US, Vallows decided, under pressure from domestic market saturation, to go beyond US borders. He bagan wholesaling in Mexico, Canada, and the UK. With the increasing fame that he had gathered, he knew that the brand "V-Star" was the fundamental source of competitive advantage. In order to finance his growth to exploit the international potential of his brand and to build the capability to distribute, Vallows hired Merrill Lynch to help him go public. In 1996 V-Star was floated on the New York Stock Exchange, with Vallows himself retaining a 46 percent share in his company. The injection of capital allowed him to create a network of flagship stores and shops-in-shops within department stores. Before its stock market listing, V-Star did not operate any outlets outside the US and had wholesale arrangements in only four foreign markets. However, within four years of going public, the number of their company-owned stores rose to over 60 in 21 countries, while the number of wholesale markets rose to 40. The company reported that international markets accounted for almost 85 percent of total sales in 1998. This unprecedented growth should be seen in the context of worldwide sales of premium-priced branded clothing, footwear, perfumery, luggage, and other products – valued at $20 billion in 1996, up from $16 billion in 1992, and with sales of $30 billion in the year 2000.

However the director responsible for international retail operations for V-Star explained how adverse trading reports affected international operations in his company: Change in ownership status and the drive to exploit international opportunities had put what he described as an "unprecedented and intolerable pressure" on many of the companies concerned. With a general recognition that companies, such as Gucci and Donna Karan and V-Star, had entered the stock market with inflated share values and unreasonable performance expectations, it was generally agreed that many fashion houses had to operate under the spotlight of intense media and financial community scrutiny, and that this pressure often had an adverse effect upon international trading. Moreover the fashion market is very well informed. At V-Star the recession that hit the world economy early 2001 prompted an alternative approach so that market share could increase even further.

George Vallows and his management team discussed some alternatives. On the one hand, they could decide to extend the range of products and move into fragrances and other luxury goods to increase revenues in the domestic US and those markets with cultural proximity. On the other hand, the money could be invested to expand further in South America, Eastern Europe, and Southeast Asia. These environments are, however, culturally remote from the domestic market. What do you think they should do?

(You can find out if you were right at the end of the chapter.)

The phases which the international market entry strategy of George Vallows and his company V-Star illustrates are characteristic of the industry. In a very well researched paper Moore, Fernie, and Burt (2000) describe four stages through which an internationalizing retail company quite normally meanders.

In the first stage wholesaling serves as a preliminary method of foreign market entry for fashion designers. Typically selling limited couture collections and ready-to-wear lines to the elite department stores located throughout the world, the internationalizing designers use wholesaling as a low-risk means of generating cash flow, customer loyalty, and market intelligence. Once demand has been established within capital cities and the designer's brand name has become better known within the market, edited versions of the ready-to-wear collections are made available through provincial department stores and other independent fashion retailers. This gives them a base in a market because wholesale is about immediate, focused distribution at low cost. Once this first step has been successfully taken, a second set of activities can be generally observed.

The second stage of market development involves the opening of flagship stores within capital cities. Typically located on premium shopping streets, such as Bond Street in London or Fifth Avenue in New York, these flagship stores have emerged as an important component of the marketing communications strategy of the design houses. Their role and function is vital to the development of the fashion brand's reputation. They are rarely about profit since the costs are very high and the turnovers are modest. But they support the wholesale business by creating allure since they are on the best streets and are beautifully presented. They are key to the marketing communications process.

While the main design houses have sought to maximize the profile of their flagship stores in order to promote their upmarket ready-to-wear collections, the marketing focus of the sector in the past decade has been the development of diffusion ranges. In this third stage of international development, the market expansion strategy adopted has involved the parallel launch of diffusion brands through the opening of diffusion flagships in capital cities, alongside a strategy of maximum brand distribution through wholesale stockists. This third stage is motivated by the recognition that diffusion lines make the designer accessible to the middle retail market, who have money to spend and who want the brand but are not too demanding.

Finally the fourth stage of fashion designers' foreign market expansion focuses upon diffusion ranges. Design houses (such as Armani, Versace, Nicole Farhi, and Donna Karan) have each developed chains of diffusion stores within the major cities of Europe, America, and Asia. And while the flagship stores for their main line, ready-to-wear collections are generally owned and controlled directly by the design house, the majority of diffusion stores within the UK, for example, are operated under franchise agreements. A number of reasons for this approach to foreign market expansion were provided by those design houses involved, not the least of which was the desire to avoid the significant start-up costs and the high levels of risk associated with the management of a national chain of diffusion stores.

It would be virtually impossible for designers to take responsibility for diffusion stores, for most fashion designer houses are relatively small companies and their resources are finite. So they develop a division of labor. Partners run the diffusion chains, and designer companies supply the product and most important of all, create the brand image through advertising, which has a high cost in terms of time and money.

There is a need for the fashion brand to have a clearly defined identity and personality, generated through the images presented as part of their advertising campaigns. Every successful fashion brand is based upon an image. The way that image is made is through advertising. Fashion thrives on advertising; advertising is what creates the identity and the attraction. Flagship stores are often part of a design house's marketing communications activity. While sustaining losses through the operation of many of these stores, the company often charges these against the company communications budget, on the basis that the function of the flagship store is to create awareness and interest, which is ultimately the role of advertising anyway.

In the 1970s fashion designers often chose a product line extension strategy. Companies such as Gucci and Pierre Cardin, through seemingly indiscriminate licensing agreements, allowed their brand name to be associated with a plethora of often non-associated products: by 1980, the Gucci brand was associated with over 22,000 product lines. Such overexposure of the brand has been avoided by those companies that recognize that this undermines the sense of exclusivity and prestige which is fundamental to the image of the fashion design brand. Nevertheless, a tension still remains, in that, through the development of diffusion clothing and lifestyle product ranges, there is the danger that the prestige and allure of the brand is lost whenever the brand becomes more accessible through lower pricing and extension into a variety of product areas.

This tension between the desire to be exclusive, while at the same time maximizing the profit potential of the brand, is perhaps most evident in relation to the fashion houses' distribution policies. As was shown above, many of the retailers have, through the development of extensive wholesale distribution networks, made their brands physically available and economically accessible to an unprecedented number of consumers. This tension has lead some commentators to suggest that the fashion brands that will have longevity will be those, such as Chanel and Dior, which have continued to restrict the availability of their distribution and have also avoided the development of diffusion ranges.

On the one hand, you cannot claim to be exclusive and charge premium prices when you are selling more jeans than, say, Marks & Spencer. The customer catches you out, and American brands in particular have been caught out already. This bubble will burst and the best brands will go back to being exclusive again. Some diffusion stores will certainly close. Exclusivity is not concerned about democracy. It is possible, therefore, to question the longevity of those companies that represent international diffusion store chains.

On the other hand, looking at the demographic trends (discussed earlier in this book) we can see that many young people have chosen to go for designer fashions big time. They are accustomed to diffusion stores and therefore there is a need to diffuse these products on

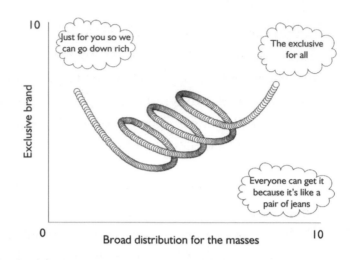

Figure 6.4 Exclusive brands versus broad distribution

a large scale while still asking for exclusivity. This dilemma is illustrated in Figure 6.4.

Levi Strauss has clearly shown what happens if you don't continue to be perceived as a unique, high-status brand. Few young people want to wear Levi's jeans nowadays because they are just too ubiquitous. Reconciliation lies in finding a path where a company seem to be exclusive for all. Brands like Replay, DKNY, and FCUK have done this smartly by combining mass distribution with selective chains and stores. And V-Star decided to go the same way.

Thus franchising across cultures is no longer the one-way export of a single business format, but a continuously looping feedback model that needs constant striving to reconcile the dilemmas which result from cultural differences.

CHAPTER 7

Marketing across ethnic boundaries

Much of this book has been focused at increasing the understanding of how to approach different cultures across country boundaries. However, we also need to give consideration to different cultures within country boundaries resulting from ethnic differences, and address issues of marketing in these multicultural societies.

Ethnicity and identity are important marketing concepts in multicultural societies but they have received relatively little attention in the literature on marketing. When the topic has been addressed the focus has been on assessing consumer behavior characteristics without reference to wider marketing debates, or drawing out any robust general model, or giving any structure to the practical marketing implications.

Research conducted by Williams, published in 1995, examined the frequency with which racial and ethnic papers were published in three consumer behavior journals over a period of twenty years. This found that only 3.4 percent of articles had a racial or ethnic focus and only 2.3 percent of the total number of subjects were identified as such. The following points have been assembled to explain why ethnicity has been relatively ignored by researchers (Burton, 2000):

- The fact that ethnic minorities account for approximately five percent of the British population and 30 percent of the US population. Marketers may have decided that it is not financially feasible to target marketing resources at these groups.
- The pervading ideology surrounding some ethnic groups. For example, Britain's Afro-Caribbean and Pakistani populations have been described as one of the foremost examples of the underclass in Europe. Much less reference is made to the Asian bourgeoisie, referred to as "Britain's hidden achievers."

- An alternative view is that members of Britain's ethnic minority community do not require any specific targeting and that they can be treated as part of the indigenous population. This approach has its roots in two possible ideologies. First, that existing methods of using the marketing mix are sufficiently accurate and appropriate without having to incorporate ethnicity as an important variable. Then another very different perspective – the postmodern arguments that suggest group boundaries have become more fluid and consumption patterns more individually centered, hence lessening the importance of ethnicity as a consumer characteristic.

DEFINITIONS

We can define an ethnic group as a social group that has a common cultural tradition, common history, and common sense of identity and which exists as a subgroup in a larger society. By implication, the members of an ethnic group differ with regard to certain cultural characteristics from other members of their broader society. The ethnic group may have its own language, religion, and other distinctive cultural customs.

Extremely important to the members of an ethnic group is their (positive) feeling of identity as a traditionally distinct social group. The term is usually, but not always, applied to minority groups. Ethnic groups should not be confused with, or taken as synonymous with, racial groups, although it is possible for an ethnic group to be a racial group as well (for example, African Americans). The concept of ethnicity is a complex process with multiple stages and multiple outcomes. It begins with contact, when newcomer ethnic groups arrive but try to maintain their old culture and identity – perhaps as a means of survival, or a means of living their lives in a familiar way because that is what they are comfortable with. They may seek out areas to live and work where they can develop a network of friends with the same value systems.

Through acculturation ethnic identities emerge amid greater exposure to the larger society and culture. Adaptation sees the group trying to maintain its ethnic identity but slowly giving way to the dominant culture. The decreasing number of foreign-born members of the group are accommodated and gradually integrated, finally being assimilated into "mainstream" society and culture. Ethnically based cultural traditions manifest in daily life, but especially on significant occasions such as weddings, births, religious festivals, and deaths. Many ethnic groups are financially disadvantaged and/or suffer other forms of prejudice.

Categorizing individuals in societies can be achieved in a number of ways ranging from a subjective approach (where individuals are asked to decide their own groupings) to more objective approaches based on factors such as lifestyle, income, etc. The aim of the traditional marketing approach is to model the structure of different classes or groups because these are ways of determining (predicting) buyer behavior. In practice, however, marketing place models are more complex and, for some businesses and services, social class or income alone may be a more important discriminator than ethnicity. For others, such as low-interest loans for example, ethnic grouping may be more important, where the lender benefits from shared equity growth or insurance premium cover.

The family is a vital frame of reference, and especially so with many ethnic groups. This may persist even after individuals have grown up and left the parental home. Accordingly, marketers use life cycle stages as a means of fine tuning their marketing strategies.

Commonly recognised American ethnic groups include American Indians, Hispanics/Latinos, Chinese, African Americans, and European Americans. Other examples from the American ethnic experience would include Italians, Jews, the Irish, Chicanos, Puerto Ricans, Poles, etc. In some cases, ethnicity involves merely a loose group identity with little or no cultural tradition in common. This is often the case with many Irish and German Americans. In contrast, some ethnic groups are coherent subcultures with a shared language and strong body of tradition.

Because several terms are used in many different ways in different situations, it is not entirely clear how "inter-ethnic" differs from "cultural difference." Ethnicity is defined by various authors with various designations: a "source of cultural meaning," a "principle for social differentiation," an act of "communicating cultural distinctiveness," a "property of a social formation," and an "aspect of interaction." However, it is commonly agreed that ethnicity is observable (through what we call the "outer layer of the onion" cultural model).

The concept of ethnicity has proven useful to domestic government agencies and international organizations trying to assist ethnic minorities in multiethnic societies to advance themselves. Rather than treating the inhabitants of a developing country as culturally homogenous, for instance, most international aid agencies now try to take into account the values, institutions, and customs of various ethnic groups, targeting relief or aid to their particular needs.

The ways people show that they are proud of their ethnic group include:

- behaving in a distinctive manner,
- living near one another,

- attending special functions (e.g., particular sports events),
- performing traditional rituals (e.g., weddings, religious festivals), and
- wearing distinctive clothing.

Ethnicity is in many contexts the single most important criterion for collective social distinctions in daily life; ethnic distinctions are rooted in perceptions of differences between lifestyles. However, even more important (and usually overlooked) is that ethnic groups often share the same meaning as their forefathers in the inner layer of culture. It is all too easy to notice the outer layers and forget that we have to respect not only these observable differences, but also everyone's right to interpret the world in the way that they choose. As with national cultures, the seven dimensional model of culture helps us to understand these deeper differences.

Consider Hispanic Americans as an example. Fifteen percent of the US population will be of Hispanic origin by 2007. Many Hispanic Americans are the descendants of Mexican people who lived in the Southwest when it became part of the United States. Almost all other Hispanic Americans or their ancestors migrated to the United States from Latin America. The three largest Hispanic groups in the United States are Mexican Americans, Puerto Ricans, and Cuban Americans. As a group, Hispanic Americans represent a mixture of several ethnic backgrounds, including European, American Indian, and African. At THT we have found in our research that those Hispanic Americans who have completed our cross-cultural diagnostic instruments have a more similar orientation on these seven dimensions to people from their areas of origin (such as Latin America) than they do to typical Caucasian Americans.

But what does this mean for the marketing manager? Looking at the demographics in both Europe and North America, we soon realize that we don't have to leave our own countries to meet the similar dilemmas that international marketing managers are facing. If we just consider the Netherlands, for example, we can observe that its major cities, Amsterdam, Rotterdam, and The Hague, are becoming truly multicultural. By the year 2020 more than 50 percent of all residents of these cities will have no Dutch roots whatsoever. And 2 million of the predicted 18 million will come from non-western cultural backgrounds, in particular the Moroccans, Turks, Surinamese, and Antilleans. In the UK census records show more than one million people of Indian heritage and over 300,000 with a Pakistani background. In the city of Leicester, where over a quarter of the population is Asian, a large number of retailers cater for the particular tastes of this ethnic minority. This can even extend to bureaux for arranged marriages, which do not form part of the society of the host culture. In Germany there are more than three million Muslims and in France the prominence of the ultra-right-wing politician le Pen shows that these changes need to be taken very seriously.

Furthermore, the composition of this ethnic diversity continues to shift. The US 1990 census counted 30 million African Americans, an increase of 13 percent over ten years. Asian Americans numbered 7.3 million, double the figure for 1980. Hispanics numbered 22.4 million, a 53 percent increase that put Latinos on course to becoming the nation's largest single ethnic group in a little more than a decade – and in 2004 the US census bureau announced that for the first time in history there would indeed be more US Americans with a Hispanic background than African Americans. President Bush's policy of allowing illegal immigrants to naturalize would accelerate this further. Among Hispanic residents, 70 percent were born abroad and an equal percentage speaks Spanish at home.

The national and international economic effects of these global trends are phenomenal. They are not only causing a change in meth-ods, types, and categories of production because of a changing and diverse workforce, but also a need for the marketing of products and services:

> In many respects, immigrants are the ideal consumers. The "need-everything" generation arrives without refrigerator, stove, washing machine, television, or automobile. They buy what they can afford, but as they adapt and move up the eco-nomic scale, they upgrade these items so that both the need and frequency of purchase is greater than in the general mar-ketplace. Moreover, there is often an overcompensation factor: they tend to make up for all the years in which acquisi-tion of such an array of material goods would have been unthinkable.   (Brandweek, 2001)

Thus it is most important for marketers to recognise that when members of any such ethnic group acquire the same disposable income as members of the dominant culture, they don't simply abandon their heritage and consume the same things or at the same rate as members of the host culture. Among the young, upwardly mobile Punjabi population in the US or young Moroccans in the Netherlands, for example, the accumulation of high-status posses-sions such as cars and designer clothing is a key marker, signifying successful assimilation, signs that they fit in. They also help as a bridge between the more traditional culture of their parents and their need to assimilate into the new society.

Annual buying power of minority customers exceeds $1 trillion and US companies now spend $2 billion each year on advertising specifically designed to attract and engage these "New American" consumers. In the Netherlands, despite enormous economic possibilities – the buying power of "New Dutch" citizens is some 20 billion euros – the literature on ethnic marketing is scarce and of a very low quality in that it is not based on data and is not conceptualized into any robust explanatory framework. Of course, this is typical of any newly developing field; it doesn't outgrow the awareness phase. Any advice that is given is based on how to segment the market differently: that is, by ethnic characteristics. This shows that Moroccans are keen to buy expensive clothing, while Turks invest in audiovisual equipment and Antilleans seek out "exotic" food.

In societies that are very segmented, where ethnic groups have clearly differentiated value orientations, a multiethnic strategy makes lots of sense. It could even be seen as a good remedy against the universal mass-consumption societies that many have become, as Halter comments:

> Though a crucial component of the rationale for the creation of ethnic pride groups and related culture-specific practices may be to protest against the ills of consumer society, the new ethnics demonstrate that they are nonetheless deeply tied to consumerist practices…In effect, the market serves to foster greater awareness of ethnic identity, offers immediate possibilities for cultural participation and can even act as an agent of change in that process.   (Halter, 2002)

The response is that, increasingly, advertising agencies such as those in the US and in Europe (to some extent) specialize to effectively focus on one of the primary New American umbrella groups – Hispanics, Asians, or African Americans – or New European groups – North Africans, Central Europeans, and citizens of former colonies.

The more sophisticated target marketers understand the limitations of too wide or too loose definitions for any groupings or clusters. For example, a crucial component of training marketing staff (in the US) is to develop an awareness of the complex intra-ethnic variations among both the Hispanic and Asian segments and to pass this knowledge on to their clients. Although both Cubans and Mexicans are classified as Hispanic by virtue of their common language, in reality their socio-cultural histories and patterns of settlement in the US are quite divergent and demand differentiated marketing approaches.

Multicultural marketing experts have proliferated and act as their companies' in-house ethnographers, learning and responding to the cultural nuances of their audiences. At the same time, ethnicity in itself is becoming increasingly optional and malleable, as individuals choose to take on certain identifying aspects of their cultural group while rejecting others.

The challenge for members of ethnic groups is to reconcile their own cultural heritage and what they prefer to retain with the norms and values and opportunities of adapting to the dominant society/culture in which they live. So we should consider two interesting questions that can be the starting point for sophisticated approaches to marketing:

- How does commercialism both enhance and make a commodity of ethnic identification?
- How do you market to groups that are not segmented but have a high degree of interaction amongst ethnic groups?

In marketing, the dilemma for considering ethnic issues is quickly apparent. On the one hand, society is faced with two dramatic and opposing forces. First, there is the advancement in communication and transportation that has given rise to a global economy, potentially moving people towards a homogenized identity. However, there is an opposing force to this one-world identity, as groups become more aware of themselves or group identity on the basis of their ethnic background (Costa and Bamossy, 1995). Media advertising has traditionally assumed that a white ethnic majority and other ethnic minorities can be reached simultaneously. Thus ads for mass audiences have tended to use white models exclusively, which is consistent with the melting-pot theory. It also leads to the assumption that ethnic minorities would gradually take on a white ethnic identity – or at least the purchasing decisions of whites (Kinra, 1997).

On the contrary, researchers have also argued that the trend is towards greater ethnic and cultural diversity. Culturally distinct segments cannot all be successfully targeted using the same marketing and advertising strategies that succeeded when society was a uniform, western market (Rossman, 1994; Berman, 1997; Kim and Kang, 2001).

The dilemma is represented in Figure 7.1.

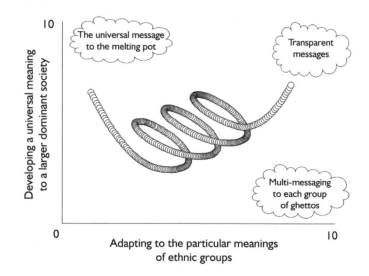

Figure 7.1 The multi- versus mono-ethnic society dilemma

Another approach is that which seeks to design promotions that find a "zone of commonality" centering on similarities rather than differences. Instead of the traditional single ethnic message, there are practitioners who develop crossover advertising in a process they call "transcreation" (Brandweek, 2001).

Berry (1990) identifies four possible models of acculturation:

1. *Integration:* individuals adopt some of the host culture while simultaneously maintaining their own culture.

2. *Separation:* consumers refuse to integrate into the host culture.

3. *Assimilation:* consumers adopt the host culture and forget their original culture over time.

4. *Marginalization:* consumers feel rejected by the host culture but do not want to maintain their original culture.

Obviously many marketing problems and suggestions for reconciliation across national boundaries apply at home as well, but some are quite specific. Different types of clients representing different cultures enter the same bank. Media channels are quite similar but aimed at a multicultural clientele.

Mono-ethnic marketing: the melting pot

An important issue is whether ethnic minorities will ultimately accept the culture of the host country, or if they will retain their own. It could be argued that if ethnic minority groups become completely assimilated then ethnicity as a variable would cease to be important and marketing discourse on the topic redundant. The whole acculturation issue is more complex and there are arguments for both approaches.

A primary reason that has been offered for a lack of ethnically diverse faces in marketing stimuli is a fear of negative attitudes from the majority white population or a so-called "white backlash." So despite the growth of ethnic minority groups in many societies, most advertisers have failed to reflect today's realities and have tended towards excluding or minimizing ethnic minorities from their advertising mix (Dunn, 1992; Marshall, 1997).

Some studies with cross-ethnic orientations, however, found that using ethnic minority actors and models raised the attitudes and purchase intentions of audiences of the same ethnicity without decreasing the attitudes and purchase intentions of the majority ethnic group (Lee et al., 2002). Further, the ethnicity of the advertising model had no significant influence on the ad, brand, attitudes, and the purchase intentions of the white majority group. While Asians showed more positive attitudes and purchase intentions towards ads that featured Asian models, the white majority's attitudes and purchase intentions were not significantly influenced by the ethnicity of the models. Thus marketers and media planners, by simply varying the ethnicity of the models featured in promotional materials, may improve their rapport with their target minority groups without endangering their position with the majority group. This opened the way to a forceful multiethnic marketing approach. Simple tokenism, whereby stratified ethnic representation is sprinkled in a mixed group, however, needs to be avoided.

Multiethnic marketing approach

More and more consumers themselves are expressing culturally distinctive desires, needs, and wants in their shopping habits, and these demands, as well as patterns of product loyalty, have prompted consulting, research, and communications firms to begin specializing in multiethnic niche marketing.

Some believe that the most effective way is to take these ethnicities seriously with significant consequences for the marketer. Thus Rosen believes:

> Each population must be communicated with on its own terms, and with an open-minded approach to the many sensitivities and possibilities each marketplace presents. The imperative for marketers is to address each ethnic group, and the many subgroups within them, in ways they find relevant and motivating.   (Rosen, 1997)

The power of ethnicity as a target variable is demonstrated implicitly by its frequent use in advertising underpinned by a wealth of prior research, documenting positive consumer responses to advertising that features similar-ethnicity actors or spokespeople.

Much attention has been given to the effectiveness of ads for different ethnic groups. For example, recent research has found that both identification and feeling similar to an ethnic spokesperson and the perception of being targeted by an advertisement are important motivators of consumer response to ethnic advertising. Both inherently involve some recognition of the match between the endorser's characteristics and the consumer's characteristics. As such, factors that increase ethnic self-awareness should increase the likelihood that a consumer will feel similar (or dissimilar) to an ethnic endorser and thereby feel targeted (or not) by an advertisement that features that ethnic endorser (Forehand and Deshpande, 2001). This type of self-referencing occurs when consumers process information by relating it to some aspect of themselves, such as their past experi-

Ethnicity and cosmetic surgery

Patients of cosmetic surgeons often have some idealized image such as Grace Kelly or Liz Hurley in their minds. Surgeons have developed reference formulae based on these stereotypical ideals and thereby define standard target measurement ratios such as the length of the nose compared to its width, or cheekbone prominence. However such standards are being revised and some surgeons need different ones because what is "beautiful" is different for different ethnic groups. White girls are more likely to base their ideal on a Barbie-doll-like figure. Black girls are more likely to base their ideal on what they perceive black men value in women, including fuller hips and larger thighs.

Increasingly surgeons are being asked by patients to make them more appealing to all men, from any ethnic background. A major reconciliation task for the surgeon!

Source: Adapted from Merrel (1994.)

ences. One of the effects of self-referencing is the generation of favorable cognitive responses, more positive attitudes towards the ad, the advertising model, and higher purchase intentions (Lee et al., 2002).

There are quite succinct differences within the US database at THT. If we look at the score on specific versus diffuse orientation across American ethnicity in our database we see significant variations, illustrated in Figure 7.2. Obviously this (as well as differences across other cultural dimensions) should be taken into account in the way

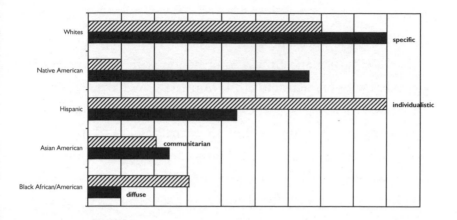

Figure 7.2 Variation of specific–diffuse and individualistic orientations amongst several US ethnic groups

advertising should be commissioned to different ethnic groups in the US.

This is illustrated by the way that the more diffuse and communitarian African American women have been approached quite differently by P&G.

Procter & Gamble

Cincinnati-based Procter & Gamble consistently tries new marketing approaches for its products even when it has a leadership position in the product category. Among feminine hygiene products, for example, P&G's Tampax is the leading brand, and the company has promoted it primarily through magazine and television advertising and through alliances with a number of women-oriented groups, such as the Women's Sports Foundation.

However P&G sought to maintain and support the brand's position among African American women by a special event marketing program aimed at that niche. The "Total You" tour combined health and fitness information with discussions of current issues of interest to black women through panel discussions with leading health experts, celebrity appearances, an expo, and other opportunities to participate. A "Total Care Tent" offered free massages and manicures. "The breakthrough is presenting these topics is a sisterly environment," says Anne Sempowski, a multicultural brand manager for P&G, noting that African American women don't have that many opportunities to gather and communicate in a group. "It's not just about providing information. We want it to be a total experience where African American women can come together and learn about topics that are important to them."

Meanwhile, the company has the chance to reinforce its brand message that "Tampax is safe, comfortable, and frees a woman up to do activities she normally might not do during her period," Sempowski notes.

Source: Sharoff (2001).

Another case of multiethnic marketing is the approach that we can learn from South Africa. During apartheid, there was a very strict separation between black and white media. Producers could easily communicate to white and black customers separately. Gaby Siera describes how the same commercial was shot twice so that it could later be distributed through both white- and black-oriented media:

A well-known brand of soap segmented its market into a white and a black target group. The commercial aiming at the white target group shows a white woman lying in a bath full of foam and singing. Her husband walks into the bathroom. She is startled and stops singing, "Feel good and feel free with this soap!" In the commercial for the black consumers we also see a singing woman – a black woman in this case. However, it is not her husband who walks into the bathroom, but her child. The woman is not startled; on the contrary, she goes on singing cheerfully, along with her child.   (Siera, 2000)

The reaction of a black staff member at the ad agency was scathing and was critical of "a poor and preposterous commercial suggesting that among black people it's prohibited to enter the bathroom when one's wife is bathing." Belittling as that is, it suggests that different commercials should be made for different groups. A white staff member spoke well of it: "It takes into consideration cultural differences of the two target groups." This is a typical example of a particularistic, multi-local approach.

After the fall of apartheid a variety of new approaches were needed in order to address the new and evolving marketplace. The separation of media for different ethnic audiences gradually disappeared so that multicultural groups saw identical commercials through one and the same medium. This led to some different solutions.

According to Siera's ethnographic research, many of the multiracial advertisements were still containing messages that were non-interactive. It was observed that advertising with no interactions, with whites and blacks still separated, was most used for family situations, showing black and white families in turn, or they were shown on separate pages, with blacks and whites never interacting across groups. As such these advertisements seem to avoid any politically risky activities.

This tendency for ethnic groups to hold fast to their roots presents both a threat and an opportunity. The opportunity in multiethnic marketing is to create a strong and lasting bond with ethnic consumers by reaching out to them in their communities and speaking to them in their native languages and with awareness of their cultural heritage. Ultimately this will express the benefits of your products and services in terms of their own value orientations. Marketing messages that fail to address consumers in terms of their own thinking and orientations are likely to miss their targets. Another, more serious, danger is that these messages can be offensive if they fail to take into account ethnic and religious sensibilities or sensitivities.

Overall there is considerable disagreement surrounding the discipline of ethnic marketing. Some protagonists believe in carefully targeted messages to each ethnic group or subgroup. Others insist on one effort that reaches down to core human values. Although ethnic values may differ, the increase of interactions between groups cannot be denied. Here a more sophisticated approach is called for, one that reconciles and creates a translucent message through what we can describe as transcreation.

THE RAINBOW CHALLENGE: TOWARDS TRANSCREATION

At first sight it makes a lot of sense to differentiate the messages to possible consumer groups when a society is highly differentiated in its ethnic groups. However, it has been noted that amongst some clusters – such as the young in particular – many interactions occur and shared core values develop that can be elicited. Some commentators also raise ethical issues, such as the role marketing and the media play and should play in making or developing the multicultural society.

When we go back to the experiences within South Africa, we observe interesting approaches to reflect the nature of interactions that developed between black and white societies. According to Siera, there are interactive ads where whites and blacks do cross-communicate. In these types of ads, children often play a central role in crossing boundaries. Obviously this is because they are unburdened by the past and have an innocent openness in their relationships. When adults come to play out their roles, it becomes an interesting picture. White men and women often represent the so-called yuppie role or other "successful" character stereotypes. Black people seem to play a much wider range of roles, ranging from unthreatening players of sports to artists or workers. In the first two categories they represent highly talented people. When blacks are represented in their traditional role of workers, white men or women doing similar jobs often accompany them. The reverse paradigm occurs hardly at all – that is where blacks play the professional roles with whites. In other words, when multiracial groups appear in South African ads, lots of attention is given to make them appear equal in either class. The overall mechanism is one whereby whites are easily "downgraded" rather than blacks upgraded. Exceptionally, a white man may be put in a stereotypical underdog position vis à vis a black person; humor takes over, so a slight reverse political correctness dominates and overcomes any potential criticism.

Consider these two examples.

Just great fun

A white journalist – obviously the "open sandals and socks" type – is sitting in the middle of the bush typing up his report. In the same room sits an imposing black man, watching silently. The journalist says to the black man in a pedantic tone: "Look, push button and type. Easy, huh?" When he has finally finished, he asks the black man the way to the post office: "Post office?" The man, still silent, points at a sign that says that the post office is thirty miles away, then gets up and asks: "Why don't you fax it?" As they are standing at the fax machine, he says, in the same pedantic tone the journalist used earlier: "Look, push button and fax it. Easy, huh?"

A second example makes the point very clear:

An old black man, who looks very neat, is selling souvenirs made from iron wire at the side of the road. A fast red car stops; its occupants are a rather unsavory-looking white man and his unattractive girlfriend. She is obviously charmed by the souvenirs. As she looks over them at length, the white man speaks to the black man in a belittling tone that implies that he thinks that he speaks Zulu fluently: "Yebo gogo." However, "yebo" is not a greeting but an answer to a greeting, and "gogo" means "grandmother" – but is insulting when you speak to an old woman you are unacquainted with, let alone when you speak to a man. In short, he is making a fool of himself. Meantime, they find out that the souvenirs cost 100 rand apiece and the white man announces that it is too much for a " piece of scrap iron." He wants to get back in his car and drive off. Then we see his car keys in the ignition and, of course, the doors are locked.

The old black man produces his mobile phone and calls the AA.

In PepsiCo, trans-creation through reconciliation is achieved by focusing on core values and interests shared across ethnic groups. Although Pepsi did its first African American ad in 1948, the cola giant has evolved from the ethnic segmentation most companies still use, into looking at young ethnic consumers as tribes (of young people) bound more by shared interests than ethnicity. Pepsi's director of multicultural marketing Giuseppe D'Alessandro says: "Race is not the unifier. The multicultural mindset is more about your interests, like music, than whether you're African American or Latino. They see their reflection in the popular culture, almost to the point of exaggeration. We call it the multicultural heart" (Wentz, 2003).

In analyzing the Pepsi spots we can see a variety of them in various languages but all uniting a common idea. They often reflect a world of imagination and passion when famous singers such as Beyoncé and Shakira sell "The Joy of Pepsi."

Joining greater ideas, however, doesn't mean that Pepsi doesn't use different language-version spots. One Shakira music spot has two versions, one sung in Spanish and one in English. And the Hispanic market was the first to be targeted for a joint promotion involving Pepsi and PepsiCo sibling Frito-Lay's Doritos. In all, relevant ads for Pepsi and Doritos were combined because it made sense for all markets, but the expression and product mix were different. The promotion was titled "El Reventon de Sabor," which loosely translates as a "huge, flavorful party," and was heavily advertised on Spanish-language TV, since Latins love a fiesta.

Another type of integration occurs in the reverse direction. Saker and Brooke (1989) found that reliance on the ethnic market (for ethnic food retailers) was insufficient to sustain many small ethnic businesses. Whilst they benefit from an initial base market in selectively selling to their own targeted group, those that survived engaged the community at large and outside of their ethnic core as a new market for growth. Eating and dining in ethnic restaurants

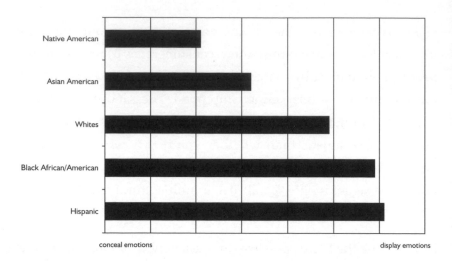

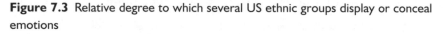

Figure 7.3 Relative degree to which several US ethnic groups display or conceal emotions

became the "thing to do" for many native residents. Successful ethnic-market-orientated businesses thus integrate their own ethnic customer businesss with the host society at large.

When comparing ethnic and non-ethnic orientation, two main differences are seen. Firstly, ethnic-market-orientated businesses tend to exploit more readily the social network of their own ethnic peers during their start-up phase – using family-funded cash flow, for example, and suppliers from the extended family. In contrast, non-ethnic-oriented businesses seek more conventional sources of support (e.g., bank business loans). Second, entrepreneurs from non-ethnic-oriented businesses tend to access business support networks to help them grow and survive, rather than an over-dependence on the extended family, as is the case with more ethnic-oriented businesses.

Thus the reconciliation approach to ethnic marketing is not about exaggerating the differences as a means of subdividing and sub-dividing into ever smaller segments, but integrating markets by appealing to common identifiers that don't challenge any one sub-group at the expense of the other. They let each ethnic subgroup retain their own passion and belief systems while at the same time being part of the greater community.

This reconciled approach is represented by US company Hallmark's highly successful Common Threads collection. Rather than trying to target a particular segment, this line was intended to broaden the ethnic market by appealing to consumers who appreciate cultural diversity. Hallmark's Ethnic Business Center oversees their popular Mahogany (African Americans), Primor (Hispanics) and Tree of Life (Jewish) lines, but the Common Threads collection is not under its auspices. The unity cards are not reflective of a specific culture, nor are they directed at a particular ethnic group. Instead, messages are chosen to represent shared truths found in poetry, proverbs, and lyrics drawn from a variety of the world's cultures, emphasizing a philosophy of global community and diverse cultural expression.

After only a few months on the market, sales tallies confirmed that the Common Threads idea was sound. Not surprisingly, the line sold particularly well among students and teachers, but especially noteworthy was that demand was strong in almost all areas of the country, not just in major metropolitan centers (Brandweek, 2001).

Ethics

As societies become more multicultural, ethnicity becomes an increasingly important factor in differentiating purchasing motives. Ethnicity can affect a range of consumer behaviors such as styles of dress, tastes in music, and leisure time pursuits, or in food and drink consumption. These socio-cultural variations can also take on a political dimension and be used to delineate differences between groups, to demarcate boundaries between ethnic groups, to mark out some as members and others as outsiders.

The above debate also reveals an ethical issue. Does marketing play a role only as reacting to societal trends or does it need to play a role to create a culture of harmony and interaction between groups? Many scholars have shown that marketing and advertising play a very important role in the creation of a culture. We suggest that reconciled values that respect differences and create a context within which these differences are shared could be the most important orientation for the future success of ethnic marketing.

CHAPTER 8

E-Marketing dilemmas across cultures

Companies have to define new paradigms for electronic commerce and enable, facilitate, sustain, and reward interaction between consumers and their organizations. With the rapid growth of the Internet, it would be foolhardy for any company to ignore its power and potential. More and more companies are jumping on the bandwagon and getting their businesses wired in order to stay afloat in today's competitive environment.

THE INTERNET AS A BUSINESS ECOSYSTEM

All businesses face the challenge of this new information economy, whether local or global. But the "global/local" distinction is less clear; the Internet knows no boundaries, except when a government tries to control access as in China, for example, where the authorities attempt to block "foreign" commercial websites on local servers.

The future belongs to those enterprises who can receive, organize, distribute, and utilize information most effectively and swiftly. And the Internet plays a crucial role in this. Moore has pointed out that we have moved beyond competition and cooperation to the creation of business ecosystems, that is to whole economic communities of interacting organizations and individuals (Moore, J., 2003). But why and how?

Because more than anything the Internet has broken the old model of marketing communication theory. Traditionally information is transferred from a producer (source) to many consumers (receivers) at one time – typically via newspaper or television advertisements – and mainly before a sale. This view of marketing was heavily influenced by what became known as the Frankfurt School whose core premise was that the media can and do exert a direct and powerful effect on the consumer.

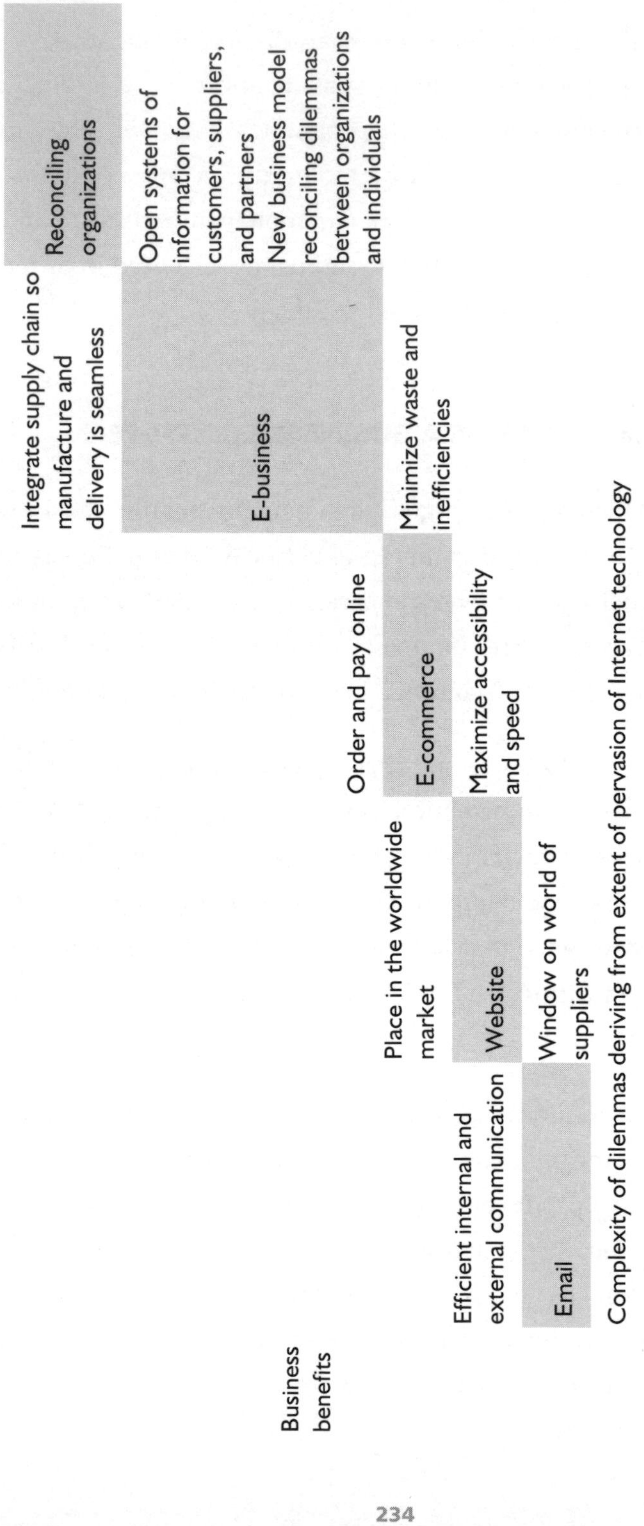

Figure 8.1 E-adoption (see Charlesworth, 2003)

The new interactionist model

But the Internet has resulted in a new interactionist model. The consumer is no longer part of a passive, mechanistic, simplex (one way) communication model. Online consumers are now interpreters. "Meaning" is no longer simply given by the producer, but is continually being refined and reinterpreted by consumers as they seek out more and more choices and offerings for themselves. The consumer is now an active, not a passive, decoder of messages. The consumer has the power now, not the media. Thus there is no longer a clear distinction between supplier and a discrete customer – there is only communication between mutual senders and receivers of messages. Web surfers may be viewing advertisements, but their behavior in terms of how long they dwell on a particular page, what they choose to click on next, whether they follow up with a pricing or delivery query also sends messages back to the producer – because the web server can be used to track the path of responses, both in time and action. In the old model, in contrast, an advertiser never knew if potential customers had looked at a newspaper advertisement nor how they had responded to it.

One of the biggest advantages the Internet has to offer is that information technology can help businesses gain competitive edge by enabling them to gather and maximize information. Porter previously used the value-chain concept back in the mid-1980s in showing the advantages of incorporating IT per se into businesses (Porter, 1985). Basically the value chain was divided into its physical and informational components. The physical component included all the steps in capturing and manipulating the data. With the help of information technology, companies could effectively improve their information-processing powers. The Internet was hailed as a good fit for those industries with information-based business activity.

The Web also offers businesses new distribution channels that enable customers worldwide to be informed and buy their products. It has the potential to create a number of opportunities. For example, an Internet-enabled distribution strategy has been heralded as a way for small and medium-sized companies to compete with larger organizations. Taking a relationship marketing perspective, Gilbert and Powell-Perry (cited in Lewis and Chambers, 2000) believe that the hotel industry must continue to use the full potential of the Web as a strategic mechanism to facilitate the development of relationships with customers .

Overall, the Internet is both an opportunity and a challenge to marketers. The opportunity lies in reaching your customers directly through websites. The challenge is to get the customers' attention to dwell long enough in order to tell your story and track their response to it.

In this brave new world, informational goods and services are produced by and for ecosystem members. The most effective strategy is to position yourself near the center of the ecosystem and make your enterprise indispensable to its major transactions. As the ecosystem develops, its principal modes of transactions grow with it – often faster than the ecosystem itself. Where an enterprise is a node in a system, every new member increases nodal transactions that grow exponentially. Thus the tenth member of a group produces nine additional relationships, all of which may pass through the nodal enterprise. The quantum leap "beyond competition" is shown in Figure 8.2.

Note that competing and cooperating have jumped to a higher level

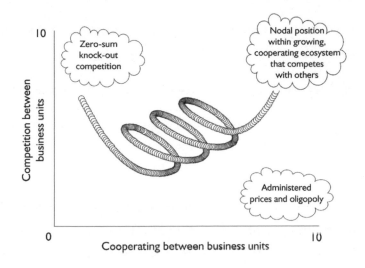

Figure 8.2 The emergence of business ecosystems

of complexity. Whereas employees once cooperated within the firm to compete with those outside it, now whole ecosystems of companies cooperate within that ecosystem to compete with outside ecosystems.

Also significant is the convergence of telecommunications and digital content, i.e., entertainment, education, business, news, etc., all of which use computers to store a wealth of data. Although marketers have been using electronic tools for many years, the Internet and other new technologies create a flood of interesting and innovative ways to provide customer value. However such new opportunities give rise to a whole series of marketing dilemmas:

- How can firms leverage new technologies to maximum benefit and still keep intimate relationships with their clients?
- How much commitment should marketers make to electronic marketing programs while at the same time using traditional approaches?

- Is your market online and do you need to serve it locally or globally?

In this chapter, we'll explore these tensions and offer reconciliations.

First let's reflect that e-marketing is not just traditional marketing using electronic methods. According to Strauss (2002) it affects traditional marketing in two ways:

- It increases efficiency in established marketing functions, but
- the technology of e-marketing also transforms many marketing strategies. These transformations result in new business models that can be used to add customer value and thereby increase company profitability.

Internet technologies have spawned a variety of innovative products for creating, delivering, and reading messages as well as services such as reverse auctions, business-to-business (B2B) market exchanges, and interactive games. Established pricing strategies are turned upside-down. Bartering, bidding, dynamic pricing, and individualized pricing are common features of online surfing. Shopping agents create transparent pricing for identical product offerings at various e-tailers. Then marketers use the Web for direct distribution of digital products (e.g., news stories and live radio) and for electronic retailing.

But tremendous value occurs behind the scenes: supply chain management and channel integration create efficiencies that can either lower customer prices or add to company profits. And the Net assists with overt two-way communication: one-to-one Web pages, email conversation, and email conferencing via newsgroups and mailing lists.

We might as well raise a flag from the start and mention that this chapter is a snapshot of e-marketing in early 2004. We all recognise that the Internet is a rapidly changing medium, that enterprising entrepreneurs constantly have cool new ideas, and thus some things in this chapter might be out of date before is is even printed – but there are some serious projections.

According to a November 2003 article on CBS MarketWatch.com internet advertising is projected to continue a strong growth pattern in 2004. After a rollercoaster ride in online advertising over the last four years, 2004 looks to be the start of stable and reliable growth over the next few years. A fresh calculation from Smith Barney pegs online advertising growth for 2004 as being between 20 and 25 percent. In 2005 this is expected to grow between 15 and 20 percent. Online advertising could potentially grow 20 percent compounded annually over the next 5 years, according to Piper Jaffray, which recently held its online advertising conference in New York. As well as the big players, a multitude of e-marketers of all sizes also use it for promotions, and sending electronic coupons and digital product samples directly to consumers.

E-MARKETING DILEMMAS

We hope to show that some organizations have been brilliant and intuitive in solving several key marketing dilemmas facing their businesses that the Internet has exposed. It is the quality of these reconciliations that have elevated organizations to their present powerful positions in global sales. Let's consider the following exemplar dilemmas:

- Global versus local approaches.
- Broad spectra of customers versus deep, personalized customer relationships.
- Face-to-face versus internet selling.

- Uniting inner and outer orientations.
- Premier Pages: the bridge between gift and sale.

Dilemma 1: global versus local approaches

This global/local dilemma manifests in many ways throughout this book, but here we'll consider the Internet version of it. One good reason that the Internet will not sweep all before it, simply by communicating data, is that every customer is different (or perhaps we should say will become different because of what the Internet will bring). As far as investors go, for example, some want high risk, others low risk; some want growth stocks, others dividends; some have specialized interests in technology, media, energy, engineering, etc., while some have ethical concerns about tobacco or armaments.

In E-Shock, Michael de Kare Silver (2000) has identified six consumer categories, based on earlier work by A C Nielsen.

1. Value shoppers – basically "mercenaries" who will purchase through the Internet whenever this offers greatest value.

2. Convenience and last minute shoppers – responsive to things that save time or make life easier (e.g., single parents of young children who work during the day).

3. Experimenters – ready to try new things and new ways of purchasing.

4. Ethical – will purchase provided it is honest and politically correct, and hence will surf to find suppliers and products that are both.

5. Die-hards – will be the last to change, preferring to use traditional means of shopping. They will come on board when the

technology is simple to use and much more convenient than their existing modes.

6.   Social shoppers – these are customers who just enjoy shopping. Now customers surf the Net for the fun of it. Some websites provide a chat room for shoppers to talk about potential purchases like holidays, to swap stories and experiences just as they would do in the store or shopping mall.

But within these categories, customers are also different.

Let's considers investors again. Some would say "I don't keep a dog and bark myself." They employ professionals to do what they do not personally want to do, or are not qualified to do. Some investors want to participate in or influence the professional's decision, and others want professional advice on choosing for themselves. Just as there are degrees of participation, there are degrees of transparency versus privacy. Some customers would like other people to know just how wealthy and successful they are, while others use professionals to keep their affairs private. They believe it boastful or dangerous to flaunt their wealth.

Whichever way you look at it, customers vary in myriad ways and may treat their broker as being anything from a Buddha to a butler. It is because customers are so individually diverse that it takes a global community to bring satisfaction to each person. It requires deep relationships of mutual respect to find, amidst that community, just those people and resources that the client requires most.

There has been a lot of discussion recently on whether the Internet can help suppliers cross borders more effectively by either ignoring cultural differences or by taking particular account of them.

Some studies indicate that marketers make too much of cultural differences and their effect on marketing, usually to the exclusion of more important issues such as "What does the customer want and need from my company and my product? What possible reason would they have to choose us over our competition?" (Flikkema, 1998). In Flikkema's study consumer and business surveys were conducted in five countries around the world: the United States, Britain, France, Australia, and Japan. It was found that cultural differences had essentially no effect on the attitudes, motivators, and needs involved in purchasing technology. A first-time PC buyer in Japan was more similar to a first-time buyer in France than to a repeat buyer in Japan. An "enthusiast" buyer was an enthusiast buyer around the world. Although regional differences were found, they didn't make any appreciable difference to the purchase process.

The main argument to explain this homogeneity is that technology is new and has given us not only common reference points, but common status and aspiration points as well. To be upscale anywhere in the industrialized world, you need a house, a car, a mobile phone, a plasma TV with DVD player, a sound system, and a sophisticated home computer. People have an innate need to believe they and their cultures are unique, and, in spiritual terms, they argue. In marketing terms, however, the world is becoming increasingly homogenous. And the use of the Internet is just making it all the more global and culturally insensitive.

On the other hand there are other research findings that conclude the opposite. They cite the US-centric approach as one of the main reasons why the Internet has not boosted overall sales worldwide, given that 65 percent of total Internet sales come from outside the US (Jastrow, 1999). Once upon a time, it was just one great, glorious space – borderless, unfettered by rules, a great virtual community. The Americans were so awestruck when developing the Web that they overlooked the fact that this was really a worldwide media platform and not just a US network. Little things – such as requiring visitors to identify themselves as "Mr," "Mrs," or "Miss" – may seem innocent, but could be perceived as insults in certain countries, as well as by certain groups of (potential) customers.

We may be seeing the end of the Web's freewheeling ways as more governments take increasingly aggressive positions on the legality (and possible taxation) of the bytes that flow across their borders. That means you could get a friendly (or not so friendly) email message from some government official telling you that you can't say or do or sell something on your website because it's being viewed in a particular country. Even buying a Dell PC online is preceded by various questions such as whether the PC will be exported to other countries and whether it is to be used for weapons of mass-destruction...In same vein, the UK Inland Revenue – the tax-collecting arm

Fons and AOL

Fons changed the credit card with which he paid his monthly bills on his AOL account. There was a way to change payment details through AOL's site; however, he was asked for his zip code and his Dutch address was immediately rejected. Fortunately there was a 1-800 telephone number for contacting AOL; unfortunately, it wouldn't work outside the US.

Fons' account and email address stopped functioning. Ludicrously, he had to call a colleague who lived in the States in order to get his account unblocked. This was the only way it was possible.

of the Treasury – is looking at ways of monitoring transactions as a means of cross-referencing declarations of income and expenditure in tax returns, and of identifying money laundering.

This may come as a surprise to some who believe that because they're moving at "web speed," the traditional rules somehow don't apply. Perhaps the most widely known example is the clothing company Lands End's recent run-in with the German government, which declared the company's "lifetime" guarantee on its products to be illegal within Germany (14 days is the maximum there). Another example concerns legal mandates, such as those in French-speaking Canada, which state that French should not only be available, but also be the dominant language on all publications and signage (Peek, 2000).

However it's not just conforming to local laws and language but to local customs that should concern contemporary web publishers. Many traditional publishers are already aware of the necessity of creating separate editions for global markets, and even though English is the language of the Web, that doesn't mean that readers will stay if an alternative is available. Forrester Research recently reported that people are twice as likely to stay at a website if it was written in their native language. While language translation programs might be adequate (an 80–90% accuracy rate is generally reported), most serious web publishers are discovering that that content must be completely rewritten in the native language of the surfing consumer.

Unfortunately, there is no simple way to translate graphics and visual elements and to ensure that they will represent the same meaning in other cultures. In the US, for example, orange is considered a warm color, but in Japan it's cool. In some cultures it may be more appropriate to show the product owned by a single individual, to emphasize individualism and individual choice. In others, it may be more effective to show a group of people enjoying or surrounding the product to emphasize collective appreciation. Here the message is to buy the product because then you can stay part of the group, or join it.

Allowing content to be controlled locally can help ensure that viewers get a cogent message (which is the whole point of publishing). But this has the potential to raise havoc with establishing or maintaining a clear corporate image or message. In addition, the integrity of data may not be maintained consistently. Information may be released in the US on Monday, but not translated for one country until Tuesday or for another until Thursday. On the other hand, it's a competitive world out there and the website that best gets the message across first wins.

Despite all the problems it will introduce, it seems inevitable that we are facing a customized future. Let's look briefly at Dell here. Dell Computer is now the world's number two. How did it achieve this? How did it bulldoze its way into a mature market, with retail outlets already stuffed with rival products?

It used a direct selling model. It first approached major corporations who would buy computers and IT in bulk, but it concentrated on discovering a corporations' particular strategy (bottom right in Figure 8.3). It then offered to assemble components accordingly (top right in the same Figure).

But what business is Dell in? Dell is an assembler, not a manufacturer. It orders key components in massive volumes, thus getting costs way down through near-universal purchasing. Finally Dell shows each unique customer how their chosen business strategy can be monitored, recorded, and expressed in terms of information tech-

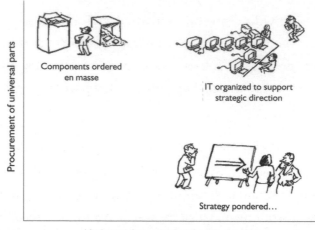

Figure 8.3 Dell – from product to solution

nology. While components of any solution are standardized, the solution itself remains unique and customized with "Premier Pages" on the Internet for each customer.

Davis and Pine have called this process mass customization, first introduced by the Japanese automobile industry and now widely imitated (Davis and Pine, 1999). By delivering components just in time to a central assembly line, thirty to forty varieties of automobiles come off at the end, with little loss of speed or momentum. Information systems define and describe each configuration in advance and components are dispatched to make their rendezvous with the vehicle in the process of assembly. This is a long way from Henry Ford's "any color provided it's black."

In short, one could say that by its very technical nature the Internet could help marketers go global with universal approaches easily. However, many private and corporate clients remain local. Solutions are not found in a choice between the two. The beauty of the sophistication of the Net is that it allows you to combine local data with global approaches and vice versa.

Take the very popular websites of BOL (A European-based web retailer), Amazon, and Google. When visiting their sites you are automatically rerouted to the closest localized version. For example, if the server detects that you are based in the Netherlands, it redirects you there. The language changes automatically, and the service localizes as well. However, the main philosophy remains global.

This is even more obvious with shops like BOL and Amazon. When you look for a book on Amazon.co.uk you are offered different categories of books for your perusal, as you are with Amazon.com or Amazon.de. Again the overall (global) philosophy remains the same and the local user can always choose to visit other Amazon sites as well.

Customer identification (and identifying their needs) has always been a fundamental requirement for presenting the right offer to the right customer at the right time. Internet marketing forces the transition of this capability from a back-office batch routine to real time in order to optimize the offer process and apply closed-loop marketing techniques. This process requires careful thinking to achieve best practice (Cameron, 2001).

Amazon has successfully used the two-way communication interactionist model (described briefly above) to learn a significant amount from local buying patterns. After five years of being successful in their market, the surfer can now see an increase in the differentiation of the items that the top-level menu offers on the home page. In addition to the core business of books, in the US this emphasizes apparel and accessories, toys and games, top sellers and today's deals, which you won't find on the French, German, and British Amazon sites. The French have "cadeaux" (presents), while the Germans have "Kueche & Haushalt" (kitchen and household) as an option on their menu. The British site had Harry Potter as a separate item.

Amazon has learned continually from local use and adjusted the universal system to fit. Furthermore, by tracking individual buyers and search pattern requests they create a client's private "box" for deals and are able to make other types of recommendations to suit the unique taste of the particular user. In this way the universal and global offering is reconciled with particular local needs.

Your personal calendar

A simpler example is an unsolicited email from Hewlett-Packard inviting recipients to "make your own unique calendar." HP offers a way to make your own personalized printed calendar completely unique by importing your own choice of pictures or photographs – either your own or those from a library provided by HP. In this way the Internet is used to offer a combination of modules that can be combined in a unique way – hence your "personal" calendar. Calendar... obviously this encourages you to use a lot of ink on your HP printer!

Let's draw from the experiences of our own organization, THT, and consider the following case, concerning a learning system across cultures delivered via the Internet.

The Culture Compass

In 2001 Trompenaars Hampden-Turner launched a new web-based tool. The Culture Compass OnLine is used for stand-alone or blended learning – that is, in combination with in-company training workshops. It is a country-specific, interactive multimedia Internet application for international managers, business travellers, expatriates, and others who regularly deal with different cultures.

A multicountry module facilitates self-paced learning through direct feedback on the user's scores and preferences. Users can match their own personal Intercultural Awareness Profile against the country profile of their choice. Business cases, anecdotes, personalized feedback, and recommendations are all part of the basic module and differ by country for each individual's scores. Apart from business topics such as meetings, management, marketing, and negotiations, users also acquire knowledge about important issues relating to a culture's history, social norms, and religion. The Culture Compass presently provides specific in-depth feedback for 12 countries, namely the US, UK, Japan, Germany, France, Netherlands, Korea, Taiwan, Singapore, Ireland, Israel, and China. Country profiles from some further 80 countries are also accessible online.

It forms part of the training kit for our workshops at THT. All workshop participants receive an access password before the workshop commences, allowing them to complete the preparatory work. Thus they work through the first modules in preparation for the workshop.

The Culture Compass OnLine consists of a number of interactive modules:

- An introduction to culture: How does culture influence

our lives? This discusses the three steps of awareness, respect, and reconciliation.

- Layers of culture: This module gives an overview of the THT model that explores the layers of culture.

- Questionnaire and dimensions of culture: Introducing the seven dimensions model and then linking to the on-line Intercultural Awareness Profiler (IAP), THT's cross-cultural questionnaire.

- Interpreting your own personal cross-cultural profile: Receive an personalized interpretation of your profile.

- Choose a country to compare with your own profile: Receive feedback on what this means to you in doing business and managing in that culture.

- Follow further country-specific advice and information about what this means for business topics including marketing, meetings, negotiations, etc.

Stage 1

After testing this application to market their own country-specific products through the Internet in six countries (US, France, UK, Germany, the Netherlands, and Japan), THT reviewed some interesting feedback. The Americans and British asked for more critical incidents and self-tests; the Japanese requested that the system be made more specific to Japanese needs, finding it too Europe-centric; the French asked for more rigor in the way we presented the models of culture and its dimensions. We took all this advice seriously and adapted our Culture Compass OnLine to accommodate the feedback.

Stage 2

After the launch of the updated Culture Compass OnLine, the same participants were asked to give THT further feedback. Criticism on content changed toward criticism on process. The French liked the order: After completing the questionnaire the system gave feedback on the generic model of culture and the seven dimensions, following which you could test yourself through some cases (particular to your country of interest) in applied areas of negotiations, meetings, marketing, management, etc. The Americans had an objection about the flow of information. They suggested that the tool should start by showing some very concrete cases and critical incidents; only thereafter would the participants be willing to go for the "harder" stuff. The Japanese would rather leave the choice to the customer while the Germans would prefer to leave out the choice. The Dutch complained about increasing development costs...

Our consultants at THT were now facing a crucial dilemma: would they prefer to go for one global system with similar content or customize the application to local cultural needs? The technical people confirmed that, technically speaking, the sky was the limit and lots of solutions were possible. In view of the above information, how would you have advised THT to develop the Culture Compass to the next level?

This case shows very clearly the first dilemma of the use of Internet: do we approach the client in a customized manner or do we benefit from economies of scale from having a universal system applied globally? If were to opt for the latter approach, the French might like it because of their love affair with deductive logic. They could start with a sound model and explore the specific applications in meetings, marketing, and management. The American learning style goes through a similar cycle but has a different starting point. They want to start with cases, to get a feel, and then see how it works in theory. This latter, inductive style is typical of American learning preferences, where you try to generalize from concrete cases; otherwise you might loose your audience too quickly. The Japanese would like to be able to give choice to the customer, while the Germans would rather go for the best system with not too many options.

That's all very well, but how can you best market this product through the Internet when in one company some (national) groups prefer this or the other style? Producing a system for every potential learning style in every country is prohibitive because of excessive development costs.

This dilemma is shown in Figure 8.4.

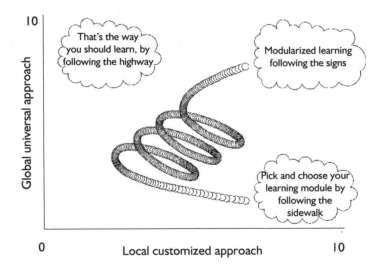

Figure 8.4 Customized versus global

We considered two approaches at THT. First of all the system could be modularized so that clients could pick and choose. But that wouldn't suffice and, in our terminology, this would only be a compromise solution.

So we accessed country-specific learning style preferences from our research database and followed the advice described above for specific nationalities. Another approach was to assess, as quickly as possible, the learning style of the individual user; we used a short, ten-item, online, interactive questionnaire. Then, depending on the assessment, the universal modules are offered in a particular sequence appropriate to that individual user. The beauty of internet technology is that it can guide the individual participant through the system in a unique way.

In either case, economies of scale were fully achieved in terms of software development, and the "local" user was given a particular structure of generalized modules. The ultimate dream we are currently exploring is one of a heuristic self-learning system that automatically adapts to a particular user's interests based on how they interact with the system from our collection of available standardized modules.

Dilemma 2: A broad spectra of customers versus deep, personalized customer relationships

The Internet obviously creates a very inexpensive way to reach millions if not billions of potential clients with the punch of one button or a single mouse click. You can do a "shotgun" broadcast to as many as possible (a.k.a. "spam"), broadly distributed across the field, or you can aim for just a few clients, with complex problems and specialized needs, who desire deep, ongoing relationships of service. The first strategy is cheap but rather superficial and may be

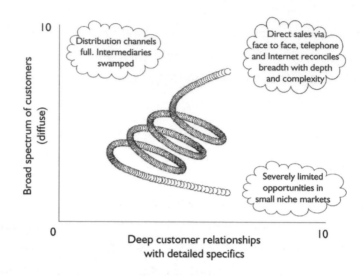

Figure 8.5 Broad spectra versus deep relationships

problematic in other ways. The second strategy is intimate and personal but typically niche-oriented and expensive, because of the detailed attention necessary. The dilemma is illustrated in Figure 8.5.

Spam has become a battleground between ISPs, filtering out unwanted emails and pop-up messages, and spammers, using increasingly innovative approaches to break through the filters. A typical way of doing the latter is to auto-generate email subject lines at random so as to appear unique and thus not be recognized by the ISP's filter.

A reconciliation that cleverly addresses this tension is based on the concept of viral marketing (see, for example, Wilson, 2000). Viral marketing describes any strategy that encourages individuals to pass on a marketing message to others, creating the potential for exponential growth in the message's exposure and influence. Like viruses, such strategies take advantage of rapid multiplication to explode the message to thousands, and on to millions. Away from the Internet, viral marketing has been referred to as "word-of-mouth," "creating a buzz," "leveraging the media," and "network marketing." But on the Internet, for better or worse, it's called viral marketing.

The classic example of viral marketing was Hotmail.com, one of the first free web-based email services. The strategy was simple: Give away free email addresses and services, attach a simple directional tag at the bottom of every free message sent out and then stand back while people emailed their own networks of friends and associates. The people who saw the message then signed up for their own free email service, and propelled the message still wider, to ever-increasing circles of friends and associates. Like tiny waves spreading ever farther from a single pebble dropped into a pond, a carefully designed viral marketing strategy ripples outward extremely rapidly.

The genius of direct selling via the Internet is that you can reach an ever-increasing spectrum of customers and you can use the net to give personalized, detailed, information-rich services to them.

So long as you assume that distributors are necessary, you are stuck with the fact that existing channels are full and that no intermediary's brain is capacious enough to hold all the details and information about several rival products and their accompanying instructions. It is only when you let go of the whole idea of using distributors that the processes of direct selling via the Internet commends itself. The Internet is uniquely suited to information-rich products, which can be embedded in an ongoing community and woven around with dialogs on details and special opportunities. You can serve the whole spectrum of net users and you can go deeply into any specific problems. This dilemma is close to the dilemma or dimension of specific versus diffuse. You can reach

Hello, Peter, did your order arrive?

When you dial some call centers, you hear may hear three rings before your call is answered. On the first ring the system checks to find out who is calling (is the calling number in the database for an existing customer or client?). The second ring looks up the database to see which customer service operator spoke to you the last time you called. If this customer service agent is not on another call, your details and your past purchases and customer record is displayed on their computer screen. The third ring is routed to this particular customer service agent, who answers. The agent can then immediately say "Hello Peter, this is Jane, I am your personal account representative, I spoke to you last week. Did your order arrive OK last Tuesday?"

Using a system that retrieves customer-specific data is perceived by the customer as personal service. The technology is programmed to reconcile the specific with the diffuse customer needs.

down to each customer's problems in specific detail, and you can serve a diffuse array or spectrum.

Let's return to Dell. Dell had to get to grips with the dilemma of selling to a broad array or to a special group with whom deep relationships were developed. This dilemma was exacerbated by Michael Dell's youth, which made him a latecomer in a maturing industry who faced the prospect of pushing into a crowded field, full of existing attachments, many well established. Could Dell push entrenched competitors out of their trenches? It turned out to be unnecessary.

In fact his newly developed direct selling model had the advantage of being simultaneously very broad and at the same time deep, personal, and customized (Trompenaars and Hampden-Turner, 2001). He broke with the conventional wisdom that you either aim for many customers or you aim for just a few with complex problems and specialized needs who need high-end service. The first strategy is cheap but rather superficial; the second is intimate and personal but typically niche-oriented and attracts premium prices. The reconciliation he created was as powerful as it was simple. By direct sales via face-to-face interaction, telephone, and the Internet he reconciled breadth with depth and complexity. Dell reconciled both this degree of involvement dilemma and the global/local dilemma through the same thinking.

Dilemma 3: High tech versus high touch: face-to-face versus Internet selling

The financial services in particular are facing a major dilemma in this arena. The struggle to integrate the specific culture of Internet-based business activity with the diffuse and deep relationships that financial consultants have developed with their clients is still ongoing, but we are confident that it will lead to success. How can it be done?

The challenge to financial service companies has come, in part, from the unbundling of services into specific pieces. You can buy information, research, trading facilities, and advice from separate sources and the combined fees may be less than those paid to six- and seven-figure professionals. While the Internet is overflowing with data, this is not the same as knowledge or information. We are informed by facts relevant to our questions and concerns. We "know" when we get answers to our propositions and hypotheses.

The larger the Internet becomes, the more customers will need a guide to what is relevant to them.

The dilemma can be analyzed as follows. On one hand we find low-cost specific data and transactions on the Internet. The risk here is that you create a high-tech solution where brokers are bypassed by technology. On the other hand, we can see the rich, meaningful, diffuse personal relationships that brokers have developed with their clients. This maintains a high-touch environment where people are (over)paying for their dependencies.

It is obvious that in specific cultures like the US and Northwest Europe, the Internet can take a lot away from traditional face-to-face business. This is true for financial services, but also for buying a dishwasher, a CD, a book, and even a car. However, people from more diffuse cultures – like Arabs, Latins, and most Asians – see the relationship as so crucial that no one would ever give it up for an anonymous service that they might get through a click.

One American Merrill Lynch consultant was working in Saudi Arabia, a country that didn't easily take to the Internet. Saudis love to have their consultant with them. However this consultant's American colleagues said that you couldn't ignore the fact that their more internet-driven competitors were gradually taking market share away. This was best pictured as the situation in Figure 8.6.

Merrill Lynch had a situation where Charles Schwab was eating away at their market share through high-level online services. Their answer was close to brilliant. They understood that instead of relationships being eclipsed by the Internet, they actually got more and more important in interpreting the possible meanings of data flows. What was available was growing ever larger, much more than was relevant to each particular client.

Figure 8.6 The unaffordable relationship

Charles Schwab's appeal goes beyond discounted fees. Indeed, compared with rival discount brokers, it is not among the cheapest. Schwab's appeal is that it transfers its own professional expertise to customers. It is that rarity among professionals, a company who educates customers in its own secrets so that they can in time, if they wish, become fully independent. This could be a losing strategy if it were not for an ever-increasing number of "pupils" eager to be taught who replace those who have "graduated." Schwab is in the "customer mentoring" business as opposed to the financial services business, but existing "graduate customers" keep coming back for more because both their needs and the market keep changing.

For many older Americans and people between jobs, managing their own share portfolios is their "last and most meaningful employment," providing funds they can leave to their families to ensure their continuing influence. Schwab was helping customers to help themselves in time-honored American tradition.

Merrill Lynch saw that this challenge would have to be met; yet they could not risk alienating their own army of professional brokers. Increasingly, however, financial services were being unbundled. You could buy top information and research and then pay as little as $5 per trade on the Internet. This was far less than the brokers' inclusive fee. Nor are brokers' judgments infallible. Given the exigencies of markets, it is not unknown for the Dow Jones average to out-perform professionally managed portfolios. Luck is quite a leveler in this game.

Merrill Lynch's response to its dilemma was to refocus its efforts on reconciling new technology with customer service. John Steffens at Forrester Conference announced its strategy in May 1999: "By combining technology with skilled advisors, clients are given the convenience of interacting when, how and where they want."

Dave Komansky, their CEO, clarified the policy. "Anyone, anywhere, anytime, can log onto the Internet to get free quotes, market data, and stock picks from a variety of chat rooms. Yet at Merrill Lynch we are confidently making unparalleled billion dollar investments in our Financial Consultants, research analysts, and in our technology and products. We're doing this because we know success in the online world – as it was in the offline world – will be defined by meaningful content for the individual. Hence in this phase we will discover that intelligent dialog about the bewildering complexity of financial markets is a formative influence on the Internet influencing the financial markets" (Steffens, 1999).

You need high tech but also high touch. The more numbers rain down upon you, the more you need to talk to someone about them. Merrill Lynch is using the Internet to give better personal service (using high technology) to its high-touch customers, but is also using it to identify those high-tech customers for whom it makes good business sense to offer high touch.

We have no hesitation in referring to Dell again as the exemplar of reconciling marketing dilemmas in internet commerce. Dell Computers had a similar high tech versus high touch dilemma. Let's look at this in more detail now.

Dell came late to the fray, as we have seen, and so had to do something entirely different, something that would distinguish the company from its competitors and something that would get around the fact that distributors were packed with rival products. It was not simply that channels of distribution were blocked. The seas of information, service, and support surrounding computing technology were ever more expansive. Even if distributors could make room for Dell products physically, could they absorb the additional information, service and support, master it and pass it on?

So Michael Dell decided to bypass distributors entirely. He would sell direct to customers, thereby establishing a unique position over other computer vendors and creating his own ecosystem apart from theirs. Direct selling had some crucial advantages.

- By manufacturing to order, capital sunk into inventory would be minimized, as would stock that became unsaleable as a consequence of technological advances.
- By speaking directly with customers instead of using intermediaries, information on changing customer needs reached the company more quickly and with greater clarity and urgency. It was possible to learn at first hand the strategic aims of major corporate customers.
- With inventory turning over every six days, innovative technologies could be introduced very swiftly, along with any needed refinements to new models. The quicker this feedback loop, the finer the adjustments to the detail of customer requirements.
- A process of mass customization became possible by which standard components were assembled in the unique configu-

rations that customers demanded. In this way economies of scope were combined with economies of scale.

- The model of direct selling received a welcome and powerful boost from the Internet, which was first used to sell a Dell computer in June 1996. Today there are more than 40,000 customized home pages, called Premier Pages, especially for corporate customers. These contain not only the details of customized configurations and instructions, but a total record of past and current transactions between Dell and each customer. One consequence of this direct link is that Dell becomes privy to far more information about its customer than would otherwise be the case. When configuring a customized package you need to know why it is wanted and how it will be used.

Dell's direct business model preceded their use of the Internet by several years, so that the almost limitless opportunities supplied by the Net came as a very welcome surprise and challenged Dell's capacity for quick adaptation.

Their salesforce initially felt threatened by the Internet. Since it was capable of creating dynamic and complete customer–client relationships, down to the purchasing of a computer, sales teams felt that their role would be drastically minimized. Field-based account managers, who "own" customer relations, were especially sensitive to how the Internet could supplant their role. Dell's management knew they had to educate their salesforce to work alongside the Internet and seize a new kind of initiative. The Internet was an inevitable and incredible development. Rather than fight it, sales representatives would need to know how to use the power of speeded-up information channels to gather better information and further enhance valuable customer relationships. And so Dell invested heavily in education and training. Michael Dell explained: "Not only did we teach them to use the Net, but we jointly invented ways to make them more effective by managing more relationships while providing value added services for the customer as well" (Trompenaars and Hampden-Turner, 2001).

The most crucial change was to start valuing and rewarding the communication of knowledge, rather than the simple registering of sales. It wasn't that sales were unimportant, but rather that knowledge applied successfully to customers was the origin of any subsequent sales. The first is prior to the second. Under the original face-to-face system in the industry, knowledge of customers' needs tended to be hoarded by the local agent and the field office. Sharing this information with others would put your own office at a competitive disadvantage. You reported your sales, not the reasons for them or the changing patterns of customer demand discovered in your territory; knowledge was considered as proprietary. After all, you had visited the customer personally and gained rare insights into how computers might be used to advance a new strategy; such knowledge is hard earned.

Sales teams were now rewarded for capturing this knowledge in machine-readable formats, accessible to all other sales teams. The more potentially valuable the information was, the more the team was rewarded. For example, a new use of software could spread rapidly through particular industries. If Dell was alerted from the moment this process started it could help spearhead the new trend elsewhere. In addition, customers are not usually confined to single sales regions. To know that District 7 of Company X has tried a new approach successfully allows you to spread the same system to all company sites. In these and many other ways, knowledge of what customers are strategizing can be systematically computerized.

Sales representatives soon stopped seeing the Internet as an adversary. They found that it could be a source of highly qualified leads, as a result of which they could close a deal with fewer calls, and have greater reach within existing accounts. Rather than being intimidated by the competition provided by the Internet, they could use it to add a dynamic dimension to unique customer relationships. The Internet became a key part of the entire business system. Dell wanted to make the Internet the first point of contact for every customer and prospect. Their information technology perspective was – and still is – to reduce obstacles to the origin and flow of information and to simplify the systems in an effort to really maximize their processes.

Brushing aside fears that employees would make "improper" use of the Net, Dell encouraged browsing and information collecting. You could make much better use of face-time if you were properly briefed (on a computer) before a meeting and if you kept careful track of the success of previous initiatives. "If you are preoccupied with the ways in which your staff might abuse technology, you're going to miss out on the benefits, while your competitors run away with the future. For us, the issue wasn't whether people would waste time on the Internet but whether they would use the Internet enough. Not to become completely familiar with a transformative business tool like the Internet is just foolish – especially when it is an integral part of the company's strategy and competitive advantage," said Michael Dell (Trompenaars and Hampden-Turner, 2001).

The dilemma Dell solved was to make personal, face-to-face knowledge, which had earlier been confined and hoarded by single sales agents, into highly relevant, networked knowledge in which the deep, personal insights of local agents become the potential inspiration for the entire community. The dilemma is set out in Figure 8.7.

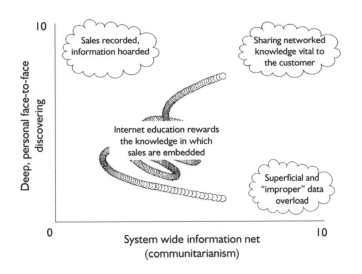

Figure 8.7 Face-to-face versus Internet selling

At top left in Figure 8.7 we have the old, competitive system where agents compete on sales but refuse to share their secrets. At bottom right we have the Internet's overload of superficial and even "improper" data. Dell was unafraid of this since his people had much important information to communicate and he was rewarding them for sharing it.

Thanks to training and education, and thanks to the emphasis given to the knowledge contexts in which sales occurred, Dell has succeeded in sharing networked knowledge, all of which was vital to at least one customer and might be generalizable to some or all customers. E-relations do not substitute for personal relationships, but record what was communicated, agreed, and planned, so that later understandings could be built on earlier ones.

In this way Dell overcame the problem identified as the basic knowledge management problem, described first by Snowden (2002), of converting from tacit sales knowledge known by "one" to explicit knowledge available to all. This is shown in the following table.

Where the knowledge is located		
Explicit	Captured in salespeople's PC database	Distributed database across the Dell Corporation
Tacit	The individual salesperson's head	Salesperson's immediate colleagues

Retail banking has similar dilemmas to those of Merrill Lynch and Dell. Let's note the typical costs of transactions. The banking industry's average cost per transaction:

at a branch, $1.07;

on the phone, 54 cents;

at an ATM, 27 cents;

on the Internet, 01 cents.

Figure 8.8 illustrates the upward oscillation between high tech and high touch in marketing financial services and how these can be reconciled using the same philosophy that Merril Lynch and Dell were able to use.

Figure 8.8 High tech and high touch in financial services

Dilemma 4: Uniting inner and outer orientation

Of crucial importance to marketing through the use of the Internet is bringing the "outside" of the company into the "inside" and letting the "inside" go "out." This perhaps exemplifies the essence of the whole marketing process.

It is a characteristic of modern business that information is increasingly stored in relationships, but where are these relationships located? Amazon's relationship with a publisher or record company is neither "inside" Amazon nor is it "inside" the supplier, but is carried via electronic impulses between the two. It is simultaneously accessible by interested parties from any point in the system. It is everywhere, yet nowhere in particular.

The real magic behind Amazon's resurgence is a bold bet by its founder and Chief Executive Officer Jeff Bezos. After all the doubts and criticism, Bezos has proved that his empire has staying power. As he states: "We're also constantly working on the website portion of the customer experience. There's still tremendous opportunity for improvement there – making it easier for customers to discover products and for products to discover customers."

And he's not limiting himself to selling Amazon's "own" goods. Bezos formed a unit to help more retailers sell to Amazon's 33 million customers, as the likes of Target and Toys 'R' Us already do. Some 19 percent of items sold on Amazon, in fact, are from other sellers. Says Bezos: "We know how to develop world-class technology to make the customer experience in e-commerce really good. It's a rapidly growing part of our business. And that goes from [large] companies that are customers all the way down to individuals using our web services to tap into the fundamental platform that is Amazon.com. They can build their own applications very effectively. It's almost closer to an ecosystem" (Bezos, 2003).

One of our champions in reconciling inner and outer direction is again Michael Dell. He observed in this respect: "One of the things that makes the Internet so exciting is that it brings the outside in. In today's market place you cannot afford to become insulated in your own activities" (Trompenaars and Hampden-Turner, 2001).

Dell's relationship with a supplier is neither "inside" Dell nor "inside" the supplier. What the Internet can do is host an entire ecosystem of suppliers, customers, partners, and subcontractors. Instead of ordering spare parts from its suppliers Dell allows them to discover for themselves the current state of inventories, by how many units and new orders from customers will draw down those inventories and make sure that Dell never runs out of components, while minimizing its carrying costs. Suppliers have the information to deliver "just in time" as their supply contracts specify. All elements in the ecosystem adjust themselves in coevolutionary patterns of mutuality.

"By virtually integrating with our suppliers in this way, we literally bring them into our business. And because our entire production is built to customer order, it requires dynamic and tight inventory control. By working virtually with our company, we challenge our suppliers to reach new heights of quality and efficiency. This improves their process and their inventory control, which creates greater value for them as well as for us and our customers," Dell explains (ibid.).

Instead of Amazon.com and Dell instructing their partners, suppliers, and subcontractors what to do, they provide and share with them the knowledge on which those instructions would have been based. The partner can then combine sources of information to make even more intelligent decisions. The ideal is to cooperate seamlessly, to use knowledge from the whole system to enable each node to behave autonomously.

Once again, both Amazon and Dell manage this cooperation with a high degree of sophistication. At Dell metrics of supplier/partner performance are agreed upon jointly every year, and these can be reviewed through Dell's secure web portal for suppliers. Through this portal each major supplier has its own equivalent of a customer's Premier Page. The portal also allows suppliers to link into Dell's own procurement orders, factory flow, etc.

At Amazon readers have an opportunity to write a review of a book and other readers can tell others how helpful the review was. "The idea of a merchant getting to know customers, introducing customers to each other, and making recommendations is, in a sense, a return to yesterday," Bezos was quoted saying in *PC World* in 2000. "In a sense, what technology has taken away from us is the ability for small-town merchants to make recommendations. But I think that what technology has taken away, maybe over time, technology can return."

Amazon.com's site currently uses two different methods:

1. Personalization, by tracking buyers' patterns and behavior to deliver recommendations for other books, and

2. Customization, by allowing users to rate different books to further refine recommendations. In using customization, Amazon's goal was to correct the misinterpretation of user behavior. Let's say you decided to buy a book for a friend. After that purchase, Amazon would base its recommendation list on your most recent buys and browsing habits – not neces-

sarily now reflecting your taste and needs since it would be distorted by the book you had bought as a gift. Registered users might find it annoying to see books that didn't match their own interests in their recommendation lists, and being able to refine the list and remove items from it would make users more confident in checking Amazon's automated recommendations in the future.

Amazon also uses collaborative filtering data mining techniques to recommend products to return visitors based on the purchases of other customers who have bought the same or similar products.

Moreover, new levels of mutual understanding and greater joint intelligence are achieved where you and your partners share the same body of information and can follow each other's reasoning. Everyone has the same "inside information" and can draw the attention of either party to something the other may have missed. This dilemma is shown in Figure 8.9.

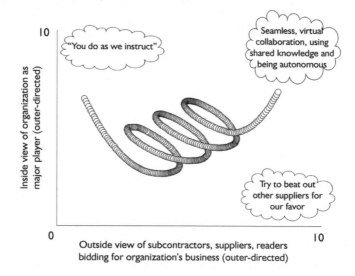

Figure 8.9 Uniting inner and outer

Economic value in this model stems from speed, effectiveness, and complexity. Instead of arguing about who is right or wrong, each party cites the information that has informed its decision. In this way mental models are shared, and conveyed to the minds of other players, in a process where decisions are mutually qualifying.

For Amazon's customers, more and more data – such as reviews – is thrust before their eyes, often promoting opposite opinions. This is now more than *caveat emptor* (let the buyer beware). On the Internet that has been replaced by a new paradigm – *caveat lector* (let the reader beware).

Dilemma 5: Premier Pages: The bridge between gift and sale

Romeo said to Juliet "The more I give you the more I have." This has always been the case of relationships based on true love, but only recently has it become more and more true of relationships between business partners. We are not talking here of well-springs of positive emotions, but of sharing important information and allowing the combinations of that information to procreate new knowledge and new synergies, usable by all parties in the interaction. Again we'll go back to Dell.

Michael Dell is typically eloquent on this topic. "The real potential of the Internet lies in its ability to transform relationships within the traditional supplier vendor customer chain. We are using the Internet to share our own applications openly with suppliers and customers, creating true information partnerships. We are developing applications internally, with an Internet browser at the front end, giving them to our customers and suppliers" (Trompenaars and Hampden-Turner, 2001).

Since Dell computers are an integral part of the information and knowledge communicated, as well as a means of storing, receiving, retrieving, and sending knowledge, the more this knowledge is "given away" the more necessary it becomes to purchase the computers to which this knowledge refers and by which it is organized. Several web entrepreneurs made their fortune by giving away programs, browsers, tools, etc. and asking users to make a donation if they found the gift useful. Their subsequent enrichment was largely or entirely the result of voluntary reciprocity. Similarly if Dell supplies you with vital information then buying their computers is a rational response and a means of keeping that information coming.

Instead of arguing whether this is "really" a gift or "really" a sale, we need to understand that co-generating knowledge on the Internet transcends this dichotomy and that gifts and sales facilitate one another. The bridge that Michael Dell has built between Dell, its customers, its suppliers, partners, and subcontractors, etc. are the Premier Pages which we've already mentioned. As described earlier, these are password-protected web pages, serving the special information needs of business customers and technology partners. There are over 40,000 of them and they serve as a dynamic interface for customers and partners to access relevant information. For a corporate customer this could include information on global accounting, preapproved pricing and configurations, technical papers, product road maps, and so on. At the click of a mouse, corporate clients have immediate access to a complete picture of their purchasing channels. For a particular client this could be the number of computer systems bought at its European operation, details of standing orders, or preapproved configurations and discounts. Of course, customers had to be willing to share information with Dell and its suppliers in the first place in order to benefit from better-informed relationships. Many purchasing departments are secretive by habit, but they learn that being more transparent can lead to more attractive and better-customized deals. What Dell does is to model the transparency it seeks from others and waits for them to reciprocate, so that confidences are mutual.

Michael Dell explains: "Driving change in your own organization is hard enough; driving change in other organizations is nearly impossible. But we believed and still believe that the Internet will become as pervasive as the phone. We know it was too important to our business and potentially to our customers' businesses to wait for them to figure it out for themselves. What teaches parties to reveal more about themselves is experience, the more that is known about your needs, the better others can serve you" (ibid.).

But the value of Premier Pages soon became evident. Companies no longer had to work through their purchasing channels every time they needed to purchase a computer. Dell made it a point to have this kind of information up and ready from the very beginning. Dell's Premier Pages have resulted in massive savings; companies have told Dell that they are saving millions of dollars by ordering their products and getting support in this way.

Michael Dell is persuasive about the economies achieved. "Early on, Ford Motor Company estimated that it saved $2 million in initial procurement costs placing orders through its Premier Page and Shell Oil saved 15 percent of its total purchasing cost. Premier Pages also allows us to deliver critical service and support information directly to our customers, based on the specific products they buy and use. This information is drawn from the same databases our own technicians and engineers use. This doesn't necessarily result in major cost savings for Dell. But it has resulted in significant cost savings for our customers, enriching their relationship with Dell."

Premier Pages are also a bridge to research and development

between Dell and its partners: "The Internet is also changing the way we work with our technology partners. We are moving to truly collaborative research and development models, using the Internet to share information openly and work together in real time. We can also engage our customers in our product development, giving them the same level of access to critical information as our own people have. For example, we were able to develop and introduce an award-winning line of notebook computers, using the Internet to keep a common set of records by engineers in the United States and Asia. By making the same information available to critical partners we were able to close the information loop. A traditional, vertically integrated company would have spent months, if not years, designing parts and building them" (ibid.).

Dell has built supplier web pages for its top 20 suppliers, covering 90 percent of its procurement needs. These pages allow Dell suppliers to provide Dell with rapid information on its capacities, upside capabilities, inventories in their supply lines, component quality as measured by Dell's own metrics, and current cost structures.

Dell passes on to the supplier direct and immediate customer feedback, gathered in part through its customer Premier Pages. This covers such areas as quality in the field, current forecasts and future demand, special technical requirements, and end-user market pricing.

This type of collaborative partnership is a starting point, or a portal, for future innovation. Any innovative process will have to begin from a point where time and distance have been shrunk and where development speed is unimpeded. The quality and directness of the relationship, the speed with which you can channel information, and the dynamic forces that you thereby create will determine the long-term sustainability of your position in an industry with notori-

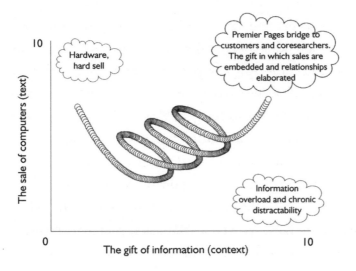

Figure 8.10 Premier Pages – the bridge between gift and sale

ously short life cycles. Like Dell, you will have blurred the traditional boundaries between buyer, seller, and supplier, and you will have created a radically new creative enterprise.

The process by which Premier Pages becomes the bridge between the gift and the sale is depicted in Figure 8.10.

What Dell has done is left behind the hard sell of hardware, and by gifting to all members of its network the relevant information, it promotes the computers and the relationships which convey that knowledge. The computers are the text within the context, helping to structure and move information across the bridges of knowledge, which join all members of Dell's ecosystem. In the progressive, mutual revelation of deep needs these bridges become preferable to all others. The wealth of knowledge that ties together members of this network would be very hard to duplicate or reconstitute. The Net binds its members by hundreds of threads.

In 2000, Victor Keegan wrote in the *Guardian* that it was difficult to move without hearing the sound of crashing dot-com companies. The expression "dot-com" had become, in itself, a sassy suffix for coolness in business. Any company that didn't embrace the Web for selling (and purchasing), would be smothered by those that did. "So what went wrong?" asked Keegan. Nearly all the early claims of the Internet were, and still are, true. Yes, it is an all-embracing change that will transform the way we do business, the way we are educated, and the way we are entertained. What the preppy-preneurs forgot, however, was the importance of two rules of the old economy and one of the new. As well as the usual problems facing start-up companies, the first generation of dot-coms failed to understand the nature of the beast they had embraced: on the Internet the consumer, not the producer, is king.

Our research and analysis of the success of organizations like Dell shows that it is essential for marketers to understand the significance of the new marketing paradigms based on the interactionist model, for them to then elicit the tensions and dilemmas that result for their own business, and to then seek creative reconcilations for each dilemma. In this way, new innovative solutions and new ways of doing business will result from the extraordinary potentialities of the Internet in marketing.

Dilemmas of strategic marketing

So far we have mainly considered aspects of "operational marketing" that deal with the problems of the application of marketing tools across cultures in order to realize the detailed marketing aims of the organization and the evaluation of the effectiveness of these activities. Because marketing is a major factor in the profitability of companies, senior management must be able to coordinate all these marketing efforts with the other aspects of the business.

We must, therefore, now turn to "strategic marketing." This is the process of formulating marketing strategy, based on examining and analyzing the environment and organization, formulating strategic aims and the ways of reaching them. The effort and necessary resourcing in strategic marketing is often proportional to the intensity of competition in the market place.

Evidence from both THT's WebCue research tools and our clients identifies key areas of most concern. These are:

1. Falling prices and thus increasing price competition.

2. An overall rise in competition as more suppliers compete for customers across the globe and as markets become increasingly oligopolistic.

3. The increasing requirement to seek higher and higher levels of customer satisfaction through the role of the customer service function.

Many of these changes owe their origin to declining product (and service) differentiation and thus the race is accelerating towards new sources of competitive advantage. In the continuous stream of innovative products and solutions, the strategic marketer has to live with the consequences of short product life cycles, rapid loss of early advantage in the market, and the corresponding fall in prices to retain market share with the ever-falling gross margins that result. In the service sector, the key issues manifest as the rising emphasis of the quality of service rather than pricing.

Already, or in only a few more years, these changes will continue to result in:

1.   fewer and larger players through consolidation of competition and mergers and acquisitions,

2.   the changing requirements and value systems of customers, and, of course,

3.   the globalization of markets and competition.

Strategic marketing has had to change – but must do so even more in the future. Already we have seen marketing shift from a (specific) separate function to being diffused throughout channels, product ranges, or technologies. Marketing as originally conceived is gone, but some new framework for marketing is essential through which organizations can survive in their increasingly hostile markets. In our language and conceptual thinking, strategic marketing faces a number of key dilemmas as a result of these transformations that we can now explore. Organizations that can continuously reconcile these dilemmas will survive in the future.

For convenience we can classify these dilemmas of strategic market-ing as:

1.   The top-down versus bottom-up dilemma.

2.   The inside-out versus the outside-in dilemma.

3.   The lateral tension between different alternative activities (such as sales and R&D).

THE TOP-DOWN VERSUS BOTTOM-UP DILEMMA

According to Al Ries and Jack Trout, notorious marketing gurus from the US, a lot of organizations follow a dead-end street. The authors of best sellers such as *Positioning*, *The Battle for your Mind*, *Bottom-Up Marketing*, and *Marketing Warfare* argue for an alternative to the path that the business in America has generally followed. Loaded with examples, everything must be turned "upside-down" (Ries and Trout, 1982, 1989, 1997). You no longer start simply with a strategy but with a tactic. It is not top-down but bottom-up that brings glory, and a broad product scale also leads to calamity. If you are focused, you can master the competition.

They make the point by representing a mirror for the overly traditional approach of top-down strategic marketing thinking. In their work one extreme approach needs to be abandoned and exchanged for another. But the more skeptical European spirit would probably be persuaded by a less extreme proposition. If we look closer, using the same lenses we use throughout this book, we can see that – once again – a series of dilemmas must be reconciled.

According to Ries and Trout's books, positioning theory in the human mind has a limited number of places available for the organization and its products to fill. This is very easy if the position is open, but very difficult if a competitor has already taken that place. General Motors, for example, never tried to take over the position of the Mercedes with the Cadillac. Repositioning of the competition, though, would be a possible approach.

Most writers take this new view that marketing is not a one-dimensional process of serving a customer. The nature of modern marketing is one of being more malignant, stronger, and richer in purpose than the competition. Marketing is war and the competitor is your enemy. The position and its ground must be conquered. How is that best done? By what Ries and Trout have called bottom-up marketing.

But just what is the value of a strategic plan if you cannot predict the movements of a competitor? Nevertheless, each day, piles of strategic marketing plans are written. They are rather like owning a surrealist painting, say one by Salvador Dali. You don't have a clue what it represents, but you'd miss it if you suddenly had a blank wall. We shouldn't start with internal matters such as strategic plans, missions, budgets, and aims. These limit the freedom of movement of the top marketer.

We quoted from the introduction to *Bottom-Up Marketing* in our parent book to this series. It is relevant enough to bear repetition here: "In almost every category, today's business arena has become warlike. We agree that this change in the environment has made the traditional "top-down" (only) approach to marketing obsolete. What good are long-term strategic plans when you cannot predict future competitive moves? How can you react to a competitor if your resources are tied up in a long-term plan?" But you do need to reconcile across this top-down, bottom-up dimension.

Based on our evidence, we argue that this dilemma for marketing is universal.

On the one hand...	Whilst on the other hand...
We need a strategy that gives us a long-term context and directions for our journey.	We need to be able to create different and unique ideas in our short-term needs to best serve our environment.

Graphically this dilemma can be presented as in Figure 9.1.

In the US Domino's Pizza has focused entirely on delivering pizzas within a thirty-minute radius of its outlets. Pizza Hut felt the compe-

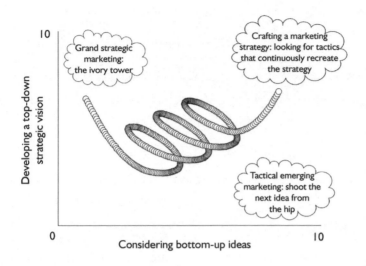

Figure 9.1 Top down versus bottom up

tition and added a fast delivery service to its normal restaurant activities. Normally Pizza Hut, with its enormous market strength, could have crunched a number of Domino's. But this did not happen because Domino's had set up a network of establishments that had but one strategic concept: delivery within thirty minutes or your money back. For Pizza Hut this was an extra activity that lacked the focus to make life difficult for Domino's.

Of course it is too naive to assume that building a strategy from a tactic is the only effective means of doing marketing. Mintzberg had already identified this dilemma by speaking of grand top-down strategy and emergent bottom-up strategy (Mintzberg, 1998). We ourselves have seen enough organizations that thread the one tactic to the other but are not able to achieve strategic harmony.

Our research data confirms that in cultures that are more specifically oriented, the crafting strategy that links "up" and "down" detail, reconciled with the larger perspective, will more likely start with the tactical experiment from which a more holistic strategy is molded. In

German cars

Germans seem to have more of a need to start from an overall, diffuse, holistic marketing strategy and to try out a number of tactics within this context.

In this way, Mercedes Benz, starting from a superior technical quality perspective, launched a diverse number of cars on the market from the very small and youthful Smart to the extravagantly large 600-series. Success speaks for itself.

Also, in recent years, Porsche launched the Boxster and the Cayenne from a strategic combination of engineering strength and speed with much success. Finally Volkswagen sold all its cars from the concept of high quality compact cars available to the masses.

contrast, more diffuse cultures make a movement from the larger whole to specific market segments. In the end it is the relationship between the two that is the crucial aspect of international marketing success, not simply the starting point.

Eventually any bottom-up marketing approach will also have to solve the dilemma between "aiming at champions" and "ensuring a broad consensus between inferior products and people representing them." The advantage of a more mundane approach is that personal agendas are pushed into the background by having such matters depersonalized. Conversely we need our gurus and champions – both in people and products – because each concept that gets maximum support will already be in use by competitors. The route to reconciling this dilemma is to have teams compete within a "champion system," such as that used in Goldman Sachs, 3M, and Intel over many years. This leads to cooperation in order to be able to act competitively. We should take them as exemplars; their marketing position needs no crown.

It is inherent in Ries and Trout's work that they believe that tactics in marketing will automatically lead to the soundest strategy. We disagree. Our evidence supports the assertion that both tactics and strategy feed into each other in a continuous crafting process. The starting point depends on your culture. Short-term cultures like to start with tactics. Conversely, long-term cultures might start with a strategy to contextualize their tactics. As always, the winners are those who can integrate the dilemma (reconcile). Which direction you start from is irrelevant.

THE INSIDE-OUT VERSUS THE OUTSIDE-IN DILEMMA

The second recurring strategic marketing dilemma is of the same nature but is nevertheless significantly different. It concerns the well-recognized tension between technology push and market pull. Do we make something we want and try to find a market to sell it in, or do we let the demands and wants of customers feedback into our product planning?

Both extreme approaches lack enough integrity once you go international. For many years, a pure push from technology worked successfully in internally controlled societies such as the UK, the Netherlands, and the US. Conversely, a focus solely on the customer worked well in externally oriented cultures such as Japan and other Asian societies. However, technology push was doomed to failure when the internationalization process accelerated in the 1960s. American-produced and conceived consumer electronics were wiped out by foreign competition and Japanese products took their place.

A push strategy can work, especially in situations of low competition. In cases where competition is strong, this push approach leads to selling your fantastic products into the ultimate niche market. As it happens, this market has no customers.

The Dutch company Philips is a splendid example of an organization that still struggles with the marketing of products such as the CD and the DVD. Philips invents and Sony sells, say the cynics. It is typically Japanese to be fully empathetic with customers. But this extreme "market pull" approach also has its restrictions as customers often have no idea what they want.

This dilemma often starts from the different ideologies of marketing and R&D. Mutual communication is very essential in making this relationship fruitful, and is a precondition for reconciling this dilemma. Bang & Olufsen are an excellent example here.

Through THT's WebCue, B&O framed this dilemmas in their own words as:

> The disconnection of Sales and Marketing from Research, Development, and Production and the elevation of the latter functions to a dominant position, so that marketing commercial considerations were largely ignored.

In terms of our conceptual framework, this was a dilemma between inner-directed push and outer-directed pull.

B&O had all the classic symptoms of technology-push by inner-directed, individualistic genius entrepreneurs, who had built a company that celebrated their own notable strengths and (after the death of Olufsen, one of the founders) played down what they lacked. The market, sales, customers, service, and effective distribution were

B&O

Bang & Olufsen faced the challenge to develop an understanding of the evolving market and patterns of demand, before aligning its own products with this knowledge. "We had to teach people how to think in business terms, without sacrificing their pride in their creativity and their products," its CEO Anders Knutsen recalled. "Beauty, style, and technical superiority were everything. No one had been paying attention to development costs or commercial success." The product had actually taken the place of the people who were supposed to lead.

Knutsen regarded this imbalance as so serious that he made himself the head of Marketing and Sales until an internationally experienced VP could be found. In this way he was able to discover facts that the company had long ignored for too long. "B&O thought communication was a one-way process and that its customers were dealers, not consumers. Of course, the dealers were passing on our arrogant treatment to the final customers." Anders Knutsen discovered that dealers used the B&O aura to upgrade the image of their dealerships, while putting most of their energies into selling rival products that were better suited to the market, including Philips, Daewoo, Sony, and Grundig. These appeared reasonably priced when compared to B&O's expensive, upmarket products. "There was a radical disconnection between the product and the market," Knutsen recalled. "It was as if we communicated to the product and not with the people."

Source: Trompenaars and Hampden-Turner (2001).

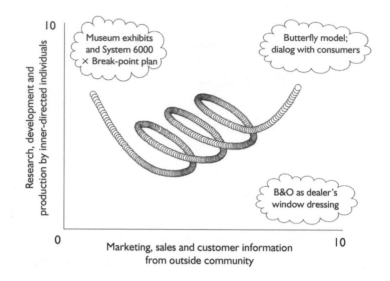

Figure 9.2 Inner-directed push versus outer-directed pull

neglected: everything that lay outside the select criteria of "brilliant professionals" was in the wider community. From these B&O took little or no direction. The dilemma is shown in Figure 9.2.

B&O's museum-type exhibits and System 6000, which was built without anything to play on it, are symptomatic of an excessive emphasis upon the vertical axis at the expense of the horizontal. The Break-point plan, point "X," is the culmination of this chronic imbalance, as B&O faced a cash-flow crisis.

Knutsen realized that he must move towards the marketing "horn" of the dilemma, that is the horizontal axis. As we've seen, he appointed himself marketing director *pro tem*, at which point he discovered that distributors were using B&O's reputation for quality as a backdrop window dressing for selling rival products. His solution was the butterfly model, with products and marketing to the final consumer as two coordinated "wings" of the same operation. Fewer, but more dedicated, distributors facilitated dialogue with consumers and the company. Consumers could order direct from retail outlets and build up a modular system over time, allowing them to spread the cost.

A form in which this dilemma can manifest itself comes from the tension between a focus on a limited number of products or an extension of the range or portfolio. The advantage of focus is depth. The disadvantage is that many opportunities can be missed with existing customers. The advantage of extending a range is that the producer can exploit existing brand reputation and distribution channels. For the customer, however, it becomes messy…look at the confusion between Classic Coke, Coke Light, Caffeine-free Coke, Cherry Coke, and Vanilla Coke – especially if they stand side-by-side on a single shelf.

There is also a related strategic marketing dilemma between product and concept. We think that Ries and Trout are going a bit too far in concluding that advertising is going into a dead end street if it focuses on the specific characteristics of a product. Marketing must be a "war of concepts," in which the whole system of values needs to be addressed. We believe that, if an organization wants to be internationally successful, it needs to choose a modular approach, in the same way that Bang & Olufsen and Lego have done. They have united the outstanding quality of their specific products with becoming growing systems or ways of life.

THE LATERAL TENSION BETWEEN DIFFERENT ALTERNATIVE ACTIVITIES

The third major area to consider concerns the relationships within the organization where marketing is situated. The main tensions here derive from the relationship between R&D and marketing/sales.

In spite of the many books and articles aimed at making their readers understand cultural differences, it is remarkable just how little attention is paid to the effects these cultural differences have within an organization. Talk at random to any employee of an innovative organization and you will receive confirmation that the relationship between its R&D and Marketing Departments is its Achilles heel. THT's extensive database of 65,000 respondents has captured such cultural constructs, and confirms that the orientation of both these functional groups differ significantly. The manifestations of this tense relationship are revealed in three main areas. Let's look at them.

Researchers often complain that Marketing rarely allows them enough time to deliver an adequate piece of work. In their view, Marketing gives them too little time to develop, test, and fine-tune a product, which often leads to discrepancies between client expectations and the delivered goods. When this happens, R&D see most of the profits as lost in upgrading the product to the originally expected standard. Marketeers, in their turn, often complain about a lack of flexibility and slow reaction speeds in R&D.

Our research into differences of time horizons between both functional groups shows that the time horizon of the marketers is significantly shorter than that of people working in R&D. Considering the exercise opposite and you can see the differences in scores between functions.

In addition, R&D employees are also much more universalistic than marketers and especially salespeople. This last group seems to move from one exceptional situation to the next in their belief that every sale is unique, which infuriates researchers.

A second source of misunderstanding seems to be in the area of com-

Exercise

Consider the relative significance of the past, present, and future. You will be asked to indicate your relative time horizons for the past, present, and future by giving a number.

7 = *Years*

6 = *Months*

5 = *Weeks*

4 = *Days*

3 = *Hours*

2 = *Minutes*

1 = *Seconds*

My past started ☐ ago, and ended ☐ ago.

My present started ☐ ago, and ends ☐ from now.

My future will start ☐ ago, and will end ☐ from now.

munication style. Here also THT's research shows that R&D people often communicate in a direct, specialized, and specific tone. Their use of language is to the point but is only understood by their own small group because of the jargon they often use. Marketers tend to use more flowery language, which is often less to the point. Sometimes the easiest solution seems to be to cease communication completely. Inevitably this leads to significant problems, and in particular to the complaint of researchers that they are involved too little in the marketing process.

Finally the lack of understanding and empathy for each other's work and culture seems to be one of the ultimate reasons for the tension in their relationship. Researchers complain that marketers

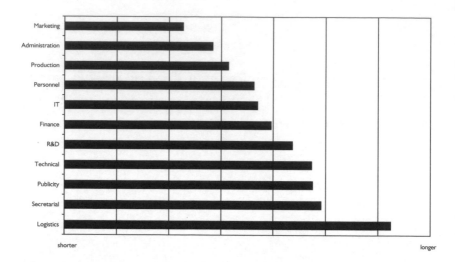

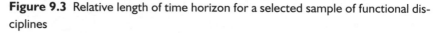

Figure 9.3 Relative length of time horizon for a selected sample of functional disciplines

fail to discover the full possibilities of specific markets while, at the same time, exploring markets that don't actually exist. Marketers see researchers as living too much in their own world. This, of course, is another fundamental difference, between external and internal views.

But what needs to be done to take better advantage of these different orientations? The Marketing Science Institute conducted interesting research, published in 1996, on how organizations can take advantage of this fundamental field of tension:

The exploration of cross-functional development groups

These so-called "skunk" groups can achieve many successes when they integrate functions on-site and, further, when they are not hindered by existing bureaucratic processes. In these groups physical, linguistic, and cultural borders are very effectively overcome. Much attention, however, needs to be given to the quality of management in these groups.

Moving people between functions

Cross-functional moves between R&D and Marketing Departments are not easy because of the specialized nature of their activities. Starting with the recruitment phase, companies need to work at attracting people who can be useful across functions and can be placed in a variety of environments. Moreover, focused internal development programs need to support the mobility of staff.

The development of informal social systems

This aim is not easily achieved because it cannot be forced upon people, but recreational activities can encourage informal social interaction in a light-hearted way. Here too, much can be achieved by minimizing the physical distance between the functions. Fruitful collaboration often occurs unexpectedly around central coffee points.

Changing the organizational design

General Electric and Philips have many coordination groups that bring together specializations in a balanced way. With good management stimulating cross-fertilization, many cultural and linguistic barriers can be crossed. The matrix organization is another option in which functional specialists carry on reporting to their particular boss and have a "dotted line" responsibility toward the project leader.

A more focused reward system

It appears that marketing staff very often have a variable reward system that is linked to market share. Developers frequently receive their bonuses on the basis of technological developments. A reward system that is very dependent on how much information is transferred across functions will have a positive effect on the revenues and profitability of a company.

Formal management processes such as project management can add much to the effectiveness of the integration between R&D and marketing

This is how Mitsubishi, for example, developed the Quality Function Deployment (QFD) process whereby the client, via a program called "Qualityhouse," was given a coordinating role between marketing and R&D. Such processes seem to decrease market uncertainties as well as having a positive effect on the innovative power of an organization. This has now been extended further to DFD – Design-Function-Deployment (see Jebb and Woolliams, 2000).

However, even in the event of an organization following all of the above advice, ultimate success will depend on the quality of leadership and the organizational culture in which these processes need to unfold. In this context, let's look further at Bang & Olufsen.

Technical excellence and the emotional climate

Anders Knutsen saw himself confronting the tension between technical excellence and emotional appeal. The latter was a subtle and diffuse concept. Beautiful audio-visual information had to be conveyed on instruments worthy of their content, in the same way that the instruments of an orchestra carry the spirit of the composer and express that composer's feeling. "Time is in our favor," Knutsen said. "The world is flooded with discount junk products that strive to become classics, and products with emotional value will be strongly placed in our 'throwaway' culture" (Trompenaars and Hampden-Turner, 2001).

In the history of B&O both technical excellence and emotional climate had been important, more so than sales or marketing, but even these leading values had not been reconciled or harmonized. First one was dominant and then the other, and their fight for dominance had made the product which resulted unaffordable. So Knutsen created "Idealand," a non-localized space where engineers, music lovers, designers, and others, both within R&D and outside the company in the community of experts, could engage in an dialog that would both stimulate ideas and balance them.

Another balance is between the audio and the visual that come together in digital sound pictures. Carl Henrik Jeppesen, B&O's chief engineer, explained to us: "We send development teams, usually to the US, to study what sounds and sights are being made and consumed. They go to concerts, music studios, discotheques, clubs. You need someone to champion the original sound picture and the emotions generated from them and someone to champion the technologies of recording and playing those sound pictures. It is this creative clash between the artists and engineers that gives you optimal integration. In the old days one competence would dominate the others but no more. There came the day when Anders Knutsen and his team refused to sponsor a prototype product because the costs were out of line. That was a real shock for all of us. It had never happened here!

"We now test our products with our customers and if they like them, sales start at once with a projected product life of ten years. We position ourselves in the market in such a way that it confirms or fails to confirm the hypotheses developed in Idealand. The latter is no private muse, but a testing laboratory for viable ideas, a set of hypotheses to which our customers say yes or no" (Private communication).

B&O elicited this dilemma, which they defined in their own words as:

On the one hand...

An aesthetic and emotional commitment to the beauty of sights and sounds recorded and played

On the other hand...

An engineering and technological commitment to brilliant scientific solutions

In our conceptual framework, this is expressed as:

On the one hand...

Particularism of art

Diffuseness of experience

Affective

On the other hand...

Universalism of science

Specificity of solution

Neutral

This is illustrated in Figure 9.4. Thus B&O's dilemma actually touches on three of our dimensions.

There is the diffuse and affective experiences of particular art forms and the specific neutrality of scientific and universal solutions. B&O

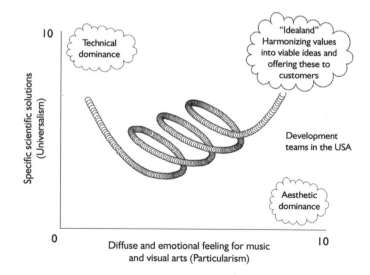

Figure 9.4 Reconciling universalism with particularism at Bang & Olufsen

had two strong traditions, often at odds with one another and hence tilting the balance of power, now this way and now that. On the vertical axis of Figure 9.4 we have the engineering commitment to specific scientific solutions and on the horizontal axis the aesthetic and emotional commitment to music and visual art forms.

As we've seen, to counterbalance the strong influence of R&D, teams were sent to the US and elsewhere to try to capture the ineffable qualities of new sounds and sights, so that these could be faithfully rendered. You have to love what you are trying to reproduce in high fidelity, in order to convey the genuine experience. It is in Idealand that these various values met, clashed, and achieved a final harmony. Each group championed their own values until these found inclusion in a larger system and in a more creative synthesis – all watched over by a principle of parsimony that sought to cut costs to the bone.

THE COST–BENEFIT ANALYSIS OF MARKETING ACROSS CULTURES

Finally the problem for marketers is that there has been no commonly accepted framework that relates models of cross culture and reconciliation to bottom-line business results. Supplier, distributor, and buyer give different emphasis to individual or team efforts, different emphasis to personal relationships within business, different emphasis to status of older, more experienced staff, different emphasis on the present and future, etc. But what does this mean in terms of marketing strategy? What are the consequences for prioritizing resource allocation and strategic decision making in marketing planning when trying to put effort and/or resource into reconciling these dilemmas? How can we synergize these models of cross culture with the marketing planning formulation process? These questions have gone unanswered for too long.

For example, an in-depth survey by Woolliams and Dickerson (1999) was conducted across Eastern Europe, the Middle East, and Africa for a major client seeking to be more effective in its global marketing effort. It revealed a need for a model to manage the complex relationships of their key customers around the world. Their employees and distributors were interviewed from the European emerging markets department of a selected company division. This was intended to uncover the existing dilemmas between the different partners and customers from the different cultures. A common need was identified for a strategic decision-making model that would enable respondents to align sales resources around the world.

The new model, based on many of these types of situations from our consulting practice over the last few years, is an extension of portfolio analysis that includes cross culture. The challenge is to find, prioritize, and quantify the cultural dilemmas that have to be reconciled. In our new model we first elicit these dilemmas and then identify from which dimension of culture they derive. We then obtain opinions from key players (e.g. supplier, distributor, and customer in the supply chain) as to how each dilemma impacts on business. Measures include the effect on short-term sales, medium-term sales, costs, time delays, etc. We then combine these data using hierarchical clustering algorithms, concordance, and correspondence analysis to produce a cultural business portfolio map. In practice the parties themselves can use the model. They follow our prescriptive approach, identifying the relevant variables for themselves in an atmosphere of collaboration and mutual respect with their business partners.

After entering the relevant variables into the computer model, a map is generated that demonstrates to a decision-maker where problems with customers exist. One axis represents an index of the relative attractiveness of each subsidiary, distributor, or customer (market potential, cultural differences) and the other represents the current or evolving business position and status of the development of the supplier–customer relationship (e.g. market share, revenues, low or high context). Now the strategist has a decision-making framework that gives a holistic view and serves as a basis for prioritizing strategic actions to gain competitive advantage.

Suppose for example that Rockwell needs to make a decision about where to invest a limited marketing budget to build relationships with major customers in Russia, Lithuania, and Turkey. Russia demonstrates a great potential for increased sales growth, but there also exists a major cultural difference with the supplier that will cost Rockwell $500,000. The cultural difference between Rockwell and the Russian customer is small (indicating that the market penetration rate may be higher and the sales budget easier to achieve) but the Lithuanian customer only distributes products within a small geographical territory. In contrast, a customer in Turkey is distributing products in the emerging markets with high prospects for sales growth, but the cultural differences will require an up-front Rockwell investment that will cost $250,000 this year and $250,000 next year before a return on the relationship (ROR) is realized. How should Rockwell prioritize market development?

Rather than just seeing cultural differences and their reconciliation as a cost, they should be seen as an investment – just like R&D. Investing this accounting period on developing the relationship and reconciling strategic dilemmas will generate increased sales growth in the next period.

Classical model	**Our new model**
Profit and Loss account	Profit and Loss account
Sales Revenue	Sales Revenue
Less costs of sales (includes reconciling dilemmas)	Less direct cost of sales
= Gross Margin	= Gross Margin
Less fixed costs	Less reconciling dilemmas
= Net Profit before Tax and Interest	Less Fixed costs
	= Net Profit before Tax and Interest
Balance Sheet	Balance Sheet
Fixed Assets	Fixed Assets
Current Assets	Current Assets
Cash	Cash
Stock	Stock
	Dilemmas reconciled
–	–
Liabilities	Liabilities
Creditors	Creditors
=	=
Total Finance	Total Finance

Our ROR index (measuring the relative return on different relationship investments) provides a means to evaluate market options. It is computed as the additional gross sales margin as a function of the discounted amount of investment required to reconcile the cultural differences in a given marketplace. This index enables the strategist to identify where the cultural differences exist with customers today and where they can be in the future. The index also provides the shareholder with an informed analysis and rationale of management's planning, as well as being a welcome addition to a

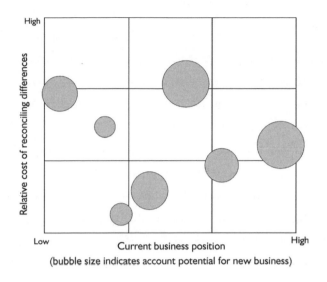

High

Relative cost of reconciling differences

Low

Current business position

High

(bubble size indicates account potential for new business)

Figure 9.5 Prioritizing reconciliations by cross referencing to business benefits

company's corporate annual report. Senior management will now have a clear picture of where to allocate resources to build the relationships in each market and to prioritize the reconciliation of strategic dilemmas as a means to sustain sales growth.

In the same way that ISO9000 provides a vehicle for quality management certification and action, our new framework provides a mechanism for undertaking a cultural audit in business strategy formulation. Management benefits from using this model to both identify the impact of cross-cultural dilemmas in their business strategy, as well as providing a decision-making framework for prioritizing action and investment.

As trading in the global village becomes the norm, market planning that can accommodate cross culture becomes mandatory. The model described here could become an essential component of Rockwell's toolkit to maximize shareholder value.

This chapter again shows how marketing, and the dilemmas of marketing, must pervade thinking at all levels. Marketing can no longer be a functional discipline that is a single, discrete arm of an organization chart. Marketing must have a diffuse relationship throughout the organization. It is no longer simply market push or pull, no longer top down or bottom up, but a different type of logic that transcends these differences to provide integrated solutions. Our new marketing paradigm thus requires a mindset that reconciles these continuing dilemmas that can arise from all of the above cultural dimensions. Today's successful marketing is the result of linking learning effort across each dimension with the contrasting orientations and viewpoints.

CHAPTER 10

Develop your capacity to reconcile dilemmas

We are very aware of the dangers of stereotyping cultures. That is not our purpose. The examples of dilemmas of marketing we have given throughout this book were chosen to help you, the reader, begin to think about some of the challenges you face when dealing with marketing across cultures. Being able to apply the methodology presented throughout this book will give you a general framework that you can apply across any culture.

Similarly we cannot obviously hope to have listed every dilemma you will face. The more you look for dilemmas the more you will realise how important they are as the root underlying cause of the problems you face – for yourself (the ideographic level) and for your organization (the nomothetic level).

Because marketing is about messages, not only about what is said but how it is said, you are faced with first eliciting the dilemmas and then reconciling: The first step is to express your problem in the form of a dilemma. Let's take an example. How should we design our advertisement? Yes, there is the old adage: "a picture is worth a thousand words," but a picture is not as effective as words in conveying factual information. So we can express the issue as:

On the one hand...	**On the other hand...**
Should our message be conveyed primarily in pictures?	Should our message be conveyed primarily in words?

Advertisers often place great emphasis on vivid and creative illustrations or photography. But ads that contain the same information, presented in either visual or verbal form, have been found to induce different reactions. The verbal versions affect ratings on the utilitarian aspects of the product, while the visual affects esthetic evaluation more (Grass and Wallace, 1994).

Verbal elements are more effective when reinforced by an accompanying picture especially if the illustration is "framed" (the message in the picture is the same as the text or audio). It requires more effort to process visual data, and that is why these are more appropriate for higher-level constructs. But verbal content also disappears more rapidly from the memory. So we also have to consider aspects of repetition.

On the one hand...	On the other hand...
Should we repeat our message to keep reinforcing it to achieve familiarity?	Should we restrict the frequency of our message to avoid boredom and oversaturation?

Familiarity breeds contempt, but people also like to see things that are familiar to them because it reinforces their value systems and makes them comfortable by giving some stability in their lives. Too much repetition gives rise to habituation, so that the consumer no longer pays attention to the stimulus (message/advertisement). We therefore have to reconcile what is normally known as the two-factor theory. This states that two separate processes are carried out when a consumer sees the repeat of an ad. This can be summarized as:

On the one hand...	On the other hand...
Should we repeat our message to keep reinforcing it to achieve familiarity?	Should we restrict the frequency of our message to avoid boredom and oversaturation?
It increases familiarity and reduces uncertainty about the product or service	Boredom increases with each exposure
There comes a point where the amount of boredom exceeds the amount of uncertainty that is reduced.	

Advertisers can reconcile this dilemma by limiting the amount of exposure per repetition – by using very short, 15-second spots for

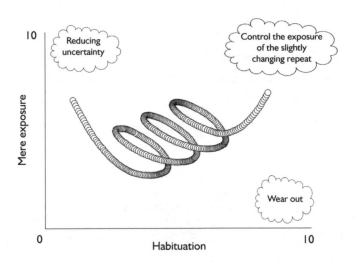

Figure 10.1 The repetition versus familiarity dilemma

example. They can also alter the content slightly so that the common theme remains but with sufficient changes to keep the viewer alert.

You can practice now by thinking about the following marketing problems and seeing if you can express these in the form of dilemmas.

In advertisements:

- Should a conclusion be drawn, or should this be left to the viewer/reader or listener?
- Should all sides of the argument be presented or just the single-sided case that "pushes" the product's benefits?
- Should explicit comparisons be made with a competitor's products?
- Should sex appeal be used?
- Should negative emotions be exploited (e.g., fear)?
- Should humor be used?
- How concrete or vivid should the imagery and arguments be (such as showing a bad crash in a drink–drive campaign)?

The point we are making is that marketers face dilemmas constantly, and these become even more significant when transferring across cultures. So not only do you need to think about these fundamental marketing issues as dilemmas, but also about how the value orientations of each culture will affect the significance of each horn of the dilemma and how the differences can be reconciled.

Marketing issues

When formulating your marketing issues as a dilemma remember that:

We define a dilemma as "two propositions in apparent conflict." In other words a dilemma describes a situation whereby you have to choose between two good or desirable options. For example, on the one hand we need flexibility whilst on the other we also need consistency. So a dilemma describes the tension that is created due to conflicting demands.

What is not a dilemma? Here are some examples:
- A description of a current and ideal state: "We have good communication tools but we need to use them better."
- An either–or option: "Should we start hiring new employees now or wait till next year?"
- A complaint: "We make good strategic plans but due to lack of leadership we are not able to follow them through."

How to formulate a dilemma?
- Avoid the above examples of non-dilemmas.
- Describe a specific situation to explain the context of the dilemma.

- Describe the positive elements of both sides of the dilemma (e.g., individual versus group; objective versus subjective; logic versus creativity; analytical versus intuitive; formal versus informal; rules versus exceptions, etc.).

TEST YOURSELF

To assist you further, we also invite you to evaluate how well you have understood the argument that we all need to recognize, respect, and reconcile cultural differences in every aspect of marketing in order to be effective. Please take some time to study the following cases and choose one of the possible options. We hope that simply reading the cases and thinking about each option will enable you to select appropriate courses of action, just through reflection.

If you are interested further, please visit our website (www.cultureforbusiness.com) for an electronic version of these cases (and others) that will also give you some feedback. You can also determine a version of your own personal cross-cultural profile there.

Good luck!

Case 1. How do we serve hot breakfasts to US passengers?

During the planning of the strategic business alliance between British Airways and American Airlines, discussions among executives of both companies dealt with the expectations of passengers and the service that the two airlines should provide.

Peter Butcher, the marketing director of American Airlines, stated his concerns: "You might say that in the US we tend to serve our passengers at the lowest cost and in a reliable way from NY to LA. Safety, being on time, and price are more important to the passenger than hot meals on short flights. In Europe people are willing to pay a higher fare for a hot meal during a one hour flight."

John Smythe, a British Airways executive, agreed. "Indeed. On BA flights passengers are served a hot breakfast from London to Amsterdam in a flight that is no longer than 40 minutes. I once had a first class flight from Detroit to Chicago of just over an hour. It took off at 6.30. a.m. and, at around 7.00 a.m., after the 'fasten safety belts' signs were turned off, I wondered when breakfast would be served. I couldn't smell anything. I asked the flight attendant when I could expect something to eat. I took her by surprise with that question. Two minutes later she came back with a big smile, saying 'Sir, we have pretzels or potato chips. Which would you prefer?' I said that a cup of coffee would do."

When passengers' expectations are so diverse around the world of travel, how would you advise John and Peter to approach their global service to their passengers?

1a. Airlines are selling seats on planes that transport passengers safely. The airline industry becomes mature and will look like a bus service. The extras don't matter. They should concentrate on providing the lowest fares available, like Ryanair or EasyJet.

1b. Passengers should be given a decent meal, which could be served according to some minimal but fair quality standards.

1c. When passengers travel they will chose the airline that provides added value to the flight. Full service, like hot meals on short flights, is one way to satisfy passengers and should be included in both the US and Europe. It is the best way to differentiate yourself from the competition. It can also act as a distraction to overcome boredom.

1d.   Passengers should be given low fares. However, if special service is needed, such as connecting flights and hotel service, the carrier should be able to give the fullest service possible.

1e.   Hot meals on short flights should be provided. However, continuous feedback should be taken from passengers and employees to monitor passenger satisfaction and possible changes in needs. When they want less, they could fly economy.

Case 2. A British supermarket's misplaced marketing strategy

A large British supermarket chain took over a successful chain of Irish supermarkets in 1997. The terms of the takeover allowed the Irish cooperative to keep a percentage of the Irish supermarkets open under their former name. Others would be redesigned and new stores would carry the British supermarket name.

The British decided to open their first branch in a prosperous midland town, in a new shopping center on the outskirts of the town. They decided to concentrate all their business in the new store and close down the older supermarket, which was located in the town center. The new store would offer Irish customers many British products that were not available locally. It would also provide a home delivery service, which would be the first in the area.

To the British management's surprise, the new store incurred huge losses in the first weeks of business. In fact local radio and newspapers carried daily complaints from people in the area about the new supermarket's unfriendly policies. The whole town was talking angrily about the home delivery vans, whizzing around the streets with their UK-registered license plates. Customers were annoyed at the disappearance of Irish products on the shelves and their replacement by British-made goods. The union set up a picket outside the new store, protesting at the closure of the original town center store, which they said was against the terms of the takeover agreement.

Management realized they had made major mistakes. How should they seek to rectify the situation?

2a. They should go "Irish" again by quickly registering vans with Irish plates and gradually reopening the supermarket under its former name. The management should apologize to local suppliers, stop importing fresh produce from Britain, and invest heavily in marketing, stressing their commitment to Irish suppliers and workers.

2b. They should communicate the advantages of being part of a British group in terms of economies of scale and logistics and thus lower prices.

2c. They should try to find a balance between Irish and UK products. Some economies of scale are won, some are lost – but that's intrinsic in international business.

2d. They should emphasize the importance of being "Irish" and underlining the strength of community and local loyalties. The strength of British logistics and being part of a larger whole should be aimed at helping to serve the Irish better.

2e. The strength of being part of a British chain will show automatically in terms of logistics and economies of scale and also by importing Irish products to the UK.

Case 3. The globalizing beer company

Frank S. is the marketing manager of a Chicago-based beer manufacturer. He is in Paris to discuss the firm's global marketing strategy with his counterpart in France, one of the company's most important local markets. The main sticking point is whether marketing should be centralized or decentralized, in particular with regard to television advertisements.

The French want the advertisements to reflect local circumstances, while the Americans prefer having one global advertising campaign. The French marketing manager insists that the advertisements be in French. But Frank is convinced that this would jeopardize the firm's global aspirations.

What do you consider the best course of action?

3a. Push for global advertisements. Beer is a global product that requires an internationally recognized brand name.

3b. Listen to the French more carefully, and leave the advertisements to a local agency. In countries like France people are very selective about their choice of beer and favor products with a local attachment.

3c. Use a global advertising campaign as a context within which local adaptations are made. In the French ads, national (French) landmarks can be included.

3d. Leave all the advertising to the local firm with the requirement that beer should shown as a global product.

3e. Agree on a globally acceptable aspect of beer consumption, such as thirst, and gear the international advertisements toward this. This becomes a superordinate value system that transcends cultural differences.

Case 4. German dairy products go sour in the Netherlands

A German dairy products company had been very successful in the domestic market and so decided to expand internationally. Their success at home was due to their consistently high quality and stylish packaging, delivering products for which the market was prepared to pay a premium price.

The first foreign market that the company chose to enter was the Netherlands. Detailed market research showed that this was a logical choice because it was both very close and had lots of milk-loving consumers. At great cost and with significant fanfare, the Germans marched into the Netherlands with their milk and yogurt.

The German company was very proud of their line of small, stylish-looking, glass yogurt containers, intended for the high end of the market. These containers were very successful with German consumers, who associated it with high quality. After some months the Germans realized that they had encountered an unqualified disaster. Nobody bought their products.

What could you do to avoid this problem next time?

4a.　　The Germans need to impress their own ideas upon the Dutch environment more and invest more money in advertising the high-class idea to the Dutch.

4b.　　 Adapt the approach to the Dutch market, where people want quality at the lowest possible price and are oriented toward buying very fresh dairy products.

4c.   It's give and take. The luxury packaging should still be retained, but for a slightly less extravagant price.

4d.   The company needs to focus on the high end of the market by advertising that it is still the best price for the higher quality delivered.

4e.   The Germans should adapt to Dutch local conditions but gradually upgrade the product so that it will tap into new market segments and niches.

Case 5. The importance of titles

An operations manager of a Korean company kept calling the director of the customer support group of an American supplier to request customer support rather than calling the American customer engineer assigned to his account. The customer support director had told the Korean manager that he should call the customer engineer directly, but the situation had not changed. The American company found out later that the customer engineer did not have enough status to be seen as the point of entry for these requests.

That's all very well, but what can be done to solve this problem, in view of the fact that everyone can't be called "director"?

5a.   The company needs to give the engineer the title of Customer Service Manager and clarify his authority to solve the customer's problems.

5b.   The company needs to communicate to the Korean that the customer engineer is technically the best equipped person to help solve his problems.

5c.   The company needs to increase the age of the customer engineers so that they are respected by the Koreans, even in cases where they lack all the technical knowledge needed.

5d.   The company needs to communicate to the Koreans that the customer engineer is one of the most educated and talented people in the organization and that if there was any doubt they could always call the director.

5e   The company needs to make the director's telephone line less accessible so calls will automatically transfer to the customer engineer.

Case 6. Silent eater

A European sales manager had invited his Chinese agent's entire staff for dinner as a reward for a well-organized seminar. Everyone seemed to be happily eating and drinking except for one person, Mr Li, who had hardly touched his food or beer. He had not spoken to anyone, and he had a very serious look on his face. The European was not sure whether he should ask about Mr Li's problems. Fortunately, the Chinese manager explained the situation on his own initiative. He began by saying that his entire staff held their European friend in high regard. The best example was Mr Li, who had a serious domestic problem but still insisted on taking part in the dinner in order to honor the host.

Later, more details were disclosed. Mr. Li's young son had caught a cold that day and was running a fever. For Europeans this is not considered a problem; in China, however, severe colds can easily lead to complications. Moreover, the Chinese live for their children, especially as each couple is only officially allowed to have one child. Leaving home for whatever reasons under such circumstances is considered quite improper in China, let alone to participate in a joyous event.

What would you do in this situation?

6a. In this case Mr Li thought it appropriate to attend the dinner but clearly showed his concern to all his colleagues. Let's leave it at that.

6b. His colleagues in their turn regarded such a display of emotions as natural. If Mr Li had been eating, drinking, and laughing like the others, his colleagues would probably have reproached him for his lack of human feeling.

6c. I would just tell him that I was concerned with the mood he was in and ask him what had happened. I'd suggest making the event a bit shorter.

6d. I would take him aside and tell him how much I appreciated his worries, but advise him to go home to his child. This would make the group happier in view of the fact that Mr Li cares about his son.

6e. I would give a little speech indicating that it is important to respect our families and children and that all those who agree should go home now; the rest could celebrate even further.

Case 7. Future/past confusion

A western company had agreed to provide financial support for some of the promotional activities of its Chinese agents, including taking part in two national exhibitions a year. The only condition was that the Chinese submitted a proposal and got consent whenever they wanted to attend a particular exhibition.

While reporting on the promotional activities of the past year and negotiating those for the coming year, the Chinese suddenly started talking about an exhibition in which they had participated. The Westerners got a little irritated because this was the first they had heard of this exhibition, so they reproached the Chinese for not having sought approval beforehand. The Chinese were confused.

After a while it became clear that the exhibition was scheduled for six months in the future, but this information had gotten lost in the translation. As the event was to take place in the near future, the agent had spoken about it as if it were a current event. He had also taken part in an exhibition a few months earlier. As this event had taken place in the near past, it was also talked about as a current event. This was confusing even for the most experienced interpreter.

The performance of interpreters during Sino–foreign negotiations is a perpetual source of jokes and complaints. Linguistic knowledge alone does not make a good interpreter. The interpreter not only has to be fluent in both languages but also has to be aware of the cultural differences and how these differences are reflected in the respective languages.

How would you address these issues? We invite you to create your own alternative options for this case.

7a.   What would be the course of action in which you had ignored the cultural differences and simply gone your own way without any attempt to reconcile the differences?

7b.   What would be the course of action in which you had abandoned your own orientations and immediately sought to behave like the other side?

7c.   What would be a compromise solution?

7d.   Finally, how could you reconcile these differences?

As explained above, you can explore the answers to these cases on our website: www.cultureforbusiness.com.

Conclusion

After reading this book it will become quite obvious that the Anglo-Saxon roots of marketing, market research, and marketing planning are both a strength and a weakness. The strength lies in the fact that thinking about a "market out there" is typically an invention by the British and Americans, if only because they have an enormous need to codify their experiences. The weakness of the Anglo-Saxon approach is that cultural complexities are often ignored. What works in New York or London will obviously not work everywhere. But we hope you now know both why and what you can do about it.

In fact the problem is now for the consumer, rather than marketer. A new trauma has been identified for consumers, which has been labeled "choice fatigue." Too much bombardment, too many suppliers, and it takes time to make sure you check out all the alternatives to ensure that you got the best bargain. So perhaps we need to write the next book to bear in mind the dilemmas faced by consumers! Already, around the corner, we can begin to see new constructs for purchasers that are being called BTO (buy to order) and OTB (order to buy), which will become the reconciliation between buying "off the peg" and "bespoke."

Watch this space!

Appendix
Accumulating and interpreting the evidence

Here we explain some of the background to the collection and analysis of evidence obtained to support the propositions of the underlying conceptual framework on which this book is based. Although the general conclusions from these studies have appeared in our other publications, some of the underlying methods have not, and this Appendix is a response to marketers and researchers asking for further detail.

Originally the investigative work on dilemma theory was inductive. In an action-learning, exploratory phase over several years, Charles Hampden-Turner undertook many interviews with senior international leaders that sought the elicitation of a number of challenges/decision options in situations with seemingly opposing views and values. Fons Trompenaars undertook similar investigations in parallel on value dilemmas leading to the construction of the main quantitative cross-cultural database. The latter required the development of a range of instruments that were originally focused at discriminating value systems at the ecological level (country specific) to derive models of cross culture and measure cultural differences. The high reliability of these instruments is well known as extensive statistical and other analytical studies have been undertaken and published extensively. This database and its principal questionnaire instruments have been used extensively in training workshops and consultancy interventions across the world. Face and content validity have been constantly improved from qualitative and quantitative studies including formal research by university PhD doctoral students.

Resulting from these activities, a number of core propositions were developed concerning the underlying significance of reconciling dilemmas. The interest was to develop an underlying robust theory to provide a model for improving professional practice in what we have described as intercultural competence.

The key premise is that at the ideographic level, senior managers and leaders become effective across cultures when they are able to reconcile dilemmas they face in their work. At the nomothetic level, dilemmas arise across organizations as soon as they start to market across cultures and/or cope with their increasingly multicultural home markets.

SAMPLING

We took most of our samples from multinational and international companies, headquartered in many different countries. The results were shared with the samples surveyed and we learned much from their comments on our questions. These samples drawn from the variety of organizations reveal functionally equivalent sets, since nearly all these organizations were pursuing similar ends. Gender, age, education, and occupation differences are being case matched, to achieve similar distributions in each subset.

Finally it should be noted that our whole approach was not based on attempting to obtain an orthogonal data set as typified in classical market research. In the latter type of study, a sample is selected (targeted) with the minimum number of cases to obtain full coverage of each attribute (country, age, gender, etc.). This full concept method is not appropriate to our quest because of practical difficulties. How, for example, would we find a young, female, senior Arab leader working in a Gulf Country? We have adopted the approach of collecting a large data set with wide internal variety and then performing a reflective analysis that we can describe as knowledge discovery by induction.

Research instruments have been developed as experimental instruments to discover how the respondents reacted to dilemmas. The dilemma methodology imagines a conflict between two principles, e.g., respect for law versus loyalty among friends. In perhaps 95 percent of all cases, the claims of law and those of friendship coincide, but by imagining a case where these clash (for example, where the terms of a business contract have become idiosyncratic due a change in market conditions), we can discover whether respondents reject reconciliation, or strive to reconcile, or simply abandon their value systems.

FINAL QUESTIONNAIRE DESIGNS

Our questionnaires, being our core instruments, have been and are continually being refined. Multiple choice questions were constructed describing alternate courses of action to respond to dilemmas. The different combinations of answers that can be selected are intended to probe constructs such as:

- whether marketers focus on trying to push their own established products in different markets with corresponding different cultures and thus reject attempts at reconciliation;
- whether they tend to abandon their attempts to market their established products or services and seek new replacement products and services appropriate to the new markets that fit the culture of these new markets. This is the "when in Rome…" approach (lose–win);
- whether marketers seek a compromise position (lose–lose);
- whether marketers develop marketing plans that reconcile the differences between the established markets and new markets that have different cultures.

The value systems underlying each dilemma that is posed owe their origin to one of the seven dimensions of Trompenaars model of cross culture. Thus the question can be used to simultaneously identify both their value orientation (e.g., preferences for rules or exceptions, individualism or communitarianism) and their propensity to reconcile.

Thus the total spectrum of dilemma questions provides gives data that is combined in different combinations to a series of scales:

- scores on each cross-cultural dimension (i.e. a full cross-cultural profile); and
- for each dimension, scores on the propensity to:
  - compromise,
  - reject reconciliation,
  - the degree of seeking reconciliation from one's own cultural orientation first and then accommodating the alternate,
  - the degree of seeking reconciliation from the alternate cultural orientation first and then accommodating one's own,

and thereby

- a total reconciliation score per dimension,

and, in summary

- a set of total scores for reconciliation across all cultural dimensions (clockwise and anti-clockwise spirals), rejection and compromise.

The accumulation of the evidence is ongoing. Recently an area of our website (www.cultureforbusiness.com) open to free access that invites online responses to versions of our models has resulted in the number of valid cases increasing exponentially.

QUALITATIVE INTERVIEW DATA

As indicated in the body of this book, we accumulated much unstructured evidence from semi-structured interviews and especially through our WebCue online interviews. We perform a number of content analyses of these texts. These include Concordance Software (Oxford Concordance Program) to obtain KWIC analysis (keyword in context) and word-frequency counts, linguistic analysis (StyleWriter), NUD*IST and similar.

These methods provided a structured approach to assist the qualitative researcher to extract key factors and findings that complemented and reinforced the questionnaire-based research.

DATA MINING

Initial interrogation and analysis of the cross-cultural dilemma database has followed convention using statistical confidence tests.

However the classical approach does not extract all the potential information waiting to be discovered. Are there hidden patterns and exciting concepts deep within the database that would only be revealed if we knew in advance what they were and could test for them? Ongoing research with the database is concerned with mining for such information by using more recent techniques of analysis including neural networks and data mining.

Because much of our primary data on cross-cultural issues of marketing contains much categorical and ordinal data, classical parametric methods could not be used and many such problems are overcome by this new approach. The technique enables the relative contribution of different factors to be determined and is easily transferable to other problems, e.g., the relative importance of attributes of products (such as price, color, style, availability) or services. It thereby achieves the same results for our categorical data as traditional conjoint analysis, so loved by marketers, can play for their parametric market research data.

Trompenaars' model of cross culture is based on seven scales (dimensions) and this serves as the basic framework for conceiving a new approach to marketing across cultures. These scales are composed of a number of combinations of smaller components. We need a method of analysis to probe the relative influence of the different items such as age, gender, religion that were collected. In this respect, even "country" can be considered as simply another categorical item.

In this discussion, our model can be considered in the following form (for each dimension):

dimension score =
$c_1 \times$ country $+ c_2 \times$ age $+ c_3 \times$ religion $+ c_4 \times$ gender $+ c_5 + \ldots$

It is tempting to "throw" established statistical techniques at the data to identify possible coefficients (c_1, c_2, c_3 etc.) using correlation and partial-correlation analysis or factor analysis. Some other authors have often done just that with their own more limited data sets or incomplete or extracted sets of our earlier data that we have previously published. This has been especially true of researchers whose skills are limited to classical parametric methods – and these are not valid for our data.

On examination of the data, we note that these parametric methods are not appropriate. Many of the data items are simply categories (nominal data) such as gender, religion, or management function. Classical statistical non-parametric methods are not readily available for our particular problem and certainty none are included in industry standard statistical software. Whilst analysis of variance and (categories) conjoint analysis can help with questionnaire design and testing, it cannot produce the analysis we require here.

In order to explore our data set we therefore need to apply a different body of mathematics which is appropriate for our cause. Recent developments in relational database technology, database mining methods, and knowledge elicitation (Expert Systems) came to our rescue. The following treatment is based on the ID3 induction algorithm. Because these new techniques may not be familiar to the reader and because of their importance in our debate, we will give a short explanation rather than simply quote the results.

For the purpose of discussion, consider a very small but typical portion of our database based on ten cases. (Note: these are for the illustration of these new methods of analysis and these cases are not intended to imply or categorize any stereotypes through these examples.)

Case	Purchasing decision = GOAL	Country (VEN = Venezuela)	Function	Gender
1	universalist	US	senior manager	male
2	universalist	UK	junior manager	male

3	particularist	UK	senior manager	female
4	universalist	US	senior manager	female
5	particularist	VEN	senior manager	female
6	particularist	VEN	senior manager	male
7	particularist	UK	senior manager	male
8	particularist	VEN	junior manager	male
9	universalist	UK	junior manager	female
10	universalist	US	junior manager	male

In the domain of data mining, the various items are called "attributes" rather than factors. This helps to differentiate between parametric factor analysis methods or variables. For simplification at this stage, the first attribute, "dimension score," has been given only two values; namely whether a respondent is likely to adopt a "universalist" or "particularist" purchasing decision. This is called the goal attribute.

We shall see later how we can use data mining where the goal attribute is not restricted in this way to two extreme values. Indeed, any of the attributes can be multistate.

The basic principle is to find the relative importance of the various attributes in determining the goal attribute. If we normalize (arrange) the data to the so-called third normal form in separate tables (as we would for representation in a relational database), we obtain:

1: Cases sorted by country

5	particularist	VEN
6	particularist	VEN
8	particularist	VEN

2	universalist	UK
3	particularist	UK
7	particularist	UK
9	universalist	UK

1	universalist	US
4	universalist	US
10	universalist	US

2: Cases sorted by manager function

3	particularist	senior
1	universalist	senior
5	particularist	senior
6	particularist	senior
7	particularist	senior
4	universalist	senior

2	universalist	junior
8	particularist	junior
9	universalist	junior
10	universalist	junior

3: Cases sorted by gender

1	universalist	male
2	universalist	male
6	particularist	male
7	particularist	male
8	particularist	male
10	universalist	male

3	particularist	female
4	universalist	female
5	particularist	female
9	universalist	female

When we look at the attribute gender in table 3, we see that we can't determine the goal attribute – i.e., whether males or females are universalistic or particularistic in their purchasing decisions – from a given gender.

Similarly, for either a junior or senior manager function, the goal attribute can't be uniquely determined from table 2. When we look at the attribute country in table 1 we find that in all cases where, for example country = US, we can correctly determine that the goal is universalistic. If we know "country," we can correctly classify six of the ten examples in our data set. In data mining terminology, the attribute "country" is therefore said to have the highest information content.

For the full database, we can compute the amount of entropy for each attribute. This gives us a measure of the uncertainty of classification of our goal by each attribute. As the entropy increases, the amount of uncertainty we gain by adding each attribute increases. However, what we really want to know is how much information there is when we know the value(s) of any particular attribute.

If HC(attribute value) is the entropy of attribute of class "c" then this is given by:

$$HC(a_j) = -\sum_{i=1}^{n} f[c_i(a_j)] \log_2 f[c_i(a_j)]$$

Thus, the entropy of classification for Management Function is 'senior manager' is:

$$
\begin{aligned}
HC(\text{function is senior}) \quad = \quad & -f(\text{particularist(function is senior)}) \\
& \times \log f(\text{particularist(function is senior)}) \\
& -f(\text{universalist(function is senior)}) \\
& \times \log f(\text{universalist(function is senior)}) \\
= \quad & -4/6\log(4/6) - 2/6\log(2/6) \\
= \quad & 0.918
\end{aligned}
$$

Similarly,

$$
\begin{aligned}
HC(\text{function is junior}) \quad = \quad & -f(\text{particularist(function is junior)}) \\
& \times \log f(\text{particularist(function is junior)}) \\
& -f(\text{universalist(function is junior)}) \\
& \times \log f(\text{universalist(function is junior)}) \\
= \quad & -1/4\log(1/4) - 3/4\log(3/4) \\
= \quad & 0.811
\end{aligned}
$$

Hence, for the overall value of H(function), we simply weight these by the ten cases:

HC(manager function) = $6/10 \times 0.918 + 4/10 \times 0.811 = 0.8752$

Repeating this procedure for the other attributes we obtain:

HC(gender) = 1.0
HC(country) = 0.4

Since HC(gender) = 1.0, i.e. maximum uncertainty, this tells us that there is no information about the goal contained in the attribute "gender." This is consistent with Table 3 which shows that half the males and half the females are of each goal.

Because HC(country) has the lowest entropy of classification, then this corresponds to the least uncertainty. In other words, "country" has the highest information content and thus "country" is the major contributor in explaining the cultural orientation on this dimension of this consumer. Manager function has a smaller contribution.

Implementing the induction algorithm

Although it is computationally intensive, it is desirable to apply the ID3 algorithm directly to the original total database. We can use as the goal attributes the complete range of responses for each dimension scale and not simply "universalistic" or "particularistic." For example, when examining the information content of the database with respect to "individualism–collectivism," we note the five contributing questions on our scale means there are 32 (=2^5) possible states for the goal attribute. This was effected using the well-established computational method of list processing which has the further advantage of being applicable to string data. For this reason it was not necessary to recode the original database with pseudonumeric codes to represent each categorical item. Furthermore, this type of analysis does not lend itself to SPSS recode like procedures readily.

Because the ID3 algorithm is concerned with the frequency of occurrence of each combination of attributes and not the value of the attributes, it is not necessary to re-scale attributes. Thus age is processed as a category, not a scaled variable. The ID3 algorithm automatically takes care of different types of variable for each attribute and enables us to explore our full database directly.

A recursive procedure, "CATEGORIZE," was constructed to process each iteration. After one iteration on our example set, this produces:

(country (USA CATEGORIZE (((universalist USA senior male) (universalist USA senior female) (universalist USA junior male)))))

(VEN CATEGORIZE (((particularist VEN senior female) (particularist VEN senior male) (particularist VEN senior male)))))

(UK CATEGORIZE (((universalist UK junior male) (particularist UK senior female) (particularist UK senior male) (universalist UK junior female)))))

The above list of lists was split by CATEGORIZE at "country" because application of the ID3 algorithm revealed that "country" had the lowest entropy.

The final list returned by CATEGORIZE is:

(country(USA(status(universalist))))

(VEN(status(particularist))))

(UK(function(senior(status(particularist))))

(junior(status(universalist)))))

In some situations there may be cases where the same attribute values produce different goals. These are known as data conflicts. Thus not every American (male) senior manager may have responded as a universalist. These are accommodated simply by weighting these cases and the basic ID3 algorithm is applied accordingly.

To explain the total variety, it would be necessary to use the same variety as there are cases. This is the same as saying that the 65,000 respondents are all individuals and we could require 65,000 attributes to describe them. Alternatively, we could use one attribute with 65,000 values (such as their name) to uniquely identify them. In the above parlance, their "name" has the highest information content and lowest entropy. However this is not our aim. We refer to earlier discussion repeated throughout this book, namely that we are seeking to develop a model based on a number of dimensions (attributes) that help structure managers' experiences. The analysis we are attempting here is intended to support this aim by exploring the relative importance of different attributes rather than containing the total variety within the data set as a ideological statistician may prefer.

The outcomes of this analysis applied to the whole database reveals the following: It is to be noted that "country" has the lowest entropy for each dimension which is very good evidence to support the main thesis of Tromepanaars' work.

Entropy	unpa	indcol	neaf	spdi	achasc	intex	time
lowest	country	country	country	country	country	country	country
	industry	religion	industry	industry	industry	industry	industry
	religion	industry	job	religion	religion	job	religion
	job	education	religion	age	job	religion	education

age	age	corporate	gender	age	gender	job
corporate	gender	age	education	education	age	age
education	job	gender	job	corporate	education	gender
highest	gender	corporate	education	corporate	gender	corporate	corporate

Whilst this discussion might be viewed as an exercise in statisticulation, it is consistent with the face validity of the dimensions and Ashby's law of Requisite Variety – too few dimensions would not account for the richness of cultural diversity we see in the world.

If we apply other methods such as factor analysis, image factoring, and Kohenen neural networks then the conclusions are identical.

LIMITATIONS OF THE CURRENT DATABASE

It is a difficult – if not an impossible – task to present in a few pages a fully-fledged, validated theory dealing with such complex issues as socially constructed systems of human relationships and systems of shared meaning. We have, however, attempted to develop sufficient conceptual and empirical evidence of the close relationship between culture and the way it affects the meaning of organization.

These analyses, however, need not be limited to between-cultural comparisons. For the attainment of supplementary information, within-cultural analyses are suggested to be added to the set of investigations. Through this procedure, however, we depart from the ecological type of comparison to an individual type of comparison. By doing so a large pool of new variety is tapped, which significantly increases the number of samples.

Consequently, the number of possible statistical procedures and levels of significance increases. Results which are derived from these operations, however, need to be interpreted as personality factors rather than as cultural factors.

FUTURE WORK AND EXTENDING THE ANALYSIS

Clearly we would wish to do more work in this whole area, to collect more data, to increase the validity of the generalizations, and extend the findings.

We are currently building a neural network that is expected to give further insights into the data.

For bona fide researchers and other interested parties, further access to our methods, tools, and data analysis is available. In particular we welcome applications from students intending to research for a PhD to extend our work.

A last comment is saved for those who have found parts of the presented discussion simplistic, and for those who have found parts rather complex. For those of the former category, we admit that parts of the analysis were relatively simplistic. It was, however, never our aim to disguise complicated realities by an apparent simplicity. The simplicity, for those of the latter category, we again have to admit that certain of our (re)presentations were indeed rather complex. The complexity of parts of our analysis, however, are the result of the fact that quite often social reality doesn't seem to care about difficulties of (re)presentation. Nature, argues Fresnel, "doesn't care about mathematical difficulties." The social reality we have analyzed sometimes just seemed to prefer complexity.

In summary, we have shown that the present research has reconciled simplicity with complexity. A reconciliation allowing the reader to follow the main arguments concerning the relationship between the meaning of organization and the organization of meaning, and at the same time stimulate the reader to do the necessary further research in this area.

Bibliography

Alker, H. R. (1966) "A Typlogy of Ecological Fallacies," in Merrit, R. and Rokkan, S. (eds), *Comparing Nations*, Yale University Press.

Allport, G. W. (1961) *Pattern and Growth in Personality*, Holt Reinhart Winston.

Bateson, G. (1980) *Mind and Nature: A Necessary Unity*, Bantam.

Berrien, P. K. (1967) "Methodological and Related Problems in Cross-Cultural Research," *International Journal of Psychology*, 1–2.

Berman, G. (1997) "Trend Spotting: Where the Ethnic Market is Heading," *Advertising Age*, 68(46).

Berry, J. W. (1980) "The Method of Cross-Cultural Psychology" in H. Triandis (ed.), *Handbook of Cross-Cultural Psychology*, Allyn and Bacon.

Berry, J. W. (1990) "Psychology of Acculturation," in Berman, J. J. (ed.), *Cross-cultural Perspectives: Proceedings of the Nebraska Symposium on Motivation*.

Bezos, J. (2003) "Fixated on the Customer," *Business Week*, September.

Blalok, H. M. (1964) *Causal Inferences in Non-experimental Design*, University of North Carolina Press.

Bohrnstedt, G. W. (1970) "Reliability and Validity Assessment in Attitude Measurement," in G. F. Summers (ed.), *Attitude Measurement*, Rand McNally.

Boyatzis, R. E. (1982) *The Competent Manager: A Model for Effective Performance*, John Wiley and Sons.

Brandweek, (2001) "The New Age of Ethnic Marketing," 42(12) (March).

Brown, C. (1992) "Same Difference:The Persistence of Racial Disadvantage in the British Employment Market," in Braham, P., Rattnasi, A. and Skellington, R. (eds), *Racism and Anti-Racism*, Sage.

Brown, S. and Burt, S. (1992) "Retail Internationalisation: Past, imperfect, future imperative," *European Journal of Marketing*, 26(8/9).

Burton, D. (2000) "Ethnicity, Identity and Marketing: A Critical Review," *Journal of Marketing Management*, 16.

Callebaut, J. and friends [*sic*] (2000) *Cross-Cultural Window of Consumer Behavior*, Censydiam and Garant.

Callebaut, J., Hendrickx, H. and Janssens, M. (2002) *The Naked Consumer Today*, Censydiam and Garant.

Cameron, D. (2001) "8 Steps to Better Customer Identification," *Intelligent Enterprise*, 4(11).

Campbell, D. T. and Stanley, J. C. (1966) *Experimental and Quasi-Experimental Designs of Research*, Rand McNally.

Campbell, N. (1928) *Measurement and Calculation*, Longmans, Green and Co.

Charlesworth, A. (2003) *The E-adoption Ladder*, IDG Publications.

Churchman, C. W. (1948) *Theory of Experimental Inference*, Macmillan.

Cicourel, A. V. (1964) *Method and Measurement in Sociology*, Free Press.

Clark, H. F. (1987) "Consumer and Corporate Values: Yet Another View on Global Marketing," *International Journal of Advertising*.

Coase, R. H. (1937) *The Nature of the Firm*, Economica.

Colebatch, H. and Lamour, P. (1993) *Market, Bureaucracy and Community: A Student's Guide to Organisation*, Pluto Press.

Costa, J. A. and Bamossy, G. J. (1995) *Marketing in a Multicultural World: Ethnicity, Nationalism and Cultural Identity*, Sage.

Crainer, S. (1998) *Thinkers that Changed the World* (Key Management Ideas), Financial Times Prentice Hall.

Crozier, M. (1980) *Actors and Systems: The Politics of Collective Action*, University of Chicago Press.

Darke, P., Chattopadhyay, A. and Ashworth, L. (2002) "Going With Your Gut," Working paper, INSEAD.

Davis, S. and Pine, J. (1999) *Mass Customization: The New Frontier in Business Competition*, Harvard Business School Press.

Dong, L. and Helms, M. (2001) "Brand Name Translation Model: A Case Analysis of US Brands in China," *Brand Management*, 9(3), November.

Douglas, S. and Craig, C. S. (1983) *International Market Research*, Prentice Hall.

Drever, J. A. (1974) *Dictionary of Psychology*, Penguin.

Drucker, P. (1973) *The Practice of Management*, HarperCollins.

Duijker, H. and Rokkan, S. (1954) "Organizational Aspects and Cross-national Research," *Journal of Social Issues*, 10.

Dunn, W. (1992) "The Move Toward Ethnic Marketing," *Nation's Business*, 80(7).

Eroglu, S. (1992) "The Internationalization Process of Franchise Systems: A Conceptual Model," *International Marketing Review*.

Evankovich, T. (2003) "Are You Ready to Go Global?" *Franchising World*, vol. 35(7), October.

Evin, S. and Bower, R. T. (1952) "Translation Problems in International Surveys," *Public Opinion Quarterly*, 16.

Farnham, D. (1999) *Managing in a Business Context*, IPD.

Flikkema, L. (1998) "Global Marketing's Myth: Differences Don't Matter," *Marketing News*, vol. 32, issue 15.

Forehand, M. and Deshpande, R. (2001) "What We See Makes Us Who We

Are: Priming Ethnic Self-awareness and Advertising Response," *Journal of Marketing Research*, 38(3).

Friedman, T. (2000) *The Lexus and the Olive Tree: Understanding Globalization*, Doubleday.

Frijda, N. and Jahoda, G. (1966) "On Scope and Methods of Cross-Cultural Research," *International Journal of Psychology*.

Frijda, N. and Jahoda, G. (1969) "On the Scope and Methods of Cross-Cultural Research," in Price-Williams, D. R. (ed.), *Cross-Cultural Studies*, Penguin.

Goldberg, M., Gorn, G., and Pollay, R. (1990) *Advances in Consumer Research*, Association for Consumer Research.

Grant, C. (1985) *Business Format Franchising: A System for Growth*, Economist Intelligence Unit.

Grass, R. and Wallace, W. (1994) "Advertising Communication: Print versus TV, *Journal of Advertising Research*, 14.

Griffiths, A. and Wall, S. (2004) as discussed in *Business Economics*, FT Prentice Hall.

Guthrie, G. M. (1972) "Unexpected Correlations and the Cross-Cultural Method," *Journal of Cross-Cultural Psychology*, 2–4.

Halter, M. (2002) *Shopping for Identity: The Marketing of Ethnicity*, Schocken Books.

Hansen, D. M. and Boddewyn, J. J. (1975) *American Marketing in the European Common Market, 1963–1973*, Marketing Science Institute.

Hofstede, G. (1980) *Culture's Consequences*, Sage.

Jastrow, D. (1999) "US Slow to Address Cultural Differences," *Computer Reseller News*, issue 866.

Jebb, A. and Woolliams, P. (2002) "Towards a Culture Free Integrated Design Methodology," Proceedings of the Engineering Design 2002 Conference, June, King's College, London.

Kaplan, A., (1963) *The Conduct of Inquiry*, Harper & Row.

de Kare Silver, M. (2000) *E-shock*, Macmillan.

Kashani, K. (1999) *Marketing Management – An International Perspective*, Macmillan.

Keegan, V. (2000) "Time to Narrow the Gap," *Guardian*, 21 October.

Kelly, T. A. F. (1961) *Language, World, and God: An Essay in Ontology*, Macmillan.

Kim, Y. K. and Kang, J. (2001) "The Effects of Ethnicity and Product on Purchase Decision Making," *Journal of Advertising Research*, 41(2).

Kinra, N. (1997) "The Communication Effectiveness of Ethnically Orientated Advertising," *International Journal of Advertising*, 16.

Kluckhohn, F. and Strodtbeck, F. L. (1961) *Variations in Value Orientations*, Greenwood Press.

Kwai-Choi Lee, C., Fernandez, N. and Martin, B. (2002) "Using Self-referencing to Explain the Effectiveness of Ethnic Minority Models in Advertising," *International Journal of Advertising*, 21(3).

Laurent, A. (1990), see Evans P., Doz, Y. and Laurent, A. *Human Resource Management in International Firms: Change, Globalization, Innovation*, Macmillan.

Law, I. (1997) "Modernity, Anti-racism, and Ethnic Managerialism," *Policy Studies*, 18(3/4).

Lazarsfeld, P. F. and Menze, H. (1961) "On the Relationship Between Individual and Collective Properties" in Etzioni, A. (ed.), *Complex Organizations: A Sociological Reader*, Holt & Winston.

Lewis, R. and Chambers, R. E. (2000) *Marketing Leadership in Hospitality: Foundations and Practices*, John Wiley & Sons

Macrae, C. and Unclex, M. (1997) "Rethinking Brand Management," *Journal of Product and Brand Management*, 6(3).

Marketing Science Institute, The (1996) Editorial, *International Journal of Physical Distribution and Logistics Management*, 26(7).

Marshall, C. (1992) "Adland's True Colours," *Management Today*.

Maruyama, M. (1963) "The Second Cybernetics: Deviation-amplifying Mutual Causal Processes," *American Scientist*.

Mayer, C. S. (1978) "Multinational Marketing Research: The Magnifying Glass of Methodological Problems," *European Research*, March.

Merrel, K. H. (1994) "Saving Faces," *Allure*, January.

Mintzberg, H., Ahlstrand, B., and Lampel, J. (1998) *Strategy Safari: A Guided Tour Through The Wilds of Strategic Management*, Simon & Schuster.

Moore, J. (2003) "The Second Superpower Rears its Beautiful Head," address to the Berkman Center for Internet and Society, Harvard Law School, March 31.

Moore, M. and Fernie, J. (2000) "Brands Without Boundaries," *European Journal of Marketing*, 34(8).

Nostradamus (1998 edn) *The Prophecies of Nostradamus*, ed. F. King and S. Skinner, Parragon.

Palmer, A. and Worthington, I. (1992) *The Business and Marketing Environment*, McGraw-Hill.

PC World, (2000) "Personalization is Key for Amazon.com," *PC World*, 19(3).

Peek, R. (2000) "Customizing the World on the Web," *Information Today*, 17(5).

Phizacklea, A. and Miles, P. (1992) "The British Trade Union Movement and Racism," in P. Braham, A. Rattnasi, and R. Skellington, (eds) *Racism and Anti-racism*, Sage.

Picard, J., Boddewyn, J. J., and Soehl, R. (1989) "US marketing policies in the European Economic Community: A Longitudinal Study, 1973–1983," in Luostarinen, R. (ed.), *Dynamics of International Business*, 15th Conference of EIBA, Helsinki.

Plotinus (270) *The Essence of Plotinus: Extracts from the Six Enneads and Porphyry's Life of Plotinus*, trans S. Mackenna (1977), Greenwood Publishing.

Porter, M. (1985) *Competitive Advantage*, The Free Press.

Porter, M. (1986) *Competition in Global Industries*, Harvard Business School Press.

Porter, M. (1995) *Competitive Advantage of Nations*, Harvard University Press.

Porter, M. (1996) "Changing Patterns of Internal Competition," *Managing Review.*

Pras, B. and Angelmar, R. (1978) "Verbal Rating Scales for Multinational Research," *European Research*, March.

Quinn, B. and Doherty, A-M. (2000) "Power and Control in International Retail Franchising," *International Marketing Review*, 17(4/5).

Rapaille, G. C. (2001) *7 Secrets of Marketing in a Multi-cultural World*, Executive Excellence Publishing.

Ricardo, D. (1817) *The Principles of Political Economy and Taxation*, reprinted edn 1996, Prometheus Books.

Ries, A. and Trout, J. (1982) *Positioning: The Battle for Your Mind*, McGraw-Hill.

Ries, A. and Trout, J. (1989) *Bottom-up Marketing*, Plume.

Ries, A. and Trout, J. (1997) *Marketing Warfare*, McGraw-Hill.

Roberts, K. H. (1977) "On Looking at An Elephant," *Psychological Bulletin*, 4–5.

Robinson, W. S. (1950) "Ecological Correlations and the Behavior of Individuals," *American Sociological Review*, VI.

Rosen, M. B.(1997) "Marketing to Ethnically Diverse Populations," *National Underwriter/Life and Health Financial Services*, 101(31).

Rossman, M. (1994) *Multicultural Marketing: Selling to a Diverse America*, Amacom.

Ryan, J. Z. and Ratz, D. G. (1987) "Advertising Standardization: A Re-examination," *International Journal of Advertising.*

Saker, R. and Brooke, P. (1989) "Ethnic Food Business, Success and Failure," *British Food Journal*, 91(2).

Sapir, E. (1929) "The Status of Linguistics as a Science," *Language.*

Satori, G. (1970) "Concept Misinformation in Comparative Politics," *American Political Science Review*, 64.

Scheuch, E. K., (1966) "Cross-National Comparisons Using Aggregate Data," in Merrit, R. and Rokkan, S. (eds), *Comparing Nations*, Yale University Press.

Sharoff, R. (2001) "Diversity in the Mainstream," *Marketing News*, 35(11).

Siegel, S. (1956) *Non-parametric Statistics for the Behavioral Sciences*, McGraw-Hill.

Siera, G. (2000) "Advertising in the Rainbow Nation", in Callebouts, J. *et al.* (eds), *Cross-cultural Window on Consumer Behavior*, Garant.

Sills, A. and Desai, P. (1996) "Qualitative Research Amongst Ethnic Minorities in Britain," *Journal of the Market Research Society*, 38.

Sly, F. (1994) "Ethnic Groups and the Labour Market," *Employment Gazette*, May.

Smelser, N. J. (1976) *Comparative Methods in the Social Sciences*, Prentice-Hall.

Snowden, D. (2002) *Third Generation Knowledge Management*, Collaboration.

Solomon, M., Bamossy, G., and Askegaard, S. (1999) *Consumer Behaviour: A European Perspective*, Prentice Hall.

Stanfield, J. H. (1993) *A History of Race Relations Research*, Sage.

Stanfield, J. H. and Dennis, R. M. (1993) *Race and Ethnicity in Research Methods*, Sage.

Steffens, L. (1999) "The Role of Online Advice," Forrester Conference, Princeton, NJ May 24.

Strauss, J. (2002) *E-Marketing*, 3rd edition, Prentice Hall.

Tatum, B. D. (1992) "Talking About Race, Learning About Racism: The Application of Racial Identity Development Theory in the Classroom," *Harvard Educational Review*, 62(1).

Trompenaars, F. and Hampden-Turner, C. (1997) *Riding the Waves of Culture*, 2nd rev. edn McGraw-Hill.

Trompenaars, F. and Hampden-Turner, C. (2001) *21 Leaders for the 21st Century*, Capstone.

Trompenaars, F. and Woolliams, P. (2003) *Business Across Cultures*, Capstone.

Usunier, J-C. (1997) *Marketing Across Cultures*; 2nd edn, Prentice Hall.

Walton, J. (1973) "Standardized Case Comparison," in Armer, M. and Grimshaw, A. D. (eds), *Comparative Social Research*, Wiley.

Wentz, L. (2003) "Pepsi Puts Interests Before Ethnicity," *Advertising Age*, 74(27).

Williams, J. D. (1995) "Review Article," [sic] *Journal of Marketing Research*, XXXII, May.

Wilson, R. F. (2000),"The Six Simple Principles of Viral Marketing," *Web Marketing Today*, 70, 1February.

Windelbrand, W. (1904, reprint 2002) *Die Geschichte der neueren Philosophie*, Reprint Lit, Philosophiegeschichtliche Darstellungen des 18. und frèuhen 19. Jahrhunderts.

Woodruffe, C. (1993) "Measuring Managers," in Boam, R. and Sparrow, P. (eds), *Designing and Achieving Competency*, McGraw-Hill.

Woolliams, P. and Dickerson, D. (1999) *Fuzio der Kulturen und Strategie*, J. Werburg und Verkauf.

Zeidman, P. (1993) "Franchising: Bridge Across Troubled Waters," *Franchising World*, 25(6), November–December.

Index

Trompenaars Hampden-Turner

Culture for Business

Trompenaars Hampden-Turner provides consulting, training, coaching, and (un)learning services to help leaders and professionals manage and solve their business and culture dilemmas. Our clients are primarily Global Fortune 500 companies. We are based in Amsterdam, the Netherlands and Boston, USA. In addition, we have a network of associates throughout the world.

We particularly focus on cross-cultural consulting services around:

- mergers and acquisitions integration
- globalization
- corporate vision and values.

We take pride in using the client's own language and discourse, although we make subtle changes to its underlying structure to render it more coherent. Topics may include diversity, communication, learning, training, teamwork, culture, coaching, knowledge management, leadership development, integrity, and balanced scorecards. For us these are all parts of a system. We also aim to introduce our clients to a paradoxical logic of human and organizational development. We aim for minimalist interventions yielding maximum results.

Introduction to our offerings

We work with all business implications of culture. These may be part of an organization's globalization process, external growth and integration strategies, corporate identity and corporate communications, international change management, or the worldwide "roll-out" of building cross-cultural competencies.

We work with organizations through a highly customized and integrated approach including:

Consulting on culture-for-business management

- Conduct cross-cultural due diligence
- Facilitate your vision and value to strengthen your corporate identity
- Surface cultural challenges and dilemmas which may be creating obstacles
- Systematically reconcile cultural differences in order to maximize the business value of cultural diversity
- Assist in creating a business climate of mutual respect and trust in order to link people from different cultures in productive and positive ways.

Global leadership development

- Create top-of-mind recognition of and respect for cross-cultural issues
- Develop culture-for-business competencies into competitive advantage
- Help leaders solve critical culture-for-business dilemmas
- Ascertain awareness of and respect for cross-cultural diversity
- Develop the ability to leverage global diversity.

Executive coaching

- Cross-cultural executive coaching helps leaders and managers with wider perspectives, cultural sensitivity, and the ability to work with diversity in a productive and innovative way to achieve organizational goals.

- Cross-cultural coaching helps the individual or team assess its own strengths and challenges. It assists with positive changes in behavior and perception. It also helps individual integration without sacrificing diversity and integrity within the organization.

Employee training and (un)learning

- Raise awareness of how culture-for-business competencies can help improve the bottom line
- Build awareness and respect for cross-culture and diversity issues
- Provide support in "unlearning" negative cultural attitudes and stereotypes
- Develop the ability to value and work with diversity.

Amsterdam Office:

A.J. Ernststraat 595D
1082 LD Amsterdam
The Netherlands
Tel: +31 20 301 6666
Fax: +31 20 301 6555
Email: info@thtconsulting.com

USA Office:

14 Arrow Street, Suite 10
Cambridge, MA 02138-5106
USA
Tel: +1 617 876 5025
Fax: +1 617 876 5026